Better Homes and Gardens®

1990 BEST-RECIPES
YEARBOOK

Our seal assures you that every recipe in the
1990 Best-Recipes Yearbook has been tested in the
Better Homes and Gardens® Test Kitchen.
This means that each recipe is practical and reliable,
and meets our high standards of taste appeal.

Better Homes and Gardens®

Every year, from month to month, *Better Homes and Gardens*® magazine publishes a potpourri of recipes and ideas to satisfy your cooking needs. Articles cover nutritious and healthy eating, quick and easy cooking, and creative yet affordable entertaining. In this, our eighth annual recipe yearbook, you'll rediscover our best recipes and ideas from 1989.

CONTENTS

JANUARY

THE MAGAZINE FOR AMERICAN FAMILIES

Better Homes
and Gardens

JANUARY 1989
$1.50

REVIVING
A '50s RANCH
PAGE 67

SPECIAL
ISSUE

AT-HOME ENTERTAINING
3 FAMILIES SHARE THEIR
DECORATING STYLES, RECIPES,
AND PARTY IDEAS

SEW-IT-YOURSELF
DECORATING
Free Pattern for
ROMANTIC
BANDBOXES

GARDENING
•OUR FAVORITES
FOR 1989

CRAFTING
•NEEDLEPOINT
•COMB
PAINTING

COOKING
•LOW-FAT
STRATEGIES

● A light, luscious party dessert: Monique's spectacular flan.

PARTIES WITH FLAIR

Monique and Leslie Bond Share Their Secrets For Fabulous Parties

By Barbara Goldman

● Three generations enjoy preparing for guests.

"I don't have any set formula—I just enjoy giving parties. I love seeing everybody having a good time!"

Bubbly toddler Noelle Bond insisted on greeting each of her guests at the door at her birthday party—her *first*! "I couldn't believe it," recalls amazed mom, Monique. But Noelle was simply following in her parents' footsteps, extending the warm welcome she'd seen so often at the Bonds' lively Atlanta get-togethers.

● Best party of all? Precious moments spent relaxing together as a family.

"How do I do it? My mother lives in the same city. She's my lifesaver!"

Party giving looks easy when Monique and Leslie do it. Yet Leslie, a corporate attorney, and Monique, vibrant mother, jewelry designer, substitute teacher, and children's store assistant, crowd more into one day than many work into a week. "Unless I plan ahead, I'm a crazy woman," says Monique.

PLANNING: AN ESSENTIAL

"But planning is part of the fun," she continues. "It's creative—and I enjoy

● Noelle samples her favorite fruit while Mom party-shops at the farmers' market.

the challenge." She credits her mother with her party-giving flair. "I entertain the way she entertains. Mom also helps with the baby while I work. She's crucial to us!" Monique emphasizes. And her Mexican party choices? Monique explains, "I learned from watching the woman who took care of me when I was little."

MONIQUE'S PLANNING TIPS

● Attempt only what you can do easily. I do everything myself for small parties. For a large fund-raiser I'll coordinate colors, napkins, flowers, and the presentation, but get help with the food.

● Give yourself enough time. I prepare what I can the night before—polish silver and set the table.

● During relaxing moments—just before bedtime, for instance—I look through magazines like *Better Homes and Gardens*® magazine for recipes. Honest!

MENU

Sangria/Margaritas

■

Chunky Guacamole

■

Quesadillas with Green Chili Salsa

■

Grilled Red Snapper With Crabmeat Stuffing

■

Spanish Rice

■

Enchiladas

■

Arroz con Pollo

■

Zucchini-Tomato Casserole

■

Flan/Banana Pudding

■

Coffee

LAST-MINUTE TOUCHES
● Four hands quickly finish up special details. The close mother-daughter duo shares a common appreciation of friends, family, and each other. They even ran a clothing shop together.

● Good food sparks good conversation in the spacious living room.

"We want people to feel comfortable. It's easiest when guests know each other or have something in common."

"Entertaining seems natural to us," Monique says. "Leslie is from St. Louis and I'm from Los Angeles, but we both grew up in 'party' houses. Our folks love having friends in." The couple met at a party of sorts—a medical convention to which their dads brought their families.

ENTERTAINING: BOND-STYLE

"My favorite way to entertain is to have four couples over for dinner. Then we can really talk," says Monique. "I enjoy using my crystal and china—and the neat things I've collected," the artwork sleuth explains, pointing to a painting spied in a secondhand store.

Because Leslie is active in politics, sometimes the couple hosts fund-raising dinners for 50 or more people. "Then we appreciate the 'stand-up' space in our living room," explains Monique. "It's easier to mix, walk around, and talk."

RELAXED CORDIALITY
● Careful party planning pays off, allowing Monique and Leslie to enjoy the good times every bit as much as their guests.

SOUTHWESTERN BUFFET

● A love of good food, an eye for detail, Mexican specialties, and a good "catch" result in a buffet of *Grilled Red Snapper, Spanish Rice, Zucchini-Tomato Casserole, Enchiladas* and *Arroz con Pollo.*

● The evening winds up with energetic talk over two favorite Bond desserts.

"Small groups are the most fun. Everyone gets to mingle and you have a lively party!"

"More often than not, we entertain casually, with just a few close friends or family," says Leslie.

THE BEST FOOD?
HOME FOOD

"The foods we serve aren't always fancy. Often, they're foods we eat every day," says Monique. "I've made enchiladas ever since I was a girl and served them to my folks, and sister, Angelique. I get a lot of recipes from my dad. He cooks like you wouldn't believe!

"Since Mom and Dad moved to Atlanta three years ago, Dad and I have cooking contests. We try to outdo each other with our recipes," she explains. "'How tender is *your* roast?' he'll ask."

LESLIE'S
SPECIALTY
● Leslie dishes up his delicious banana pudding to an appreciative guest. He makes the pudding nearly once a week—when the bananas Noelle adores become overripe. Leslie, Monique, and guests reap the benefits.

TIME OUT
FOR FUN
● Monique pauses over dessert to share a humorous moment with one of her guests.

MONIQUE'S MEXICAN FLAN

● Caramelized sugar pools float over this inviting baked custard. Served with slices of papaya, strawberries, oranges, and limes, it's almost too beautiful to sample—but try it!

● Noelle helps stir the seasonings for Daddy's catch.

THE BONDS COOK

GRILLING THE CATCH
● Leslie uses a grill basket especially designed for fish. This red snapper is one that "didn't get away" during Leslie's annual spring fishing expedition with friends in Destin, Florida.

EASY DOES IT
● Monique uses tongs to place the succulently browned *pollo* (chicken) of the *Arroz con Pollo* atop the rice, broth, and seasonings. The chicken will cook to a delectable tenderness.

"Leslie's quite a cook," Monique says. "You should taste his specialties!" Leslie admits that he makes a mean venison stew with carrots and peppercorns. "I like to serve it with steamed vegetables and wild rice," he explains, as he hunts for the recipe in his recipe file. Leslie brings home the venison from October hunting trips with Monique's dad and some friends. "After they go on a trip," says Monique, "we have meat for the whole year."

FOODS THAT MAKE HER DAY

And Monique's favorite foods? "Unfortunately, practically everything!" she replies, with her characteristic peal of laughter.

"I'm crazy about pizza, and on Friday nights we go to the farmers' market, buy ready-made pizza dough and lots of fresh vegetables. Then we go home and make pizza with everything on it.

"But my very favorite food? It has to be Mexican! I love enchiladas and soft-shell tacos. Noelle takes after me. She may be a toddler, but she knows what a taco is!"

FABULOUS PARTY RECIPES
(Pictured on pages 8–13.)

CHUNKY GUACAMOLE
2 large ripe avocados, halved, pitted, peeled, and chopped
2 green onions, sliced (¼ cup)
1 small onion, chopped (¼ cup)
1 teaspoon lemon juice
1 teaspoon olive oil *or* salad oil
Dash salt
Dash pepper
1 medium tomato, chopped
Chopped tomato (optional)
Fresh cilantro sprig (optional)
Tortilla chips (optional)

● **In medium mixing bowl** combine avocados, onions, lemon juice, oil, salt, and pepper. Stir in medium tomato. Transfer to serving bowl. Garnish with additional tomato and cilantro. Serve with tortilla chips. Makes 2 cups.

Note: To make ahead, increase lemon juice to 1 tablespoon; cover and chill till serving time.

Nutrition information per tablespoon: 25 cal., 0 g pro., 1 g carbo., 2 g fat, 0 mg chol., 6 mg sodium, 95 mg potassium.

QUESADILLAS
3 cups shredded Monterey Jack cheese (12 ounces)
1 4-ounce can diced green chili peppers, drained
12 7- *or* 8-inch flour tortillas
Green Chili Salsa (optional) (see recipe, *opposite*)

● **Place** ¼ *cup* of cheese and about *1 teaspoon* peppers over *half* of *one* tortilla. Fold in half, then in half again to form triangle. Place on baking sheet. Repeat with remaining ingredients. Overlap slightly on sheet, if necessary.

● **Bake in 300° oven** 3 to 4 minutes or till cheese melts. Serve with salsa. Makes 12 appetizer servings.

Note: To make ahead, prepare quesadillas; chill, covered, till serving. Bake 2 to 3 extra minutes to melt cheese.

Nutrition information per serving: 171 cal., 9 g pro., 14 g carbo., 9 g fat, 25 mg chol., 236 mg sodium. U.S. RDA: 23% vit. A, 27% calcium.

GREEN CHILI SALSA

Serve with the Bonds' Quesadillas (see recipe, opposite)—

     1 large tomato, chopped
     1 small onion, chopped
     3 green onions, finely chopped
     2 tablespoons finely chopped
       pickled jalapeño
       chili peppers
     2 tablespoons vinegar
     1 tablespoon pickled jalapeño chili
       pepper juice (optional)
Sliced pickled jalapeño chili
       peppers (optional)

● **In a small bowl** combine tomato, onion, green onions, and chopped chili peppers. Stir in vinegar and pepper juice, if desired. Cover and chill till serving time. Garnish with pepper slices, if desired. Makes about 2 cups.

Nutrition information per tablespoon: 3 cal., 0 g pro., 1 g carbo., 0 g fat, 0 mg chol., 10 mg sodium, and 17 mg potassium.

GRILLED RED SNAPPER WITH CRABMEAT STUFFING

     3 to 4 cups mesquite wood chips
     1 cup sliced fresh mushrooms
     2 tablespoons margarine *or* butter
     1 pound lump crabmeat *or* two
       7-ounce cans crabmeat, drained,
       flaked, and cartilage removed
     1 3-pound *or* two 1½-pound
       scaled, drawn red snapper
       (with head and tail)
     2 tablespoons olive oil
     1 tablespoon lime juice
    ⅛ teaspoon garlic powder
Caribbean Seasoning
     1 tablespoon Old Bay seasoning
Spanish Rice (optional)
Tomato wedges (optional)
Fresh cilantro sprigs (optional)

● **At least 1 hour before cooking,** soak mesquite chips in water to cover.
● **For filling,** in a large skillet cook mushrooms in hot margarine or butter till tender; stir in crabmeat.
● **Spoon filling** into the fish cavity. Skewer the cavity opening closed with wooden toothpicks.
● **In a small mixing bowl** combine olive oil, lime juice, and garlic powder. Brush on both sides of fish.
● **Rub fish** on both sides with Caribbean Seasoning and Old Bay seasoning.
● **Drain wood chips.** In a covered grill arrange preheated coals around a foil drip pan; test for *medium-hot* heat above the pan. Sprinkle the drained chips over the preheated coals.
● **Place fish** in a well-greased grill basket over pan. *Or*, place fish on grate lined with greased heavy-duty foil that has several slits for drippings.
● **Lower grill hood.** Grill for 20 minutes. Turn fish over. Grill for 10 to 20 minutes or till fish just flakes with a fork. Serve with Spanish Rice, and garnish with tomato wedges and cilantro, if desired. Makes 6 servings.

Caribbean Seasoning: Mix 1 teaspoon *sugar*, ¾ teaspoon *onion salt*, 1 teaspoon *black pepper*, ¾ teaspoon *ground ginger*, ¾ teaspoon *ground cinnamon*, ¾ teaspoon *crushed red pepper*, ¼ teaspoon *salt*, and ⅛ teaspoon *ground cloves*.

Nutrition information per serving: 302 cal., 37 g pro., 3 g carbo., 15 g fat, 74 mg chol., 1,043 mg sodium.

SPANISH RICE

     1 large green pepper, coarsely
       chopped
     1 large tomato, coarsely chopped
     1 medium onion, chopped (½ cup)
     2 tablespoons margarine *or* butter
     2 cups cooked rice
    ⅓ cup water
    ½ teaspoon salt
    ¼ teaspoon pepper

● **Cook** green pepper, tomato, and onion in hot margarine or butter till tender. Stir in cooked rice, water, salt, and pepper. Heat through, stirring occasionally. Makes 6 side-dish servings.

Microwave directions: In a 1-quart microwave-safe casserole, microcook the green pepper, tomato, onion, and margarine or butter, covered, on 100% power (high) for 5 to 6 minutes or till vegetables are tender, stirring once. Add cooked rice, water, salt, and pepper. Cook, covered, on high for 3 to 4 minutes or till the mixture is heated through, stirring once.

Nutrition information per serving: 122 cal., 2 g pro., 19 g carbo., 4 g fat, 0 mg chol., 227 mg sodium, 115 mg potassium, 2 g dietary fiber.

ARROZ CON POLLO

     1 2½- to 3-pound broiler-fryer
       chicken, cut up
     3 tablespoons olive oil
    1¼ cups long grain rice
     1 14½-ounce can chicken broth
     1 12-ounce can beer
     1 tablespoon ground cumin
     2 cloves garlic, minced
    ½ teaspoon salt
    ¼ teaspoon ground saffron
    ¼ teaspoon pepper
Salt
Pepper
     2 10-ounce packages frozen peas

● **Rinse chicken;** pat dry. In a 12-inch skillet cook chicken, uncovered, in hot oil over medium heat for 10 to 15 minutes or till brown, turning to brown evenly. Remove chicken. Add uncooked rice to skillet. Cook and stir over medium heat till rice is light brown. Stir in broth, beer, cumin, garlic, ½ teaspoon salt, saffron, and ¼ teaspoon pepper.
● **Place chicken** on top of the rice mixture. Season lightly with salt and pepper. Bring to boiling; reduce heat. Simmer, covered, for 30 to 35 minutes or till rice and chicken are tender.
● **Remove the chicken;** keep warm. Stir the peas into the rice mixture; heat through. Transfer the rice mixture to a serving bowl. Arrange the chicken on top of the rice mixture. Serves 6.

Nutrition information per serving: 447 cal., 30 g pro., 47 g carbo., 13 g fat, 65 mg chol., 452 mg sodium, 454 mg potassium, 3 g dietary fiber. U.S. RDA: 12% vit. A, 11% vit. C, 32% thiamine, 16% riboflavin, 53% niacin, 24% iron.

ENCHILADAS

1½ pounds ground beef
½ cup sliced green onions
1 to 2 tablespoons chili powder
2 10-ounce cans enchilada sauce
1½ teaspoons garlic salt
¼ to ½ teaspoon pepper
2 tablespoons cooking oil
12 corn tortillas
1 cup shredded cheddar cheese
  (4 ounces)
1 cup shredded Monterey Jack
  cheese (4 ounces)
Sliced green onion (optional)
Dairy sour cream (optional)

● **For meat filling,** in a large skillet cook the ground beef and the ½ cup green onions till the meat is brown and green onions are tender. Drain off fat.
● **Add** chili powder to meat mixture. Cook and stir for 1 minute.
● **Stir in** *one* can of the enchilada sauce, the garlic salt, and the pepper. Bring to boiling; reduce heat. Cover and simmer for 20 minutes, stirring occasionally.
● **Meanwhile,** in a heavy 10-inch skillet heat cooking oil.
● **Using tongs,** dip tortillas, one at a time, in hot oil for 10 seconds or just till limp, adding more oil, if needed. Drain on paper towels.
● **To assemble,** spoon a scant ¼ *cup* of the meat filling onto *each* tortilla. Sprinkle *each* with *2 teaspoons* of the cheddar cheese and *2 teaspoons* of the Monterey Jack cheese.
● **Fold the tortilla sides** over the meat filling to overlap slightly; secure with a wooden toothpick.

Top each tortilla with meat mixture and cheese.

● **Arrange tortillas** in a 13x9x2-inch baking dish.
● **Combine** the remaining meat filling and remaining can of enchilada sauce; pour over tortillas.
● **Bake, covered, in a 350° oven** about 20 minutes or till heated through.
● **Remove the cover.** Sprinkle with remaining cheese and bake about 5 minutes more or till cheese melts.
● **Remove the toothpicks** from tortillas before serving. Garnish with additional sliced green onion, if desired. Serve with sour cream, if desired. Makes 12 servings.
   Microwave directions: For meat filling, in a 2-quart microwave-safe casserole, crumble the ground beef. Stir in the ½ cup green onions. Micro-cook, covered, on 100% power (high) for 5 to 7 minutes or till the meat is brown and green onions are tender. Drain off fat. Stir in chili powder. Cook, covered, on high for 1 minute. Stir in *one* can of enchilada sauce, garlic salt, and pepper. Cook, covered, on high for 4 to 5 minutes or till bubbly, stirring once. Prepare the tortillas, assemble, and bake as directed.
   Nutrition information per serving: *271 cal., 18 g pro., 18 g carbo., 14 g fat, 58 mg chol., 695 mg sodium, 275 mg potassium, 3 g dietary fiber.*

ZUCCHINI-TOMATO CASSEROLE

4 small zucchini, sliced
1 small onion, chopped
2 tablespoons olive oil
1 16-ounce can stewed tomatoes
1 8-ounce can tomato sauce
¼ cup snipped fresh oregano *or*
  1 tablespoon dried oregano,
  crushed
4 ounces cheddar cheese
4 ounces Monterey Jack *or*
  mozzarella cheese

● **In a large skillet** cook zucchini and onion in hot oil for 2 minutes or till crisp-tender. *Do not overcook.* Add cut-up *undrained* tomatoes, tomato sauce, and oregano. Bring to boiling; reduce heat. Simmer, uncovered, 5 minutes.
● **Meanwhile,** slice *two* or *three* ¼-inch slices from *each* of the blocks of cheese; reserve slices for garnish. With a sharp knife cut remaining cheese into ¾-inch cubes. Stir cubed cheese into zucchini-tomato mixture. Transfer vegetable mixture to a 1½-quart casserole.
● **Bake in a 350° oven** about 10 minutes or till heated through. Arrange cheese slices on top. Let stand for 5 to 10 minutes or till the cheese melts. Makes 8 to 10 servings.
   Microwave directions: In a 2-quart microwave-safe casserole, micro-cook zucchini, onion, and oil, covered, on 100% power (high) for 6 to 9 minutes or till just tender. Add cut-up *undrained* tomatoes, tomato sauce, and oregano. Cook, covered, on high for 3 to 4 minutes or till mixture bubbles, stirring once. Slice and cube cheese as directed above. Stir cubed cheese into zucchini-tomato mixture. Cook, covered, on high for 2 to 4 minutes or till cheese just melts. *Do not stir.* Arrange reserved cheese slices on top. Cook, uncovered, on high for 45 seconds to 1½ minutes or till cheese melts. *Do not stir.*
   Nutrition information per serving: *174 cal., 9 g pro., 8 g carbo., 13 g fat, 27 mg chol., 481 mg sodium.*

FLAN

For six servings, halve the recipe and bake in an 8-inch round pan for 30 to 35 minutes. (Pictured on page 6.) —

1¾ cups sugar
8 eggs
4 cups milk
3 inches stick cinnamon
1½ teaspoons vanilla
Orange sections (optional)
Peeled papaya slices (optional)
Strawberry slices (optional)
Lime slices (optional)

● **To caramelize sugar,** in a small heavy skillet heat *¾ cup* of the sugar over medium heat till the sugar begins to melt *(do not stir).* Cook and stir for 4 to 5 minutes more or till the sugar turns a rich brown.
● **Remove skillet from heat** and immediately pour caramelized sugar into an oval 3-quart shallow casserole (approximately 13x9-inch oval dish).
● **Holding dish** with pot holders, quickly rotate dish so sugar coats the bottom and sides evenly. Cool.
● **Meanwhile, in a large mixing bowl** beat eggs with a rotary beater, gradually adding remaining 1 cup sugar.
● **In a saucepan** heat milk and stick cinnamon over medium heat till mixture bubbles. Remove cinnamon stick. Slowly add milk to egg mixture, stirring constantly. Stir in vanilla.
● **Place caramel-coated dish** in a 14x10x2-inch or 15½x10½x2-inch baking pan on an oven rack. Pour egg mix-

ture in dish. Pour the hottest tap water available into the baking pan around the dish to a depth of 1 inch.
● **Bake, uncovered, in a 325° oven** about 40 minutes or till a knife inserted halfway between the center and edge comes out clean.
● **Carefully remove dish** from hot water. Cool flan on a wire rack. Cover and place in the refrigerator.
● **To unmold flan,** loosen edges with a spatula. Slip end of spatula down sides to let air in. Invert flan onto a serving platter. Spoon caramel mixture that remains in dish on top.
● **Arrange** orange sections, papaya slices, strawberry slices, and lime slices beside the flan, if desired. Serves 12.
Nutrition information per serving: *190 cal., 7 g pro., 29 g carbo., 5 g fat, 189 mg chol., 87 mg sodium, 215 mg potassium. U.S. RDA: 10% vit. A, 24% vit. C, 15% riboflavin, 12% calcium.*

BANANA PUDDING

1½ cups milk
½ of a 14-ounce can (⅔ cup) *sweetened condensed* milk
½ cup margarine *or* butter
1 4-serving-size package *regular* vanilla pudding mix
36 vanilla wafers
5 ripe medium bananas, sliced
3 cups tiny marshmallows

● **In a medium saucepan** combine milk, sweetened condensed milk, margarine or butter, and vanilla pudding mix. Bring to boiling, stirring constantly. Reduce heat. Cook and stir for 4 to 5 minutes or till mixture is thick. Remove from heat; set aside.

● **Line** the bottom of a 2- or 2½-quart casserole with *12* of the vanilla wafers and *one-third* of the bananas. Top with about *1 cup* of the pudding mixture.
● **Repeat layers** 2 more times. Sprinkle the marshmallows over the top.
● **Bake in a 350° oven** for 12 to 15 minutes or till the marshmallows are light brown. Serve warm. Serves 10 to 12.
Nutrition information per serving: *393 cal., 5 g pro., 65 g carbo., 15 g fat, 16 mg chol., 270 mg sodium, 402 mg potassium, 1 g dietary fiber.*

Invite friends to share this scrumptious layered cookie and banana dessert.

GOOD FOOD, GOOD HEALTH

By Barbara Goldman

LOW-FAT STRATEGIES

Positive steps toward action

Smart choices for healthful eating: low-fat, high-nutrition foods

Learn to cook, eat, *and* enjoy low-fat foods! Because what you eat can cut your risk of heart disease and certain cancers. And, it can keep you slim. Here's how to translate the recommendation into good food choices.

Concentrate on plant foods

Rutgers University nutritionist Dr. Paul LaChance suggests a simple way to begin your quest for a more healthful diet: Eat meals with two-thirds plant foods to one-third animal foods. Now, that's an easy ratio to eat by.

Plant foods encompass fruits, vegetables, grains, and legumes. Animal foods include meats, poultry, fish, and dairy products, and they are important, too.

However, plant foods contain no cholesterol, virtually no fat, and are loaded with vitamins, minerals, and fiber. When they comprise the greater share of your diet, it's easier meeting nutrition guidelines of the American Heart Association, American Cancer Society, and other health organizations. Their guidelines suggest a maximum of 30 percent of daily calories from fat (at most 10 percent from saturated fat), and no more than 300 milligrams of cholesterol per day.

BEST FOODS FOR BEATING FAT

● **Eat five vegetables and fruits each day.** This simple step reaps complex benefits. Packed with vitamins and minerals, fruits and vegetables also are low in fat. Because they're filling, you're less likely to eat high-fat foods.

Some fruits (grapefruit, strawberries, and apples) also are high in soluble fiber, which has been shown to lower blood cholesterol levels. Vegetables, like carrots, potatoes, and broccoli, are great fiber providers, too.

● **Heap your plate high with legumes and grains.** Whole-grain breads and cereals, oat bran, brown rice, barley, dried peas, beans, and lentils are important—and underused by many Americans. They are excellent sources of complex carbohydrates and fiber.

● **Choose low-fat dairy products.** Dairy products are rich in protein and calcium, but low-fat versions are a smart choice for older children and adults. They contain far less saturated fat and cholesterol. One cup whole milk has about 8 grams fat; skim, only half a gram.

● **Choose small portions of fish, skinless chicken, and lean meat.** A 3-ounce cooked portion provides good amounts of protein, vitamins, and minerals, but is low in fat and cholesterol.

A fat and cholesterol primer

● **Cholesterol:** Essential in moderate amounts for good health, your body manufactures an adequate supply. It is carried in the blood in "packages" called lipoproteins. There are two types of lipoproteins:

LDL: Often referred to as "bad" cholesterol, LDL tends to clog arteries, leading to heart disease and stroke.

HDL: Usually called "good" cholesterol, HDL appears to clear fat and excess cholesterol from the blood.

Cholesterol in foods can raise your blood cholesterol level. Only animal foods contain cholesterol.

Fats in foods also influence your blood cholesterol. This includes:

● **Saturated fats:** Studies suggest these **raise** blood cholesterol. They're found in butter, milk, cheese, meat, palm and coconut oil, and shortening.

● **Polyunsaturated fats:** Found in some vegetable oils, these appear to **lower** blood cholesterol.

● **Monounsaturated fats:** These may be beneficial because some studies show that when they replace saturated fats, they **lower LDL without lowering HDL.** They're in vegetable sources such as olives and peanuts.

FISH FOR A HEALTHY HEART
Omega-3-rich seafood is the smart choice

It sounds crazy, but the fattier the fish, the better it is for you! Studies suggest that omega-3, the fatty acid found in fish oil, helps to protect your body from heart disease. Two to three servings of fish such as tuna or salmon per week should provide positive results.

POACHED TUNA WITH JULIENNE VEGETABLES
Poach tuna and vegetables in wine for a great-tasting omega-3-rich recipe—

- 1 medium red, yellow, *or* green sweet pepper, cut into thin strips (2½ cups)
- 2 medium carrots, cut into thin strips (2 cups)
- ¾ cup dry white wine
- 1½ teaspoons instant chicken bouillon granules
- ½ teaspoon dried dillweed
- 2 tuna steaks *or* salmon steaks (8 to 12 ounces total)
- ⅓ cup plain yogurt
- 1½ teaspoons cornstarch
- Cooked pasta (optional)

For poaching liquid, in a medium skillet combine peppers, carrots, wine,

Healthful eating made oh-h-h so good!

bouillon granules, dillweed, and ½ cup *water*. Bring to boiling; reduce heat. Cover and simmer for 5 minutes. Add fish to skillet; spoon poaching liquid over fish. Simmer, covered, for 4 to 6 minutes for each ½-inch thickness of fish or just till fish flakes easily with a fork. Using a slotted spatula, transfer fish and vegetables from skillet to dinner plates; cover and keep warm.

Strain poaching liquid using a strainer or cheesecloth; return ½ *cup* of the liquid to skillet. Combine yogurt and cornstarch; stir into liquid in skillet. Cook and stir till thickened and bubbly. Cook and stir for 2 minutes more. Spoon atop fish and vegetables. Serve with pasta. Makes 2 servings.

Nutrition information per serving: 296 cal., 29 g pro., 19 g carbo., 4 g fat, 60 mg chol., 377 mg sodium, 824 mg potassium, and 3 g dietary fiber. U.S. RDA: 475% vit. A, 141% vit. C, 16% riboflavin, 73% niacin, 17% iron.

WHERE TO FIND OMEGA-3
These fish are some of the best sources of omega-3 (more than 1 gram per each 4-ounce serving).
- Mackerel
- Herring
- Lake trout
- Albacore tuna (fresh and canned)
- Pink salmon
- Rainbow trout
- Swordfish

Source: Seafood and Health by Joyce A. Nettleton.

SOLUBLE FIBER: GOOD FOR ALL
Especially cholesterol watchers, diabetics

Suddenly, oat cereals are the hottest foods in the supermarket. Here's why: oats contain fiber, which is healthful for all of us. More important, however, oats (and other grains, fruits, beans, and vegetables) contain a significant amount of *soluble* fiber, which recent studies show lowers blood cholesterol and blood sugar levels.

The cholesterol connection
Research shows that soluble fiber reduces total cholesterol in the blood, especially LDL cholesterol (the "bad" cholesterol), thus reducing the risk of heart disease. The studies found that people who consumed a very high-fiber diet (up to 47 grams of dietary fiber daily) based on oat bran or beans re-

One a day for good reason.

duced their cholesterol levels by 13 to 19 percent. Although this daily fiber intake is quite high, the studies suggest that these foods, even when consumed in lesser amounts, can be beneficial.

The blood sugar connection
Soluble fiber slows the absorption of carbohydrates through the small intestine into the blood. For diabetics, this means that blood sugar may not rise and fall as drastically.

Soluble fiber sources
For most adults, 25 to 35 grams of total dietary fiber per day is recommended, with 25 to 30 percent of it soluble fiber (about 8 grams). The amount of soluble fiber is listed here.

½ cup peas, canned ....2.7 grams
½ cup kidney beans ....2.5 grams
⅓ cup dry oat bran ....2.0 grams
4 prunes...................................1.9 grams
½ cup lentils or corn ....1.7 grams
¾ cup cooked oatmeal...........1.4 grams
1 apple ....0.9 grams

COD CLASSICS
CATCH YOUR FAMILY'S FANCY

SPUNKY COD SANDWICH is a meal-in-a-roll.

PHOTOGRAPHS: SCOTT LITTLE

SERVE POACHED ITALIAN COD over corkscrew pasta.

SPUNKY COD SANDWICHES

- 12 ounces fresh *or* frozen cod fillets
- ¼ cup finely chopped celery
- ¼ cup mayonnaise *or* salad dressing
- 2 tablespoons sliced green onion
- 1 to 2 tablespoons horseradish mustard
- 1 tablespoon lemon juice
- ¼ teaspoon pepper
- Dash ground red pepper (optional)
- 4 individual French rolls
- 1 cup shredded lettuce

Thaw fish, if frozen. In a microwave-safe 8x8x2-inch baking dish arrange fillets with thicker portions toward edges of dish. Turn under any thin portions for an even thickness. Cover with vented microwave-safe clear plastic wrap. Micro-cook on 100% power (high) for 4 to 6 minutes or till fish just flakes with a fork, giving dish a half-turn after 2 minutes. (*Or*, pour ¾ inch of water into a large saucepan or Dutch oven. Place a steamer basket atop; bring water to boiling. Gently lay fish in basket, cutting to fit, if necessary. Cover; steam 6 to 8 minutes or till fish just flakes with a fork.)

Drain off liquid. Pat fish dry with paper towels. Place cod in a large bowl and flake with a fork. Stir in celery, mayonnaise, green onion, horseradish mustard, lemon juice, and peppers. Mix till combined. Cover; chill 1 hour.

Slice buns. Place ¼ *cup* of the lettuce inside *each* bun. Top *each* with about ⅓ *cup* of cod mixture. Makes 4 servings.

Nutrition information per sandwich: *289 cal., 19 g pro., 24 g carbo., 13 g fat, 52 mg chol., 403 mg sodium, 431 mg potassium, and 1 g dietary fiber. U.S. RDA: 15% thiamine, 10% riboflavin, 16% niacin, 10% iron.*

TODAY'S BEST: COD

- Cod, a saltwater fish, is firm and delicately flavored. The versatile fish makes a tasty meal poached, simmered in soup, crisp-fried, baked, or micro-cooked.
- This white fish, like most other fish, is right in step with good nutrition—it's low in fat and high in protein.
- When shopping for fresh fish, rely on your nose and eyes. Avoid fish with a strong fishy odor. Frozen fish should be frozen solid. Avoid packages with torn wrappers, or those with frost or blood visible inside or out.

POACHED ITALIAN COD

- 1 pound fresh *or* frozen cod fillets
- ¼ cup water
- 2 teaspoons cornstarch
- 2 tablespoons olive oil *or* cooking oil
- 2 cloves garlic, minced
- 2 large tomatoes, chopped
- 1 onion, cut into wedges
- 1 small green pepper, cut into thin strips
- ¼ cup dry white wine
- 1 teaspoon snipped fresh basil
- ¼ cup sliced, pitted ripe olives
- 2 cups hot cooked pasta
- Grated Parmesan cheese (optional)

Thaw fish, if frozen. Cut into 1-inch pieces. For sauce, stir together water and cornstarch; set aside. Preheat a large skillet over medium heat; add oil. Cook garlic in hot oil for 15 seconds. Add tomatoes, onion, green pepper, wine, basil, ¼ *teaspoon salt*, and ¼ *teaspoon pepper*. Cook and stir about 5 minutes or till onion and green pepper are tender.

Add the fish to the skillet. Bring to boiling; reduce heat. Cover and simmer gently for 4 to 6 minutes per ½-inch thickness of fish or till fish just flakes with a fork. Stir cornstarch mixture; add to skillet. Cook and stir till thickened and bubbly. Cook and stir for 2 minutes more. Stir in olives. Serve immediately over hot cooked pasta. Pass Parmesan cheese. Makes 4 servings.

Nutrition information per serving: *308 cal., 25 g pro., 28 g carbo., 10 g fat, 82 mg chol., 293 mg sodium, 764 mg potassium, and 4 g dietary fiber. U.S. RDA: 25% vit. A, 65% vit. C, 18% thiamine, 12% riboflavin, 21% niacin, 14% iron.*

FEBRUARY

THE MAGAZINE FOR AMERICAN FAMILIES

HOME SPIFF-UP ALMANAC

Better Homes and Gardens

FEBRUARY 1989
c$1.50

OUR 30 BEST RECIPES FROM 60 YEARS

10 PRIZEWINNING NEW HOUSES
NEW TRENDS, STYLES, AND IDEAS

AFFORDABLE REDECORATING
• A BEAUTIFUL BEDROOM GETAWAY
• FANCIFUL PAINTED FURNITURE FOR KIDS

•COLLEGE
PAYING FOR YOUR KIDS' EDUCATION

•GOOD FOOD GOOD HEALTH
EATING FOR TWO

THE KITCHEN YOU WANT TO COME HOME TO
APPLIANCES AND DESIGN FOR THE 1990s

30 BEST RECIPES FROM 60 YEARS

UPDATED FOR TODAY'S TASTES!

How do you say "Happy 60th birthday"? By remembering the best of the years! Here are the all-time greatest recipes to come out of our Test Kitchen. Come celebrate and enjoy them all!

By Barbara Johnson

THE '20s

Prosperity marked the early years of this rip-roaring decade. People reveled in a booming economy. Fun, frolic, and an interest in recipes abounded; this prompted our Test Kitchen's birth.

◀ APPLE DUMPLINGS DELUXE

One of the first recipes to be perfected in our spanking-new Testing-Tasting Kitchen, it's as homey and good today as it was back in 1929.

'20s TRENDS

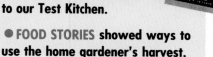

● **MORE PRECISE RECIPES** became the norm, thanks to our Test Kitchen.

● **FOOD STORIES** showed ways to use the home gardener's harvest.

22

THE '30s

Family life thrived in these lean, simple years.

'30s TRENDS

- **REFRIGERATORS** debuted, opening a new, modern world of cooking.

▲ ORANGE ICEBOX CAKE

Chilled gelatin recipes, like this light custard-filled dessert, became popular with the advent of "iceboxes."

▲ CHICKEN À LA KING

This homey family dish is as comforting today as in 1937. Smother chicken in sherry cream sauce; serve over toast.

THE '40s

Patriotism and rationing were the watchwords of the 1940s. The war years tried our nation's strength, and we proved steadfast. Home and family became more dear than ever. Victory gardens proliferated.

'40s TRENDS

- **POPULAR RECIPES** included waffles, canned soup casseroles, hearty breakfasts, chiffon cakes and pies, and dishes that stretched meat or saved sugar.
- **TIMESAVING MEALS** appealed to the many women who now began working outside the home.

▲ HAMBURGER PIE WITH LATTICE CHEESE CRUST

One of our most requested recipes originally topped with mashed potatoes. The lattice crust is a later version.

▲ CORNFLAKE WAFFLES WITH HONEY BUTTER SAUCE

Waffles were common supper fare in the '40s. This one is tender, light, and airy, with a toasty corn flavor.

▲ NO-KNEAD FAN ROLLS

Like cooks of the '40s, today's cooks want shortcuts. This sweet yeast bread has them! There's no kneading; plus, you can mix the dough the day ahead.

▲ LEMON CHIFFON PIE

A family restaurant in Iowa supposedly served the first "mile-high" chiffon pie. Before long, this smooth, light dessert caught on across the country.

▲REGAL CHEESECAKE

This cheesecake may well be the best ever published! So rich and creamy, yet airy and fluffy. As the editors said in 1953: "It's absolutely luscious!"

THE '50s

Happy days were here again! People had time and money to experience novel foods. Grocery stores blossomed. Eating was fun and exciting.

'50S TRENDS

● RAGE FOODS: sour cream, cheesecake, chips and dip, pizza, and salads.

● ELECTRIC APPLIANCES (such as blenders, mixers, can openers, and skillets) bloomed.

◀HAWAIIAN LEMONADE

Hawaii became a state in 1959. Eager to sample the new state's cuisine, folks on the mainland tried recipes like this refreshing, triple-fruit cooler.

STOCKHOLM POTATO SALAD▶

Americans were fascinated with Scandinavian cooking in the '50s. Apples, potatoes, and dill were common ingredients, as this salad reveals.

◀PAPRIKA CHICKEN WITH SOUR CREAM GRAVY

When commercial sour cream was introduced, enterprising cooks stirred it into recipes, such as this gravy.

AVOCADO DIP▶

Thanks to the electric blender, creamy dips could be mixed up in jig time, as they said in the '50s!

THE '60s

Americans fervently searched out and embraced the new and different: far-out clothes, alternate lifestyles, exotic foods and cooking.

'60s TRENDS

- **FOREIGN FOODS** and cooking became popular as Americans traveled abroad.

- **MORE MEN** began stepping into the kitchen. Their specialties were likely to be barbecues and salads.

▲DEVILED SWISS STEAK

Round steak was a popular family feast in the '60s. This piquant dinner is liberally seasoned with dry mustard, then simmered to tender, juicy perfection.

◀SWISS CORN BAKE

"This creamy corn is bound to become a vegetable 'classic,'" the '67 recipe read. It has! Full of cheese, it's one of our editors' favorite recipes today.

CARAMEL PECAN ROLLS▶

Cooks of the '60s could have fresh breakfast rolls without last-minute hassle. The shaped buns rise in the refrigerator up to 24 hours.

◀TRI-LEVEL BROWNIES

Two moist chocolate layers over a chewy oat base add up to triple goodness. It's no wonder a cookie this irresistible has stood the test of time!

COBB SALAD▶

As interest in eating out grew, people wanted to try restaurant recipes at home. This classic salad is from the renowned Brown Derby in California.

THE '70s

An energy crisis and inflation made economy uppermost in consumers' minds—especially when it came to shopping for food and cooking. Consumers took on the challenge with gusto: They were out to get the most for their money.

◀FETTUCCINE ALLA CARBONARA

Pasta's fame rose to an all-time high with the likes of this recipe. The smooth sauce delicately coats every tender strand of noodle. It's divine!

◀CHOCOLATE REVEL BARS

Our Test Kitchen home economists cherish the '70s for nurturing this decadent recipe. It's such a favorite, they still can't have a party without it!

'70s TRENDS

● **SMART SHOPPING** and cooking ideas to stretch meat and other expensive foods dominated our food stories.

● **THE "DO-YOUR-OWN-THING"** generation had food hobbies: making yogurt, wine, and liqueur.

● **INTEREST IN NUTRITION** began with low-calorie cooking, whole grain recipes, and such "natural" foods as granola and carob.

▲ STIR-FRY PORK AND JICAMA

Almost simultaneously, Chinese cooking and the wok became hot. As Americans learned to stir-fry, they also experimented with unusual ingredients: jicama, gingerroot, and Chinese cabbage in this case.

◄ ZUCCHINI STUFFING CASSEROLE

Vegetable gardening was "in." When gardeners discovered prolific zucchini, they were hungry for new recipes. This easy side dish was an instant hit.

SPAGHETTI PIE ►

The novel spaghetti crust caused this main dish to become a "rage" recipe. Readers requested it from us over and over, and shared it with many friends.

◄ RAINBOW FRUIT COMPOTE

More varieties and better qualities of fresh fruit became available in supermarkets. That spurred more fruit recipes, like this layered creation.

EARLY COLONIAL BREAD ►

As in the early days of our nation, multigrain breads were commonplace in the '70s. This wholesome loaf has cornmeal, whole wheat, and rye.

THE '80s

We've come back home. We spend free time there, giving our families priority. Yet, dedicated to careers, we find ourselves ever juggling home, family, and job. We want the best of all things—and the way we eat is no exception.

◄ CHOCOLATE MOUSSE CAKE

Exquisite chocolate is "in." Next time you deserve a chocolate reward, sink your teeth into this torte. It's the ultimate—sinful, rich, and indulgent.

'80s TRENDS

● **MICROWAVE COOKING** reigns supreme, making meal preparation faster and easier than ever.

● **DESIRE FOR GOOD HEALTH** affects the decisions we make about what to eat and how to live.

● **QUICK AND EASY MEALS** are a must, whether it's a 20-minute dinner, frozen food, or take-out item.

● **GRANDMA'S HOME COOKING** enchants us again. We embrace the comfort these foods give.

● **WE LIKE TO COOK,** and often create extravagant meals as a means of relaxing on the weekend.

▲TURKEY FAJITAS WITH GREEN PEA GUACAMOLE

Before Tex-Mex cooking became popular, most Americans hadn't heard of fajitas. Suddenly they were all the craze. In our healthful version of the trendy dish, turkey and peas replace beef and avocado.

◄WINE-SAUCED SALMON AND RICE MEDLEY

During the '80s, we discovered you *can* serve great-tasting, nutritious dinners that take 30 minutes or less to make. This meal for six is one of them.

SIZZLING CHEESE SALAD▶

When there's time to cook, we like to go all out. This classy salad is a real show-stopper with a heavenly flavor. It's worth every ounce of effort.

◄MUSTARD-GLAZED PORK CHOPS

We like it hot and spicy! Team hot oriental dry mustard *and* ground red pepper for a glaze with kick. It'll leave your taste buds tingling with delight.

CARROT CAKE▶ WITH PINEAPPLE

Home-style cake with cream cheese frosting—now microwave easy.

APPLE DUMPLINGS DELUXE

A lot faster and easier to make than classic dumplings: Roll up apples, sugar, and spice in a tender sour-cream pastry for an all-American treat—

- 1 beaten egg
- 1 8-ounce carton dairy sour cream
- 2 cups all-purpose flour
- 2 tablespoons sugar
- 2 teaspoons baking powder
- ¼ teaspoon baking soda
- ¼ teaspoon salt
- 4 cups thinly sliced, peeled cooking apples
- ¼ cup sugar
- ½ teaspoon ground cinnamon
- ¼ teaspoon ground nutmeg
- 1½ cups water
- 1¼ cups packed brown sugar
- 1 cup sugar
- 2 tablespoons cornstarch
- 2 tablespoons lemon juice
- 2 tablespoons margarine *or* butter
- Light cream *or* ice cream (optional)

● **For dough,** in a medium mixing bowl combine egg and sour cream. In a small mixing bowl stir together flour, the 2 tablespoons sugar, baking powder, baking soda, and salt; add to sour-cream mixture. Mix well.
● **On a lightly floured surface, roll** dough into a 12-inch square. Spread apples atop dough. In a small mixing bowl combine the ¼ cup sugar, cinnamon, and nutmeg; sprinkle atop the apples. Carefully roll up the dough. Cut into twelve 1-inch-thick slices.
● **Place slices,** cut side down, in a greased 13x9x2-inch baking pan. Stir together water, brown sugar, the 1 cup sugar, cornstarch, and lemon juice; pour over slices in pan. Dot with margarine or butter.
● **Bake,** uncovered, in a 350° oven for 35 to 40 minutes or till golden. To serve, spoon warm dumplings and juices into individual dessert dishes. Serve with light cream or ice cream, if desired. Makes 12 servings.

Nutrition information per serving: 341 cal., 3 g pro., 69 g carbo., 7 g fat, 31 mg chol., 163 mg sodium, 179 mg potassium, 1 g dietary fiber. U.S. RDA: 10% thiamine, 10% iron.

ORANGE ICEBOX CAKE

- 1 cup sugar
- 2 envelopes unflavored gelatin
- 4 teaspoons cornstarch
- 2¼ cups milk
- 2 beaten eggs
- 1 teaspoon finely shredded orange peel
- 2 cups orange juice
- 2 3-ounce packages (24) ladyfingers, split
- Whipped cream (optional)
- Peeled orange slices, halved, *and* unpeeled orange slices, quartered (optional)

● **For filling,** in a 3-quart saucepan stir together sugar, gelatin, and cornstarch. Stir in milk. Cook and stir over medium heat till gelatin dissolves and mixture is thickened and bubbly. Cook and stir for 2 minutes more. Remove from heat.
● **Gradually stir** about *1 cup* of filling into eggs. Return all of the mixture to saucepan. Cook and stir 2 minutes more. Remove from heat. Stir in orange peel and juice. Transfer to a bowl. Cover surface with clear plastic wrap. Chill till partially set (consistency of unbeaten egg whites), stirring occasionally.
● **Line** bottom and sides of an 8-inch springform pan with about *32* of the ladyfinger halves. Spoon in *half* of the filling. Top with a layer of ladyfinger halves (about *eight*). Repeat layers with remaining filling and ladyfinger halves. Cover and chill in the refrigerator for several hours or overnight.
● **To serve,** remove sides of springform pan. Garnish with whipped cream and orange slices, if desired. Serves 8 to 12.

Microwave directions (not recommended in low-wattage microwave ovens): In a 3-quart microwave-safe casserole mix sugar, gelatin, and cornstarch. Stir in milk. Micro-cook, uncovered, on 100% power (high) for 8 to 10 minutes or till thickened and bubbly, stirring after every minute. Cook, uncovered, on high 1 minute more. Gradually stir about *1 cup* of hot mixture into eggs; return all of mixture to casserole. Cook, uncovered, on high for 1 minute, stirring after 30 seconds. Stir in orange peel and juice. Cover surface with clear plastic wrap. Continue as directed.

Nutrition information per serving: 265 cal., 7 g pro., 50 g carbo., 4 g fat, 150 mg chol., 69 mg sodium, 257 mg potassium, 1 g dietary fiber. U.S. RDA: 42% vit. C, 14% riboflavin, 11% calcium.

CHICKEN À LA KING

We think this version tastes even better than the original, with less egg and light cream in place of heavy cream—

- ½ cup sliced fresh mushrooms
- ¼ cup chopped green pepper
- 2 tablespoons margarine *or* butter
- 4 teaspoons all-purpose flour
- ¼ teaspoon salt
- 1 cup light cream *or* milk
- 1 beaten egg yolk
- 1½ cups chopped cooked chicken
- 1 tablespoon sliced pimiento
- 1 tablespoon dry sherry
- 1½ teaspoons lemon juice
- ¼ teaspoon paprika
- 3 English muffins, split and toasted, *or* 6 slices toasted bread

● **In saucepan cook** mushrooms and green pepper in hot margarine or butter till just tender. Stir in flour and salt. Add cream or milk all at once. Cook and stir till thickened and bubbly.
● **Gradually stir** ½ *cup* of the hot mixture into egg yolk; return all of the mixture to the saucepan. Cook and stir over medium heat just till mixture returns to boiling. Add chicken, pimiento, sherry, lemon juice, and paprika; cook and stir till heated through. Serve over English muffins. Makes 3 servings.

Microwave directions: In a 1½-quart microwave-safe casserole micro-cook mushrooms, green pepper, and margarine or butter, covered, on 100% power (high) for 2 to 4 minutes (low-wattage oven: 3 to 5 minutes) or till tender. Stir in flour and salt. Stir in cream or milk. Cook, uncovered, on high 2 to 4 minutes (low-wattage oven: 3 to 5 minutes) or till thickened and bubbly, stirring after every minute.

Gradually stir ½ *cup* of the hot mixture into the egg yolk; return all of the mixture to the casserole. Cook, uncovered, on high for 30 seconds. Stir in chicken, pimiento, sherry, lemon juice, and paprika. Cook, uncovered, on high for 1½ to 3 minutes (low-wattage oven: 3 to 5 minutes) or till heated through, stirring after every minute. Serve as directed above.

Nutrition information per serving: 596 cal., 29 g pro., 45 g carbo., 32 g fat, 208 mg chol., 409 mg sodium, 426 mg potassium, 4 g dietary fiber. U.S. RDA: 27% vit. A, 26% vit. C, 18% thiamine, 24% riboflavin, 42% niacin, 12% calcium, 16% iron.

HAMBURGER PIE WITH LATTICE CHEESE CRUST

     1 pound ground beef
     1 large onion, chopped (1 cup)
    ¾ cup chopped celery
    ⅓ cup chopped green pepper
     1 clove garlic, minced
     2 teaspoons chili powder
    ⅛ teaspoon pepper
     1 10¾-ounce can condensed tomato soup
     1 cup loose-pack frozen cut green beans
     1 cup all-purpose flour
     1 teaspoon baking powder
    ⅛ teaspoon salt
    ¼ cup finely shredded American cheese
     2 tablespoons shortening
    ⅓ cup milk

● **In a large skillet cook** beef, onion, celery, green pepper, and garlic till beef is brown and vegetables are tender. Drain off fat.
● **Stir in** chili powder and pepper; cook for 1 minute. Add soup and green beans; bring just to boiling. Transfer to an 8x1½-inch round baking dish.
● **Meanwhile, for crust,** in a mixing bowl stir together flour, baking powder, and salt. Cut in cheese and shortening. Add milk; mix well. Form into a ball.
● **On a lightly floured surface roll** crust into a 9-inch square. Cut into eighteen ½-inch-wide strips. Weave strips atop casserole, forming a lattice crust. Trim strips at the casserole edge; press down slightly.
● **Bake,** uncovered, in a 425° oven 15 minutes or till golden. Serves 4.

Microwave directions: In an 8x1½-inch microwave-safe round baking dish crumble beef; add onion, celery, green pepper, and garlic. Cover; micro-cook on 100% power (high) 5 to 7 minutes (low-wattage oven: 6 to 8 minutes) or till no pink remains; stir once. Drain fat. Stir in chili powder and pepper. Cover; cook on high 1 minute. Stir in soup and green beans. Cover; cook on high 4 to 6 minutes (low-wattage oven: 6 to 8 minutes) or till bubbly; stir twice. Continue with crust as directed.

Nutrition information per serving: 528 cal., 28 g pro., 43 g carbo., 27 g fat, 85 mg chol., 867 mg sodium, 695 mg potassium, 3 g dietary fiber. U.S. RDA: 26% vit. A, 78% vit. C, 28% thiamine, 26% riboflavin, 37% niacin, 18% calcium, 33% iron.

CORNFLAKE WAFFLES WITH HONEY BUTTER SAUCE

    1¼ cups all-purpose flour
    ¾ cup finely crushed cornflakes
     1 tablespoon baking powder
    ¼ teaspoon salt
     2 slightly beaten egg yolks
    1¾ cups milk
    ½ cup cooking oil
     2 egg whites
Sliced strawberries and bananas (optional)
Honey Butter Sauce

● **In a mixing bowl combine** flour, cornflakes, baking powder, and salt. In a small bowl combine egg yolks, milk, and oil; stir into flour mixture.
● **In a small mixer bowl beat** egg whites till stiff peaks form (tips stand straight); fold into the flour mixture. (*Do not* overmix.)
● **For each waffle, pour** batter onto grids of a preheated, lightly greased waffle baker. Close lid quickly; *do not* open during baking. Use a fork to help lift the baked waffle off of the grid.
● **Repeat with remaining batter.** To keep waffles warm, place in a single layer on a wire rack set on a baking sheet in a warm oven. Serve with strawberries, bananas, if desired, and Honey Butter Sauce. Makes 4 (8-inch round) waffles.

Honey Butter Sauce: In a small heavy saucepan warm 1 cup *honey* over low heat. Stir in ¼ cup *margarine or butter,* ¼ teaspoon *ground cinnamon,* and dash *ground nutmeg* till margarine is melted. Serve warm. Makes 1¼ cups.

Nutrition information per waffle with 2 tablespoons Honey Butter Sauce: 684 cal., 12 g pro., 77 g carbo., 37 g fat, 144 mg chol., 696 mg sodium, 270 mg potassium, 1 g dietary fiber. U.S. RDA: 25% vit. A, 11% vit. C, 35% thiamine, 39% riboflavin, 25% niacin, 30% calcium, 19% iron.

NO-KNEAD FAN ROLLS

    3¼ cups all-purpose flour
     1 package active dry yeast
     1 cup milk
    ¼ cup sugar
    ¼ cup shortening
     1 egg
    ½ teaspoon finely shredded lemon peel
    ½ cup packed brown sugar
    ½ cup raisins
     1 teaspoon ground cinnamon
     2 tablespoons margarine *or* butter, softened
Powdered Sugar Icing

● **Mix** *1¼ cups* of the flour and the yeast. Heat milk, sugar, shortening, and 1 teaspoon *salt* just till warm (120° to 130°) and shortening almost melts; stir constantly. Add to flour mixture with egg and lemon peel. Beat on low ½ minute, scraping bowl constantly. Beat on high 3 minutes. Stir in remaining flour. (Dough will be soft.) Place in greased bowl. Cover; chill 2 to 24 hours.
● **To shape,** let dough stand at room temperature 10 minutes.
● **For filling, combine** brown sugar, raisins, and cinnamon.
● **On a lightly floured surface roll** dough into a 16x12-inch rectangle. Cut in half lengthwise, forming two 16x6-inch rectangles. Spread *half* of the margarine over *each* rectangle. Sprinkle *half* of the filling down the center third of *each* rectangle. Fold edges of dough over filling so each rectangle is three layers thick. Pat lightly to flatten. Cut *each* into four 4-inch-wide rolls.
● **Place** rolls on a greased, foil-lined baking sheet. Using kitchen shears, cut 5 crosswise slashes in *each* roll from one long edge to, but not through, opposite edge. Spread slashes apart slightly, forming fans. Cover; let rise in warm place till double (about 45 minutes).
● **Bake** in a 350° oven for 20 minutes or till golden. Transfer to a wire rack. Drizzle with Powdered Sugar Icing. Serve rolls warm or cool. Makes 8 rolls.

Powdered Sugar Icing: Stir together 1¼ cups sifted *powdered sugar* and enough *cream or milk* (2 to 3 tablespoons) to make icing for drizzling.

Nutrition information per roll: 464 cal., 8 g pro., 83 g carbo., 12 g fat, 39 mg chol., 332 mg sodium, 245 mg potassium, 2 g dietary fiber. U.S. RDA: 25% thiamine, 20% riboflavin, 16% niacin, 18% iron.

LEMON CHIFFON PIE

Chill the filling before spooning it into the pastry shell so it mounds high for a fluffy pie—

- ½ cup sugar
- 1 envelope unflavored gelatin
- ⅛ teaspoon salt
- 4 well-beaten egg yolks
- ½ cup cold water
- 1 teaspoon finely shredded lemon peel
- ½ cup lemon juice
- 4 egg whites
- ½ cup sugar
- 1 baked 9-inch pastry shell
- Lemon slices, quartered (optional)

● **For filling,** combine ½ cup sugar, gelatin, and salt. Stir in egg yolks, water, lemon peel, and juice. Cook and stir over medium heat till gelatin dissolves and mixture is thickened and bubbly. Remove from heat. Chill to consistency of corn syrup, stirring occasionally. Remove from refrigerator (mixture will continue to set).
● **Beat** egg whites till soft peaks form (tips curl). Gradually add ½ cup sugar, beating till stiff peaks form (tips stand straight).
● **When filling is partially set** (consistency of unbeaten egg whites), fold in beaten egg whites. Chill till mixture mounds when spooned. Spoon into pastry shell. Chill for several hours or till firm. Garnish with lemon slices, if desired. Makes 8 servings.

Microwave directions: In a 1½-quart microwave-safe casserole stir together ½ cup sugar, gelatin, and salt. Stir in water, lemon peel, and lemon juice. Micro-cook, uncovered, on 100% power (high) for 3 to 5 minutes (low-wattage oven: 5 to 8 minutes) or till the gelatin is dissolved and the mixture boils, stirring once. Gradually stir about *half* of the hot mixture into egg yolks; return mixture to the casserole. Cook, uncovered, on high 1½ to 2½ minutes (low-wattage oven: 3 to 5 minutes) or till thickened, stirring every 30 seconds. Chill and continue as directed.

Nutrition information per serving: 255 cal., 5 g pro., 36 g carbo., 10 g fat, 136 mg chol., 201 mg sodium, and 62 mg potassium.

REGAL CHEESECAKE

Loosening the pan sides after baking helps keep the cheesecake edges from cracking, though sometimes the top will still crack. That's normal—

- 1 6-ounce package zwieback
- ¼ cup margarine *or* butter, melted
- 2 tablespoons sugar
- 2 8-ounce packages cream cheese
- 1 cup sugar
- 2 eggs
- 3 egg yolks
- 2 8-ounce cartons dairy sour cream
- 1 teaspoon lemon juice
- 1 teaspoon vanilla
- 3 egg whites
- 6 to 8 whole strawberries, hulled and halved
- ½ cup red currant jelly

● **Finely crush** zwieback; stir in margarine and the 2 tablespoons sugar. Press onto the bottom and 1½ inches up sides of a greased 9-inch springform pan.
● **In a large mixer bowl beat** cream cheese till smooth. Add the 1 cup sugar; beat till fluffy. Add whole eggs and egg yolks; beat on low speed just till mixed. Stir in sour cream, lemon juice, and vanilla. Transfer sour cream mixture to another large bowl. Thoroughly wash the large mixer bowl and beaters.
● **In the large mixer bowl beat** egg whites till stiff peaks form (tips stand straight). Fold beaten whites into sour cream mixture. Transfer to prepared pan. (Filling is higher than crust.)
● **Bake** in a 350° oven 60 to 65 minutes or till center is almost set. Cool on wire rack 5 to 10 minutes. Using a thin metal spatula, loosen cheesecake from sides of pan. Cool 30 minutes more; remove sides of pan. Cool completely. Cover; chill several hours or overnight.
● **About 1 hour before serving,** arrange strawberries in a circle on top of cheesecake. In a small saucepan heat jelly over low heat just till melted; spoon over strawberries and center of cheesecake. Chill 30 to 60 minutes or till jelly sets. Halve another whole strawberry and use as a garnish, if desired. Makes 16 servings.

Nutrition information per serving: 337 cal., 6 g pro., 31 g carbo., 22 g fat, 131 mg chol., 179 mg sodium, 147 mg potassium, 1 g dietary fiber. U.S. RDA: 17% vit. A, 11% riboflavin.

HAWAIIAN LEMONADE

- 1 6-ounce can frozen lemonade concentrate
- 1 12-ounce can apricot nectar, chilled
- 2 6-ounce cans unsweetened pineapple juice, chilled
- 1 12-ounce can ginger ale, chilled
- Fresh pineapple wedges, quartered lime slices, *and* maraschino cherries

● **In a large bowl or pitcher combine** lemonade concentrate and 1 can *water.* Add apricot nectar and pineapple juice. Slowly pour ginger ale down side of bowl or pitcher. Stir gently with an up-and-down motion to mix.
● **Serve** over ice with pineapple, lime, and cherries skewered on toothpicks. Makes 5 (8-ounce) servings.

Nutrition information per serving: 208 cal., 1 g pro., 54 g carbo., 0 g fat, 0 mg chol., 4 mg sodium, 251 mg potassium, 2 g dietary fiber. U.S. RDA: 19% vit. A, 111% vit. C.

STOCKHOLM POTATO SALAD

- 1 8-ounce carton dairy sour cream
- ¼ cup finely chopped onion
- ¼ cup light cream *or* milk
- 2 tablespoons snipped fresh dillweed *or* 2 teaspoons dried dillweed
- 2 teaspoons prepared mustard
- ½ teaspoon salt
- 1 cup chopped red apple
- 1 tablespoon lemon juice
- 3 cups sliced cooked potatoes
- ½ cup sliced celery

● **For dressing,** stir together the sour cream, onion, light cream or milk, dillweed, mustard, and salt.
● **In a bowl sprinkle** chopped apple with lemon juice. Halve any large potato slices; stir potatoes and celery into apple. Pour dressing over; toss lightly.
● **Cover and chill** at least 2 hours. Serve in a bowl lined with romaine leaves and garnish with apple slices and dill sprigs, if desired. Makes 5 or 6 side-dish servings.

Nutrition information per serving: 225 cal., 4 g pro., 27 g carbo., 12 g fat, 28 mg chol., 286 mg sodium, 528 mg potassium, 2 g dietary fiber. U.S. RDA: 10% vit. A, 20% vit. C.

PAPRIKA CHICKEN WITH SOUR CREAM GRAVY

    1   2½- to 3-pound broiler-fryer
        chicken, cut up
    ¼   cup all-purpose flour
    2   tablespoons cooking oil
    ¾   cup water
    ½   cup chopped onion
    2   teaspoons paprika
    ½   teaspoon salt
    1   tablespoon all-purpose flour
    1   8-ounce carton dairy sour cream
    1   teaspoon finely shredded
        lemon peel
Hot cooked spaetzle *or* rice

● **Rinse chicken;** pat dry. Place the ¼ cup flour in a plastic bag. Add chicken pieces, a few at a time, shaking to coat.
● **In a large skillet cook** chicken in hot oil about 10 minutes or till brown, turning to brown evenly. Drain off fat. Add water, onion, paprika, and salt. Cover; cook 35 to 40 minutes or till no pink remains in chicken. Transfer chicken to platter, reserving juices; cover chicken to keep warm.
● **For sour cream gravy, stir** the 1 tablespoon flour into sour cream. Stir mixture into reserved juices in skillet. Cook and stir till thickened and bubbly. Cook and stir for 1 minute more. Stir in lemon peel. Serve gravy over chicken and spaetzle or rice. Makes 6 servings.

Nutrition information per serving: *387 cal., 27 g pro., 28 g carbo., 18 g fat, 82 mg chol., 265 mg sodium, 328 mg potassium, 2 g dietary fiber. U.S. RDA: 15% vit. A, 16% thiamine, 17% riboflavin, 40% niacin, 12% iron.*

AVOCADO DIP

    3   slices bacon, crisp-cooked
        and drained
    ½   cup mayonnaise *or* salad
        dressing
    1   small onion slice
    1   tablespoon lemon juice
    5   drops bottled hot pepper sauce
Dash salt
    1   medium avocado, halved,
        pitted, peeled, and cut up
        (about 1 cup)
Zucchini slices *and/or* sweet red
    pepper strips

● **Place** bacon in a blender container or food processor bowl; cover and pulse on/off till bacon is coarsely chopped. Remove bacon; set aside.
● **In same container** combine mayonnaise, onion, lemon juice, hot pepper sauce, and salt. Cover; blend or process about 10 seconds or till combined. Gradually add avocado, blending or processing till smooth.
● **Transfer** to a serving bowl; sprinkle with bacon. Cover; chill up to 1 hour, if desired. Serve with zucchini and sweet pepper. Makes about 1½ cups.

Nutrition information per 2 tablespoons: *108 cal., 1 g pro., 2 g carbo., 11 g fat, 7 mg chol., 96 mg sodium, 131 mg potassium, 1 g dietary fiber.*

DEVILED SWISS STEAK

For the photograph on page 25, we served this hearty entrée with steamed baby vegetables and broccoli flowerets—

    2   tablespoons all-purpose flour
    1   tablespoon dry mustard
    ½   teaspoon pepper
    1½ to 2 pounds beef bottom round
        steak, cut 1-inch thick
    2   tablespoons cooking oil
    1   tablespoon Worcester-
        shire sauce
    1   teaspoon instant beef
        bouillon granules
    2   4-ounce cans whole mushrooms,
        drained

● **Combine** flour, mustard, and pepper. Sprinkle *half* of the flour mixture over one side of steak; cover with clear plastic wrap and pound with flat side of meat mallet. Repeat on other side with remaining flour mixture.
● **In a large skillet brown** steak on both sides in hot oil. Drain off fat. Combine Worcestershire sauce, bouillon granules, and 1 cup *water;* pour over steak. Spread mushrooms over steak. Bring to boiling; reduce heat. Cover and simmer for 1¼ to 1½ hours or till tender.

● **Transfer** steak and mushrooms to a serving platter. Skim fat from juices; spoon *some* of the juices over steak. Pass remaining juices. Serves 6 to 8.

Nutrition information per serving: *255 cal., 28 g pro., 4 g carbo., 13 g fat, 82 mg chol., 269 mg sodium, 316 mg potassium. U.S. RDA: 14% riboflavin, 21% niacin, 19% iron.*

SWISS CORN BAKE

If you're using frozen corn, use the ¼ teaspoon salt. For fresh corn, use ½ teaspoon salt or season to taste—

    3   cups fresh cut corn (from 6 ears)
        or one 16-ounce package frozen
        whole kernel corn
    2   beaten eggs
    1½ cups shredded process Swiss
        cheese (6 ounces)
    2   5-ounce cans (1⅓ cups)
        evaporated milk
    ¼   cup finely chopped onion
    ¼   to ½ teaspoon salt
Dash pepper
    ¾   cup soft whole wheat *or* white
        bread crumbs (1 slice)
    2   tablespoons margarine *or* butter,
        melted
Sweet red pepper rings
    (optional)
Celery leaves (optional)

● **If using fresh cut corn, cook** in a medium saucepan in 1½ cups boiling *water* 5 to 8 minutes or till crisp-tender; drain. (If using frozen corn, cook according to package directions; drain.)
● **In a medium mixing bowl combine** eggs, *1 cup* of the cheese, evaporated milk, onion, salt, and pepper. Stir in cooked, drained corn.
● **Transfer** mixture to a 9-inch quiche dish or an 8-inch round baking dish. Place dish on a baking sheet. Bake in a 350° oven for 20 minutes.
● **Toss** bread crumbs with remaining cheese and margarine or butter; sprinkle the mixture in a ring over the corn mixture. Bake 5 to 10 minutes more or till golden and bubbly. Let stand 5 minutes. Top with sweet pepper and celery leaves, if desired. Makes 8 servings.

Nutrition information per serving: *245 cal., 13 g pro., 19 g carbo., 14 g fat, 101 mg chol., 318 mg sodium, 350 mg potassium, 2 g dietary fiber. U.S. RDA: 13% vit. A, 11% thiamine, 17% riboflavin, 33% calcium.*

CARAMEL PECAN ROLLS

Treat yourself to the tantalizing aroma and flavor of fresh-baked sticky buns. Simply mix and shape the night before; bake the next morning—

  6 to 6½ cups all-purpose flour
  2 packages active dry yeast
2¼ cups milk
  3 tablespoons shortening
  2 tablespoons sugar
  2 teaspoons salt
  ½ cup margarine *or* butter
  1 cup packed brown sugar
  2 tablespoons light corn syrup
  1 cup pecan halves
  ¼ cup margarine *or* butter, softened
  ½ cup sugar
  1 teaspoon ground cinnamon

● **In a large mixer bowl stir together** 2½ cups of the flour and all of the yeast.
● **In a small saucepan heat** milk, shortening, the 2 tablespoons sugar, and salt just till warm (120° to 130°) and shortening is almost melted, stirring constantly.
● **Add** the milk mixture to the flour mixture. Beat with an electric mixer on low speed for 30 seconds, scraping sides of bowl constantly. Beat on high speed for 3 minutes. Using a wooden spoon, stir in as much of the remaining flour as you can.
● **Turn out** onto a lightly floured surface. Knead in enough of the remaining flour to make a moderately soft dough that is smooth and elastic (3 to 5 minutes). Shape into a ball. Cover and let rest for 20 minutes.
● **In a small saucepan melt** the ½ cup margarine or butter; stir in brown sugar and light corn syrup. Cook and stir just till combined.

● **Distribute** brown sugar mixture evenly in bottoms of 36 well-greased muffin pans. Sprinkle pecans evenly on bottoms of pans. Set aside.
● **Divide** dough in half. On a lightly floured surface, roll *one* dough half into an 18x10-inch rectangle.
● **Spread** with *half* of the ¼ cup margarine or butter.
● **Combine** the ½ cup sugar and cinnamon; sprinkle *half* of the sugar mixture over dough.
● **Roll up,** starting from one of the long sides. Seal edges.
● **To cut into 1-inch slices,** place a piece of thread under the roll where you want to make the cut. Pull the thread up around the sides. Crisscross the thread across the top of the roll, pulling quickly as though tying a knot. Place rolls, cut side down, in prepared muffin pans.
● **Repeat** with the remaining half of the dough, margarine or butter, and sugar mixture.
● **Cover** with lightly oiled waxed paper, then with clear plastic wrap. Chill in the refrigerator for 2 to 24 hours.
● **To bake,** let stand, covered, 20 minutes at room temperature. Puncture any surface bubbles with a greased wooden toothpick. Bake in a 375° oven for 20 minutes or till golden. Invert onto a wire rack. Serve warm. Makes 36 rolls.

Nutrition information per roll: 189 cal., 3 g pro., 28 g carbo., 8 g fat, 1 mg chol., 174 mg sodium, 87 mg potassium, and 1 g dietary fiber. U.S. RDA: 12% thiamine.

TRI-LEVEL BROWNIES

Moist, gooey, and good! Serve with a scoop of your favorite ice cream—

  1 cup quick-cooking rolled oats
  ½ cup all-purpose flour
  ½ cup packed brown sugar
  ¼ teaspoon baking soda
  ½ cup margarine *or* butter, melted
  1 egg
  ¾ cup sugar
  ⅔ cup all-purpose flour
  ¼ cup milk
  ¼ cup margarine *or* butter, melted
  1 square (1 ounce) unsweetened chocolate, melted and cooled, *or* 1 envelope (1 ounce) premelted unsweetened chocolate product
  1 teaspoon vanilla
  ¼ teaspoon baking powder
  ½ cup chopped walnuts
  1 square (1 ounce) unsweetened chocolate *or* 1 envelope (1 ounce) premelted unsweetened chocolate product
  2 tablespoons margarine *or* butter
1½ cups sifted powdered sugar
  ½ teaspoon vanilla
Walnut halves (optional)

● **For bottom layer,** stir together oats, the ½ cup flour, brown sugar, and baking soda. Stir in the ½ cup melted margarine or butter. Pat mixture into the bottom of an 11x7x1½-inch baking pan. Bake in a 350° oven 10 minutes.
● **Meanwhile, for middle layer,** stir together egg, sugar, the ⅔ cup flour, milk, the ¼ cup melted margarine or butter, the square of melted chocolate, the 1 teaspoon vanilla, and baking powder till smooth. Fold in chopped walnuts. Spread batter over baked layer in pan. Bake about 25 minutes more or till a toothpick inserted in center comes out clean. Set on a wire rack to cool.
● **For top layer,** in a medium saucepan heat and stir the second chocolate square and the 2 tablespoons margarine or butter till melted. Stir in powdered sugar and the ½ teaspoon vanilla. Stir in enough *hot water* (1 to 2 tablespoons) to make a mixture that is almost pourable. Spread over brownies. Arrange walnut halves on top, if desired. Cool completely; cut into bars. Makes 32 brownies.

Nutrition information per brownie: 144 cal., 2 g pro., 19 g carbo., 8 g fat, 9 mg chol., 74 mg sodium, 57 mg potassium, and 1 g dietary fiber.

COBB SALAD

- 6 cups shredded lettuce
- 3 cups chopped cooked chicken
- 3 hard-cooked eggs, chopped
- 2 medium tomatoes, seeded and chopped
- ¾ cup crumbled blue cheese (3 ounces)
- 6 slices bacon, crisp-cooked, drained, and crumbled
- 1 medium avocado, halved, pitted, peeled, and cut into wedges

Small Belgian endive leaves
Brown Derby French Dressing

● **Place** lettuce on six individual plates. Evenly divide chicken, eggs, tomatoes, cheese, and bacon among plates, arranging each in a row atop lettuce. Place avocado wedges and endive leaves to the side. Serve with Brown Derby French Dressing. Serves 6.

Brown Derby French Dressing: In a screw-top jar combine ⅓ cup *red wine vinegar*, 1 tablespoon *lemon juice*, 1 teaspoon *Worcestershire sauce*, ½ teaspoon *salt*, ½ teaspoon *sugar*, ½ teaspoon *dry mustard*, ½ teaspoon *pepper*, and 1 clove *garlic*, minced. Cover and shake to mix well. Add ½ cup *olive oil or salad oil*; cover and shake vigorously. Chill thoroughly. Shake before serving. Makes 1 cup dressing.

Nutrition information per serving: *509 cal., 31 g pro., 8 g carbo., 40 g fat, 216 mg chol., 618 mg sodium, 731 mg potassium, 20 g dietary fiber. U.S. RDA: 28% vit. A, 26% vit. C, 15% thiamine, 21% riboflavin, 41% niacin, 13% calcium, 15% iron.*

FETTUCCINE ALLA CARBONARA

- 4 eggs
- ¼ cup whipping cream
- ¼ cup margarine *or* butter, cut up
- ½ pound bacon, cut up
- 1 cup grated Parmesan cheese (4 ounces)
- 16 ounces fettuccine *or* linguine
- ¼ cup snipped parsley

Coarsely ground pepper (optional)

● **Let** eggs, cream, and margarine or butter stand at room temperature for 2 to 3 hours.

● **In a skillet cook** bacon till crisp. Remove and drain on paper towels.

● **In a medium** mixing bowl beat together eggs and cream just till combined. Stir in Parmesan cheese; set aside.

● **In a large kettle** or Dutch oven cook pasta according to package directions. Drain and immediately return to hot kettle or Dutch oven. Toss pasta with margarine or butter till melted. Add bacon and cheese mixture. Toss gently till well mixed. Transfer to a warm serving dish. Sprinkle with parsley and pepper, if desired. Serve immediately. Makes 6 main-dish servings.

Nutrition information per serving: *592 cal., 25 g pro., 59 g carbo., 28 g fat, 222 mg chol., 687 mg sodium, 297 mg potassium, and 2 g dietary fiber. U.S. RDA: 18% vit. A, 53% thiamine, 30% riboflavin, 28% niacin, 31% calcium, and 19% iron.*

STIR-FRY PORK AND JICAMA

- ½ cup cold water
- ¼ cup dry sherry
- ¼ cup soy sauce
- 4 teaspoons cornstarch
- 1 teaspoon grated gingerroot
- 1 clove garlic, minced
- 2 tablespoons cooking oil
- 1 pound lean boneless pork, cut into thin strips
- ½ of a medium jicama, peeled and cubed (1 cup)
- 1 cup sweet red *and/or* green pepper strips
- 2 tablespoons sliced green onion
- 2 cups chopped Chinese cabbage *or* fresh spinach

Hot cooked rice

● **In a small bowl stir together** water, sherry, soy sauce, and cornstarch; set the mixture aside.

● **In a wok or large skillet cook** gingerroot and garlic in hot oil for 30 seconds. Add *half* of the pork and stir-fry for 3 to 4 minutes or till no longer pink. Remove from wok. Stir-fry the remaining pork till no longer pink.

● **Return** all of the pork to the skillet; add jicama, pepper strips, and green onion. Stir-fry about 1 minute more or till pepper strips are crisp-tender. Stir cornstarch mixture; stir into meat mixture. Cook and stir till thickened and bubbly; cook and stir for 2 minutes more. Stir in cabbage or spinach; heat through. Serve with rice. Serves 4.

Microwave directions: In a small bowl stir together water, sherry, soy sauce, and *5 teaspoons* cornstarch; set mixture aside.

In a 2-quart microwave-safe casserole combine gingerroot, garlic, and pork. (*Omit oil.*) Micro-cook, covered, on 100% power (high) for 5 to 7 minutes (low-wattage oven: 7 to 9 minutes) or till no pink remains in meat, stirring once. Drain off fat.

Add jicama, pepper strips, and green onion. Cook, covered, on high for 3 to 4 minutes or till the pepper strips are crisp-tender (low-wattage oven: 6 to 8 minutes).

Stir cornstarch mixture; stir into pork mixture. Cook, uncovered, on high for 2½ to 4 minutes (low-wattage oven: 4 to 6 minutes) or till thickened and bubbly, stirring after every minute. Stir in cabbage or spinach. Cook on high for 30 to 60 seconds more or till heated through. Serve as directed.

Nutrition information per serving: *479 cal., 34 g pro., 37 g carbo., 19 g fat, 94 mg chol., 1,103 mg sodium, 577 mg potassium, 4 g dietary fiber. U.S. RDA: 59% vit. A, 108% vit. C, 62% thiamine, 18% riboflavin, 39% niacin, 18% iron.*

CHOCOLATE REVEL BARS

If desired, substitute 1 cup whole wheat flour for 1 cup of the all-purpose flour—

  1 cup margarine *or* butter, softened
2½ cups all-purpose flour
  2 cups packed brown sugar
  2 eggs
  4 teaspoons vanilla
  1 teaspoon baking soda
  3 cups quick-cooking rolled oats
1½ cups semisweet chocolate pieces
  1 14-ounce can (1¼ cups) *sweetened condensed* milk
  2 tablespoons margarine *or* butter
  ½ cup chopped walnuts

● **In a large mixer bowl beat** the 1 cup margarine or butter with an electric mixer on medium speed for 30 seconds. Add about *half* of the flour, all of the brown sugar, eggs, *2 teaspoons* of the vanilla, and baking soda. Beat on low speed till thoroughly combined. Beat in remaining flour. Stir in oats.

● **In a medium saucepan cook** chocolate pieces, sweetened condensed milk, and the 2 tablespoons margarine or butter over low heat till the chocolate is melted, stirring occasionally. Remove from heat. Stir in remaining vanilla and walnuts.

● **Pat** *two-thirds* of the oat mixture (about 3⅓ cups) into the bottom of an ungreased 15x10x1-inch baking pan. Spread the chocolate mixture over the oat mixture. Dot with the remaining oat mixture.

● **Bake** in a 350° oven about 25 minutes or till the top is lightly golden. (Chocolate mixture will still look moist.) Cool on a wire rack. Cut into bars. Makes 60 bars.

Nutrition information per bar: 145 cal., 2 g pro., 20 g carbo., 7 g fat, 12 mg chol., 72 mg sodium, 93 mg potassium, and 1 g dietary fiber.

ZUCCHINI STUFFING CASSEROLE

  2 pounds zucchini *and/or* yellow summer squash, sliced ⅜ inch thick (7 cups)
  ¼ cup chopped onion
  1 10¾-ounce can condensed cream of chicken soup
  1 8-ounce carton dairy sour cream
  1 cup shredded carrot
  2 cups herb-seasoned stuffing mix
  ¼ cup margarine *or* butter, melted

● **In a large saucepan cook** zucchini and onion in boiling salted water for 5 to 10 minutes or till crisp-tender. Drain zucchini mixture well.

● **In a large bowl combine** soup and sour cream; stir in carrot. Fold in zucchini mixture.

● **Toss** stuffing mix with margarine or butter. Spread *half* of the stuffing mixture in a 12x7½x2-inch baking dish. Spoon zucchini mixture atop. Sprinkle with remaining stuffing mixture. Bake in a 350° oven for 25 to 30 minutes or till heated through. Makes 6 servings.

Nutrition information per serving: 401 cal., 11 g pro., 46 g carbo., 21 g fat, 23 mg chol., 1,142 mg sodium, 620 mg potassium, 4 g dietary fiber. U.S. RDA: 130% vit. A, 19% vit. C, 19% thiamine, 16% riboflavin, 15% niacin, 15% calcium, 14% iron.

SPAGHETTI PIE

If you make this pie with ground beef, it will have a mild flavor. For more zip, use sausage—

  6 ounces spaghetti
  2 tablespoons margarine *or* butter
  2 well-beaten eggs
  ⅓ cup grated Parmesan cheese
  1 pound ground beef *or* bulk pork sausage
  ½ cup chopped onion
  ¼ cup chopped green pepper
  1 7½-ounce can tomatoes, cut up
  1 6-ounce can tomato paste
  1 teaspoon sugar
  1 teaspoon dried oregano, crushed
  ¼ teaspoon garlic salt
  1 cup cream-style cottage cheese (8 ounces), drained
  ½ cup shredded mozzarella cheese

● **Cook** spaghetti according to package directions; drain. (You should have about 3¼ cups spaghetti.) Stir margarine or butter into hot spaghetti. Stir in eggs and Parmesan cheese. Press spaghetti mixture into a buttered 10-inch pie plate, forming a crust.

● **In a large skillet cook** beef or sausage, onion, and green pepper till meat is brown and vegetables are tender. Drain off fat. Stir in *undrained* tomatoes, tomato paste, sugar, oregano, and garlic salt. Heat through.

● **Spread** cottage cheese over bottom of the prepared spaghetti crust. Top with the meat mixture.

● **Bake,** uncovered, in a 350° oven for 20 minutes. Sprinkle with mozzarella cheese. Bake about 5 minutes more or till cheese melts. Makes 6 servings.

Microwave directions (not recommended in low-wattage microwave ovens): Cook spaghetti and prepare crust as directed above.

Meanwhile, in a 1½-quart microwave-safe casserole, crumble beef or sausage. Add onion and green pepper. Micro-cook, covered, on 100% power (high) for 4 to 6 minutes or till meat is no longer pink and vegetables are tender, stirring once. Drain off fat. Stir in *undrained* tomatoes, tomato paste, sugar, oregano, garlic salt, and 1 tablespoon *all-purpose flour.* Cook, uncovered, on high for 6 to 8 minutes or till bubbly, stirring every 3 minutes. Cook on high for 1 minute more. Cover and set aside.

Cover spaghetti crust with vented microwave-safe plastic wrap. Cook on 50% power (medium) 5 to 7 minutes or till just set, giving dish a half-turn once.

Spread cottage cheese over bottom of the prepared spaghetti crust. Top with the meat mixture. Cover with vented microwave-safe plastic wrap. Cook on medium for 3 to 5 minutes or till heated through, giving the dish a half-turn once. Sprinkle with mozzarella cheese. Let stand for 5 minutes.

Nutrition information per serving: 447 cal., 30 g pro., 33 g carbo., 21 g fat, 155 mg chol., 764 mg sodium, 659 mg potassium, 3 g dietary fiber. U.S. RDA: 27% vit. A, 31% vit. C, 27% thiamine, 27% riboflavin, 30% niacin, 22% calcium, 24% iron.

RAINBOW FRUIT COMPOTE

- 2 medium oranges
- ⅓ cup sugar *or* honey
- ½ teaspoon finely shredded lemon *or* lime peel
- 1 tablespoon lemon *or* lime juice
- ⅛ teaspoon ground cinnamon
- 1 cup fresh blueberries
- 1½ cups cubed papaya, honeydew melon, *or* cantaloupe
- 1 cup peeled and sliced kiwi fruit *or* sliced carambola (star fruit)
- 1 cup halved strawberries
- Toasted coconut *or* slivered almonds

● **Over a small bowl peel** and section oranges, reserving juice. Stir sugar or honey, lemon or lime peel, lemon or lime juice, and cinnamon into oranges and reserved juices. Cover and chill for several hours or overnight.

● **Use a slotted spoon to transfer** oranges to a 1½-quart glass compote, reserving syrup. Layer blueberries, papaya or melon, kiwi fruit or carambola, and strawberries atop oranges. Drizzle reserved syrup over all. Top with a carambola slice, if desired. Sprinkle with coconut or almonds. Makes 4 servings.

Nutrition information per serving: *183 cal., 2 g pro., 45 g carbo., 1 g fat, 0 mg chol., 7 mg sodium, 517 mg potassium, 6 g dietary fiber. U.S. RDA: 26% vit. A, 223% vit. C.*

EARLY COLONIAL BREAD

- ½ cup cornmeal
- ⅓ cup packed brown sugar
- 1 teaspoon salt
- 2½ cups boiling water
- ⅓ cup cooking oil
- 4¼ to 4¾ cups all-purpose flour
- 1 package active dry yeast
- 1 cup whole wheat flour
- ½ cup rye flour

● **In a small mixing bowl stir together** the cornmeal, brown sugar, and salt. In a medium mixing bowl gradually stir the cornmeal mixture into the boiling water. Stir in the oil. Cool cornmeal mixture just till warm (120° to 130°), stirring occasionally (cooling should take about 40 to 45 minutes).

● **In a large mixer bowl stir together** *2 cups* of the all-purpose flour and yeast. Add cornmeal mixture. Beat with an electric mixer on low speed for 30 seconds, scraping sides of bowl constantly. Beat on high speed for 3 minutes. Using a wooden spoon, stir in whole wheat flour, rye flour, and as much of the remaining all-purpose flour as you can.

● **Turn out** onto a lightly floured surface. Knead in enough of the remaining all-purpose flour to make a moderately stiff dough that is smooth and elastic (knead 6 to 8 minutes total).

● **Shape** dough into a ball. Place in a lightly greased bowl; turn once. Cover; let rise in a warm place till double (about 60 minutes).

● **Punch dough down;** turn out onto a lightly floured surface. Divide dough in half. Cover and let rest for 10 minutes. Shape dough into loaves. Place in 2 greased 8x4x2-inch loaf pans. Cover and let rise till nearly double (30 to 45 minutes).

● **Bake** in a 375° oven about 45 minutes or till bread sounds hollow when tapped lightly with a finger. Cover with foil the last 20 minutes to prevent overbrowning. Makes 2 loaves, 12 to 16 slices each.

Nutrition information per slice: *152 cal., 4 g pro., 27 g carbo., 3 g fat, 0 mg chol., 91 mg sodium, 66 mg potassium, and 2 g dietary fiber. U.S. RDA: 13% thiamine.*

CHOCOLATE MOUSSE CAKE

The next best thing to eating this dessert is knowing you can make it ahead. Simply cover it and chill. Let stand 30 minutes at room temperature before serving—

- 1¾ cups whole hazelnuts (filberts)
- 3 tablespoons margarine *or* butter, melted
- 2 8-ounce packages semisweet chocolate squares, cut up
- 1 cup whipping cream
- 6 eggs
- 1 teaspoon vanilla
- ⅓ cup all-purpose flour
- ¼ cup sugar
- Chocolate Whipped Cream
- Whole hazelnuts (filberts) (optional)

● **Butter** a 9-inch springform pan. Place the 1¾ cups hazelnuts in a blender container or food processor bowl. Cover and blend or process till coarsely ground. In a small bowl stir together the ground hazelnuts and the melted margarine or butter. Press mixture onto the bottom and 1½ inches up the sides of the prepared springform pan.

● **In a medium saucepan combine** semisweet chocolate and whipping cream; cook and stir over low heat till chocolate melts. Remove from heat. (*Or,* place semisweet chocolate and whipping cream in a 4-cup glass measure or medium-size microwave-safe bowl. Micro-cook, uncovered, on 100% power (high) for 3 minutes or till melted, stirring after 2 minutes.)

● **In a large mixer bowl beat** eggs and the vanilla with an electric mixer on low speed till well combined. Add flour and sugar; beat with an electric mixer on high speed for 10 minutes or till slightly thick. Stir about *one-fourth* of the egg mixture into the chocolate mixture to lighten. Then fold all of the chocolate mixture into the remaining egg mixture. Transfer all of the mixture to the prepared springform pan.

● **Bake** in a 325° oven about 40 minutes or till the cake is slightly puffed on the outer third of the top. (The center will be slightly soft.) Cool on a wire rack for 20 minutes. Remove the sides of the springform pan. Cool completely for 3 to 4 hours more.

● **Before serving,** use a decorating bag and star tip to pipe on Chocolate Whipped Cream. Top with whole hazelnuts, if desired. Serve at room temperature. To store, cover and chill in refrigerator; let stand at room temperature for 30 minutes before serving. Makes 16 to 20 servings.

Chocolate Whipped Cream: In a small saucepan combine ½ cup *whipping cream* and ½ square (½ ounce) *semisweet chocolate.* Cook and stir over low heat till chocolate melts. Remove from heat and stir till no chocolate specks remain. Pour into a small mixer bowl; cover and chill completely. Just before serving, beat cream mixture with an electric mixer on low speed till stiff peaks form.

Nutrition information per serving: *395 cal., 6 g pro., 25 g carbo., 33 g fat, 136 mg chol., 68 mg sodium, 206 mg potassium, 2 g dietary fiber. U.S. RDA: 11% vit. A, 10% iron.*

TURKEY FAJITAS WITH GREEN PEA GUACAMOLE

You can grill or broil your fajitas—

  1 **pound turkey breast tenderloin steaks (3 to 4)**
  ½ **teaspoon finely shredded lime peel**
  ½ **cup lime juice**
  2 **cloves garlic, minced**
  ½ **teaspoon salt**
  ½ **teaspoon dried oregano, crushed**
  ½ **teaspoon ground cumin**
Few drops bottled hot pepper sauce
  3 **sweet red, yellow, *and/or* green peppers, cut into thin strips**
  1 **medium onion, sliced**
  8 **6- *or* 7-inch flour tortillas**
Shredded lettuce
  ¼ **cup sliced pitted ripe olives**
Green Pea Guacamole
Plain low-fat yogurt (optional)

Grilling directions:
● **Rinse turkey; pat dry.** For marinade, in a shallow baking dish combine lime peel, lime juice, garlic, salt, oregano, cumin, and hot pepper sauce. Add turkey, peppers, and onion. Cover and chill for 2 hours, turning turkey once.
● **Remove turkey from marinade,** reserving marinade. With a slotted spoon, remove peppers and onion from marinade; wrap in an 18-inch square piece of heavy-duty foil. Stack tortillas and wrap in an 18x12-inch piece of heavy-duty foil.
● **Grill** pepper-onion packet and turkey directly over *medium* coals for 8 minutes. Add tortilla packet to grill. Turn turkey; continue grilling for 4 to 6 minutes or till turkey is no longer pink, brushing turkey occasionally with reserved marinade.
● **Transfer** turkey to warm platter; cover to keep warm. Continue grilling foil packets for 4 to 6 minutes more or till vegetables are tender and tortillas are heated through.

● **To serve,** cut turkey into thin bite-size strips; return to warm platter. Arrange pepper-onion mixture, tortillas, lettuce, and olives on another serving platter. To assemble fajitas at the table, place *some* of the lettuce, pepper-onion mixture, turkey, and olives in center of *each* tortilla. Top with *some* of the Green Pea Guacamole and yogurt. Roll up tortillas. Makes 6 servings.

Broiling directions:
● **Marinate** turkey and vegetables as directed for grilling. Wrap tortillas in foil. Set aside.
● **Remove turkey from marinade,** reserving marinade. With a slotted spoon, remove peppers and onion from marinade; set aside. Place turkey on the unheated rack of a broiler pan. Broil 3 inches from heat for 10 to 12 minutes or till tender, turning once and brushing occasionally with reserved marinade. During the last 5 to 6 minutes of broiling, place wrapped tortillas on broiler rack next to turkey. Broil till heated through, turning once.
● **Meanwhile,** spray a large skillet with *nonstick spray coating.* Preheat skillet over medium-high heat till a drop of water sizzles. Stir-fry peppers and onion for 4 to 5 minutes or till crisp-tender. Serve as directed.

Green Pea Guacamole: In a blender container or food processor bowl combine 2 cups cooked *peas or* cooked *green beans,* drained and chilled; 2 tablespoons chopped *onion;* one 4-ounce can *diced green chili peppers,* drained; 1 clove *garlic,* minced; ¼ teaspoon *pepper;* and few drops *bottled hot pepper sauce.* Cover and blend or process till smooth. Transfer to a serving container. Cover; chill. Just before serving, stir in 2 tablespoons *lime juice.*

Nutrition information per serving: *243 cal., 23 g pro., 33 g carbo., 2 g fat, 47 mg chol., 295 mg sodium, 515 mg potassium, 4 g dietary fiber. U.S. RDA: 109% vit. A, 158% vit. C, 19% thiamine, 13% riboflavin, 31% niacin, 12% calcium, 22% iron.*

WINE-SAUCED SALMON AND RICE MEDLEY

  3 **large *or* 6 small frozen salmon steaks (2 to 2¼ pounds total), cut ½ to ¾ inch thick**
  2 **tablespoons margarine *or* butter (optional)**
  2 **7-ounce packages frozen long grain rice with peas and mushrooms**
  ¼ **cup chopped onion**
  ½ **teaspoon dried rosemary, crushed**
  3 **tablespoons margarine *or* butter**
  1 **tablespoon cornstarch**
  ½ **cup water**
  ½ **teaspoon instant chicken bouillon granules**
  ¼ **cup dry white wine**
Lemon slice twists (optional)
Fresh rosemary sprigs (optional)

● **Place** salmon in a lightly greased 15x10x1-inch baking pan. Season with salt and pepper; dot with the 2 tablespoons margarine or butter, if desired. Bake in a 450° oven for 13 to 15 minutes or till fish just flakes with a fork.
● **Meanwhile, cook** rice according to package directions.
● **While rice and salmon cook,** prepare wine sauce: Cook onion and dried rosemary in 3 tablespoons hot margarine till tender. Stir in cornstarch. Add water and bouillon granules. Cook and stir till thickened and bubbly. Stir in wine. Cook and stir 1 minute more.
● **To serve, arrange** salmon over rice on a warm platter. Spoon *some* of the wine sauce over salmon. Garnish with lemon and fresh rosemary, if desired. Pass remaining wine sauce. Serves 6.

Microwave directions: Prepare salmon and rice as directed. Meanwhile, in a 2-cup glass measure combine onion, dried rosemary, and the 3 tablespoons margarine or butter. Micro-cook, uncovered, on 100% power (high) for 2 to 3 minutes or till onion is tender. Stir in cornstarch. Stir in water and bouillon granules. Cook, uncovered, on high for 2 to 3 minutes or till thickened and bubbly, stirring after every minute. Stir in wine. Cook on high for 1 minute more. Serve as directed.

Nutrition information per serving: *369 cal., 31 g pro., 16 g carbo., 19 g fat, 84 mg chol., 506 mg sodium, 572 mg potassium, 2 g dietary fiber. U.S. RDA: 11% vit. A, 27% thiamine, 13% riboflavin, 43% niacin.*

SIZZLING CHEESE SALAD

    4 cups torn mixed greens
    ¼ cup pitted ripe olives
    6 whole sun-dried tomatoes *or* 6
       tomato wedges
    2 teaspoons sliced green onion
    ¼ cup salad oil
    ¼ cup tarragon vinegar
    1 tablespoon walnut oil
    2 teaspoons Dijon-style mustard
    1 egg
    2 tablespoons cornmeal
    1 tablespoon fine dry bread
       crumbs
    1 tablespoon sesame seed,
       toasted
    2 teaspoons grated Parmesan
       cheese
    4 ounces Neufchâtel cheese,
       cut up
    1 cup shredded gjetost cheese
       (4 ounces)
    2 tablespoons margarine *or* butter
    6 small pita bread rounds, split
       horizontally and toasted

● **On a serving platter arrange** greens, olives, and tomatoes; sprinkle with green onion. Cover and chill.
● **For dressing,** in a screw-top jar combine salad oil, tarragon vinegar, walnut oil, mustard, and 2 tablespoons *water.* Cover and shake. Chill.
● **In a small bowl combine** egg and 1 tablespoon *water.* In a shallow bowl combine cornmeal, bread crumbs, sesame seed, and Parmesan cheese.
● **In a small mixer bowl beat** Neufchâtel and gjetost cheeses with an electric mixer till combined. Divide mixture into 12 equal portions; shape into balls. Flatten balls to form 2-inch patties. Dip each patty into egg mixture; coat with the cornmeal mixture. Cover; chill.
● **At serving time,** in a 10-inch skillet melt margarine or butter. Add cheese patties; cook over medium heat for 3 to 5 minutes or till golden, turning once.
● **Arrange** cheese patties atop salad; place pitas to the side. Shake dressing and serve with salad. Makes 6 side-dish servings.

Nutrition information per serving: 410 cal., 10 g pro., 31 g carbo., 28 g fat, 78 mg chol., 319 mg sodium, 441 mg potassium, 2 g dietary fiber. U.S. RDA: 27% vit. A, 13% vit. C, 15% thiamine, 24% riboflavin, 14% calcium, and 10% iron.

MUSTARD-GLAZED PORK CHOPS

    4 pork loin chops, cut ¾ inch thick
    1 pound whole tiny new potatoes,
       sliced ¼ inch thick
    ½ cup water
    ¼ cup snipped dried apricots
    2 tablespoons brown sugar
    2 tablespoons vinegar
    1 green onion, sliced
    1 teaspoon instant chicken
       bouillon granules
    ¼ teaspoon ground turmeric
    ¼ teaspoon ground red pepper
    2 tablespoons cold water
    2 teaspoons cornstarch
    ¼ cup water
    4 teaspoons hot oriental dry
       mustard *or* dry mustard

● **Preheat broiler.** Trim fat from chops. Place chops on unheated rack of a broiler pan. Broil 3 inches from heat for 12 to 14 minutes or till no pink remains, turning once halfway through cooking.
● **Meanwhile,** place potatoes in a steamer basket; sprinkle lightly with salt and pepper. Place over boiling water. Cover and steam for 10 to 12 minutes or till tender.
● **For glaze,** in a 1-quart saucepan combine the ½ cup water, apricots, brown sugar, vinegar, green onion, bouillon granules, turmeric, and red pepper. Bring to boiling; reduce heat. Cover and simmer for 5 to 10 minutes or till apricots are tender. Stir together the 2 tablespoons cold water and cornstarch; stir into apricot mixture. Cook and stir till thickened and bubbly. Cook and stir 2 minutes more. Remove from heat. Stir together the ¼ cup water and mustard; stir into glaze (*do not* cook).
● **To serve,** arrange potatoes on individual dinner plates; top *each* with a pork chop. Spoon glaze over each chop. Makes 4 servings.

Nutrition information per serving: 357 cal., 30 g pro., 37 g carbo., 10 g fat, 83 mg chol., 167 mg sodium, 959 mg potassium, 2 g dietary fiber. U.S. RDA: 13% vit. A, 18% vit. C, 74% thiamine, 18% riboflavin, 34% niacin, 11% iron.

CARROT CAKE WITH PINEAPPLE

    1 cup all-purpose flour
    1 cup packed brown sugar
    1 teaspoon baking powder
    ½ teaspoon ground cinnamon
    ¼ teaspoon baking soda
 1½ cups finely shredded carrot
    ⅓ cup cooking oil
    ⅓ cup milk
    1 beaten egg
    ¼ cup finely chopped pecans
    1 8¼-ounce can crushed
       pineapple
 1½ teaspoons cornstarch
Creamy Pineapple Frosting

● **Grease** the bottom of an 8x1½-inch microwave-safe round baking dish. Line bottom with waxed paper.
● **Mix** flour, sugar, baking powder, cinnamon, soda, and ⅛ teaspoon *salt.* Stir in carrot, oil, milk, and egg just till combined. Stir in nuts. Spread in dish.
● **Micro-cook,** uncovered, on 50% power (medium) 13 to 15 minutes, giving dish a quarter-turn every 5 minutes. (Low-wattage oven: micro-cook on 100% power [high] 8½ to 9½ minutes, giving a quarter-turn every 2 minutes.) To test for doneness, scratch the surface with wooden toothpick. The cake should be cooked underneath. If not done, cook on high 30 seconds to 2 minutes more. Cool 5 minutes. Remove from dish. Remove waxed paper. Cool.
● **For filling,** drain pineapple, reserving juice. Reserve ¼ *cup* pineapple for frosting. In 2-cup glass measure mix reserved juice, cornstarch, and remaining pineapple. Micro-cook, uncovered, on high 2 to 3½ minutes or till bubbly, stirring after every minute. Cook on high 30 seconds more. Cover and cool.
● **Cut** cake in half crosswise. Spread *one* half with filling. Top with remaining cake half. Frost with Creamy Pineapple Frosting. Makes 6 to 8 servings.

Creamy Pineapple Frosting: Beat 2 cups sifted *powdered sugar* and 3 tablespoons softened *margarine or butter* till well mixed. Add reserved ¼ cup crushed pineapple; beat till fluffy. Add additional sifted *powdered sugar* (¼ to ½ cup) to make frosting spreadable.

Nutrition information per serving: 625 cal., 5 g pro., 100 g carbo., 25 g fat, 47 mg chol., 247 mg sodium, 339 mg potassium, 2 g dietary fiber. U.S. RDA: 161% vit. A, 17% thiamine, 10% riboflavin, 11% calcium, 16% iron.

EAT WELL! FEEL GREAT!

THE WOMACKS SHOW YOU HOW
- HELPFUL RECIPES - WORKOUT HINTS

By Barbara Goldman

▲ PARTNERS, PLUS
Mike and Ellen Womack view their health-oriented lifestyle as pretty ordinary.

"I've always been nutrition- and health-conscious. I learned it young, from my mother."

"I'm just an everyday cook," Ellen Womack told me when we first met. "You must think we do something extraordinary."

I did—and they do. Ellen and Mike, both 47, who managed to elope the day after high school graduation, also manage to do what many families find tough—weave healthful eating into their everyday lives in a natural way.

They don't eat strange foods or feel deprived. They just incorporate plenty of high-fiber, low-fat foods into a healthful eating plan.

Photographs: D. Randolph Foulds. Field editor: Estelle Guralnick. Food stylist: Janet Herwig

FEEL-GREAT TIPS
◄ FAMILY WALK-OUT
The Womacks combine fitness and fun on weekend family jaunts near their Massachusetts home. From left, daughter-in-law Donna, son Paul with Sarah, 1, "little" Michael, 7, Ellen, "Pop," and son Adam with friend Tracy. Daughter Liz is at work.

"I haven't let anyone leave home without breakfast in 29 years. It's been important to me ever since I can remember."

An early beginning

"I became aware of the importance of good nutrition very young," Ellen explains. "Because my dad had heart disease, Mom paid attention to saturated fat at a time when few others did.

"And I remember learning in high school that men in the Korean War were testing high for arterial problems, possibly because of eating habits."

Recalling those high school days, Ellen laughingly told me, "We were such typical '50s kids! Mike played basketball and football, and I was a cheerleader. We married young, but we worked Mike's way through college—and we've defied the statistics. We'll celebrate our 30th anniversary June 6."

Hearty and heart-healthy

Once married, the Womacks concentrated on nutritious, low-fat meals; Ellen wanted Mike to avoid the trouble her father had. When their children arrived, Ellen and Mike were even more diligent. "I think kids need to eat carefully, too," says Ellen. "But I have to consider 'hearty' as well as heart-healthy. Food has to fill 'em up without clogging the arteries. My sons like food that sticks to the ribs!"

Starting the day right

Mike and Ellen are emphatic about eating a good breakfast. Like most busy folks, they prefer fast-to-fix foods. Cereal with fruit and skim milk and Ellen's Whole Wheat Pancakes made in minutes from a homemade mix are popular choices.

For another fast breakfast, the Womacks top whole wheat bread with sliced bananas and a light spreading of peanut butter.

▲ A GREAT BEGINNING
Ellen, Mike, and Adam enjoy breakfast in their sunny kitchen.

▲ HURRY UP, DAD
Adam squeezes fresh orange juice with a restaurant-type juicer.

◄ QUICK-FIX PANCAKES
Ellen keeps homemade mix in a plastic bag, then adds milk and egg.

◄ MORNING STRETCH
Liz, home for the weekend, points out a tip in a health magazine, while Ellen goes through her daily yoga routine.
● "I like to do yoga for about 15 minutes each morning after I wake up so that I feel really stretched out. It keeps me flexible, and it helps with posture."

● Ellen, who taught yoga when the family lived in Chicago, thinks it's a great way to begin the day, especially for someone who is stressed or overprogrammed at work.
● Later she does the more vigorous part of her exercise routine—speed-walking. She usually walks about 4½ miles in an hour.

◀ MIKE'S ROUTINE

A brother-in-law's treadmill sparked Mike's enthusiasm a couple of years ago. Now he has one in his own basement—and walks it regularly.

- "I use it to relieve stess," says Mike. "My 25-minute walking sessions make me feel much better, and help keep my weight down."
- Later, Adam assists him with weights. Mike lifts weights for about an hour four times each week.

Lunch at the Womacks'

Saturday lunches are *the* get-together time for the family. That's when Adam (a freshman attending Boston College), Paul, Donna, and the grandkids relax and enjoy each other. Paul and his family live about an hour away, and Liz comes when she can from Philadelphia where she started a new job last year.

Saturdays Paul makes up a batch of his special-formula chili. His great-tasting low-fat chili combines lean ground beef with lots of beans, tomatoes, and plenty of green chili peppers.

Healthful, and oh-so-good!

If chili isn't on the menu, the family enjoys one of Ellen's homemade soups. She's especially fond of split pea and lentil soups. A salad and bread or rolls round out the lunches. Ellen usually serves the split pea soup with brown rice for a complete-protein dish. Healthful and filling, the high-carbohydrate, low-fat lunches are low in cost, too—one of the nicest things about serving plenty of grains, legumes, and vegetables.

All in the family

The Womacks serve their big group buffet-style, from the dining room buffet that Mike built. They're likely to spoon the soup from heirloom soup bowls. Rho Rho's Rolls, another family tradition, sometimes accompany the soup. These rolls are always on Womack holiday menus. Ellen's great-grandmother first made the rolls, but Rho Rho, Ellen's mother, adapted the recipe, substituting oil for lard to lower cholesterol. Often, the family splits the rolls and makes turkey sandwiches.

continued on page 110

"We love getting together as a family. It's as often as twice a week in summer, and on all holidays and birthdays."

▲ CHILI CHECKOUT
Chili-maker Paul samples a spoonful.

BONUS WEEKDAY RECIPE

ADAM'S LOW-FAT FETTUCCINE

Liz teases "little" brother as he makes his low-fat version of Fettuccine Alfredo.

● **Adam's** football coaches also tout a high-carbohydrate, low-fat diet. So Adam eats the fettuccine after workouts, and serves it to his parents for supper.
● **Adam substitutes** evaporated skim milk for cream, and uses just one-third cup grated cheese, far less than in typical versions. The recipe makes six side-dish servings—for *non*-football players.
● **Fettuccine** is one of Adam's favorite foods. Breakfast Muffins are another. Says Ellen, "My family panics if there's only one muffin left. Adam eats one each morning."

▲ DONNA AND SARAH
Even little Sarah loves Rho Rho's Rolls.

▲ GRANDMA'S OTHER MIKE
No boy's too big for Grandma's kiss!

◄ AN ATHLETE WORKS OUT
Other family members work out to stay fit, Adam trains to keep a football scholarship. His friend, Tracy, assists him on weights.
● Adam does an hour of aerobics four times a week in addition to a high-intensity Nautilus program at a health club. At home, he uses the rowing machine and treadmill.

● One day a week, Adam does plyometrics (which is a lot of jumping in the air) for quickness and power on the football field.
● A running and conditioning program fills out Adam's routine, and he frequently runs and cycles along the country roads near his Framingham, Massachusetts, home.

LUNCH

A healthful, homey, great-tasting lunch—

- Paul's Chili
- Pea Soup
- Three-Lettuce Salad
- Rho Rho's Rolls

"We've always tried to eat dinner together in the dining room. Sometimes it's difficult, but our family dinners are important."

The family dinner

"Pass the pasta" is a likely call at dinners for the extended Womack family. "I combine pasta with whatever I have on hand—chicken, fish, vegetables, white clam sauce—that kind of thing," Ellen explains. A vegetable or salad is passed with the pasta. One family favorite is a broccoli, carrot, leek, and garlic stir-fry. The family also eats lots of chicken and fish.

Ellen strives to serve low-fat, high-fiber foods, but she's not compulsive. "I think it's a mistake for people to avoid certain foods. I don't. You just have to be moderate, eat a wide variety of foods, and be sensible. I never say, 'I won't eat that food.' If you set up rigid eating routines, you're likely to break the rules."

Plenty of tuna

From July through September, tuna often tops the Womack menu. Avid fishers, Mike and Ellen spend many summer and early fall weekends out at sea on their tuna boat. Mike distributes materials-handling equipment, so Paul dubbed the boat *Deep Reach* after one of Mike's specialized forklift trucks..

The Womacks were disappointed that they couldn't provide their own fresh-caught tuna for our dinner—but who can blame a 500-pound bluefin for not cooperating?

Fortunately, when the fish aren't biting, fresh tuna steaks are available from many supermarkets and most seafood shops in and around Boston, and around the country. Tuna from a local market, grilled the Womack way, was great!

▲ DINNER FOR EIGHT
"Pop" does the honors, while Grandma tends baby Sarah.

Mike and Ellen enjoy a family joke as she prepares to serve a favorite weeknight entrée.

BONUS DINNER RECIPE

POPPY SEED CASSEROLE

- **"Twenty-five years ago** I adapted this from a recipe much higher in fat. It's my sons' favorite dish," says Ellen.
- **Perfect** for a weeknight supper, the casserole is a proven hit at potlucks, too. It's easy to put together, and the taste—wonderful.
- **Just brown** ground turkey and vegetables, stir in tomato sauce, toss the hot cooked noodles with low-fat cheeses and yogurt, layer in a baking dish—and bake. Don't forget the poppy seed!

◀ EXERCISE, FAMILY-STYLE

What do the Womack men do for fun when they get together? They wrestle and play basketball, that's what.

"Sometimes I'm amazed at the competition," says Ellen. "But they've developed a great camaraderie from these informal games. Why, even little Mike gets into the action."

DINNER
Mike's specialty:
grilled fish—
- Tuna Steaks
- Vegetables with Pasta
- Romaine Salad
- Whole Wheat Baguettes

"Popcorn is our middle name—and our main snack. We make it each night in a commercial popcorn popper."

▲ **BIG AND LITTLE MIKE**
They both love popcorn! Little wonder that the popper occupies such a prominent place on the kitchen counter.

How about dessert?

I'll vouch for it—the Womacks really do eat mostly fresh fruit for dessert.

How did it happen? They never got used to eating sweet desserts, so fruit satisfies them. And, Ellen says, "The rewards are so obvious. You don't gain weight, you feel better, and nutritionally you're ahead of the game because you don't fill up with empty calories."

Ellen feels that eating habits can be changed, but adds that no one should expect to do so overnight. Try not to get discouraged, she says, if high-calorie desserts are hard to pass up at first. With time, you'll prefer the natural sweetness of fruit.

What about company?

Occasionally the Womacks splurge, of course. Ellen makes a rich pecan loaf for the holidays. Mostly, however, she serves ice milk topped with coffee liqueur, or fruit with a dollop of yogurt. And, she follows a friend's advice:

"When you entertain, do what you know how to do and what you feel comfortable with. If you serve lasagna, be sure it's the best lasagna in the world."

Ellen adds one more thought, "Make it healthful!"

LITTLE THINGS THAT HELP A LOT

TIPS FROM ELLEN

◀ **SHE MAKES 'HEALTHFUL' FUN**
The Womacks' approach to healthful eating is positive. They don't talk about what shouldn't be eaten. They just see that healthful food is available.

● **Ellen says:** I definitely believe that our healthful lifestyle has paid off. Mike and I feel good because we eat well and follow our physical fitness routines. It gives us more energy—mentally as well as physically. In more concrete terms, both Mike and I have blood cholesterol levels under 200.

● **You can start** changing your lifestyle at any time. I don't care how old you are, or how sedentary. In respect to both eating and exercise, I think the biggest problem at first is that you tend to try too hard. It's better to start out moderately.

● **I keep** everyday meals simple. It's easier to create healthful meals over the long haul if you don't go to extraordinary lengths to prepare special foods or buy special ingredients.

● **I serve** only a few foods at each meal. Dinner might be roast chicken, pasta, and a salad or vegetable, or soup and salad, plus bread or spaghetti. But our food plan balances out over the day.

● **If you eat snacks,** it's important that they're healthful. We don't butter popcorn, for instance, so it's low fat and low calorie. Many prepare healthful meals, then eat lots of fat and calories during the rest of the day.

● **We're big on whole grains,** salads, and vegetables. These provide plenty of fiber, vitamins, and minerals. We steam our vegetables or cook them in the microwave.

● **I use** low-fat dairy products. After their first few years of life, our kids were brought up on low-fat milk.

● **We never use** butter or margarine on bread. We also eliminate or cut down on butter and margarine as spreads or toppings for other foods. We just use real maple syrup on pancakes, for instance. Although pancakes aren't exactly low calorie, without butter, margarine, or whipped cream toppings, they make a filling, healthful, high-carbohydrate breakfast.

● **When I'm cooking,** I substitute egg whites for yolks as often as possible. I may leave one or two whole eggs in a large recipe if they don't add up to too much cholesterol per serving. I also find that one egg in my pancake recipe prevents sticking. But unless we eat a food only infrequently, such as during the holidays, I try to alter the recipe.

● **I prefer** to make my own low-fat chicken broth for soups. When I do, I always place the broth in the refrigerator, then skim off all the fat after it congeals.

48

BREAKFAST MUFFINS

These great-tasting cholesterol-free muffins are good either hot or cold—

1½ **cups unbleached all-purpose**
   flour
½ **cup regular rolled oats**
2 **teaspoons baking powder**
1 **teaspoon ground cinnamon**
½ **teaspoon salt**
½ **teaspoon ground ginger**
½ **teaspoon ground mace**
¼ **teaspoon baking soda**
⅛ **teaspoon ground cloves**
2 **slightly beaten egg whites**
1 **cup canned pumpkin**
½ **cup light molasses**
½ **cup orange juice**
¼ **cup cooking oil**
½ **cup chopped walnuts**
¼ **cup regular rolled oats**
Nonstick spray coating *or*
   shortening
Walnut halves (optional)

● **In a large mixing bowl stir** together the all-purpose flour, the ½ cup rolled oats, baking powder, cinnamon, salt, ginger, mace, baking soda, and cloves.
● **In a medium mixing bowl combine** egg whites, pumpkin, molasses, orange juice, and oil. Add liquid mixture all at once to flour mixture.
● **Stir just till moistened;** batter should be lumpy. Fold in chopped walnuts.
● **Spray 12 muffin cups** with nonstick spray coating. Fill almost full with batter. Sprinkle with the remaining oats.
● **Or,** lightly grease muffin cups with shortening. Coat the sides of the muffin cups with the remaining oats; fill almost full with batter. Top *each* with a walnut half, if desired.
● **Bake in a 375° oven** for 20 to 25 minutes or till a wooden toothpick inserted in centers comes out clean. Remove from pans. Makes 12 muffins.
  Microwave directions: Prepare muffin batter as directed, *except* omit the ¼ cup oats. Line 6-ounce custard cups or a microwave-safe muffin pan with paper bake cups. Fill *each* cup ⅔ *full* with batter. Top *each* with a walnut half. (If using custard cups, arrange in a ring on a microwave-safe plate.) Micro-cook, uncovered, on 100% power (high) 30 to 60 seconds for 1 muffin, 1 to 2 minutes for 2 muffins, or 2½ to 3½ minutes for 6 muffins, or till done, giving plate or pan a half-turn every minute. To test for doneness, scratch the slightly wet surface with a wooden toothpick. Muffins should be cooked underneath. If using custard cups, remove each cup from microwave as muffin is done. Makes 18 muffins.
  Note: Microwave muffins do not get a crust on top and have a lighter texture than the conventional version.
  Nutrition information per muffin (¹⁄₁₂ of recipe): 197 cal., 4 g pro., 28 g carbo., 8 g fat, 0 mg chol., 179 mg sodium, 280 mg potassium, 2 g dietary fiber. U.S. RDA: 90% vit. A, 13% thiamine, 12% iron.

Breakfast Muffins

ELLEN'S WHOLE WHEAT PANCAKES

Ellen triples the dry ingredients and stores the mixture in a plastic bag. When ready to cook, she combines 1 cup mix with egg, milk, and margarine—

⅔ **cup unbleached all-purpose flour**
⅓ **cup whole wheat flour**
2 **tablespoons sugar**
2 **teaspoons baking powder**
¼ **teaspoon salt**
1 **beaten egg**
⅔ **cup milk**
2 **tablespoons margarine, melted**
Maple syrup

● **In a medium bowl stir together** the unbleached flour, whole wheat flour, sugar, baking powder, and salt.
● **In another bowl mix** the beaten egg, milk, and melted margarine; add all at once to flour mixture, stirring till batter is combined but still slightly lumpy.
● **For** *each* **4-inch pancake, pour** about ¼ cup of the batter onto a hot, lightly greased griddle or heavy skillet.
● **Cook** till golden, turning once when pancakes have a bubbly surface and slightly dry edges. Serve with maple syrup. Makes 6 pancakes, 3 servings.
  Nutrition information per serving (2 pancakes with 2 tablespoons maple syrup): 401 cal., 9 g pro., 68 g carbo., 11 g fat, 96 mg chol., 523 mg sodium, 265 mg potassium, 2 g dietary fiber. U.S. RDA: 10% vitamin A, 24% thiamine, 17% riboflavin, 11% niacin, 26% calcium, and 14% iron.

PAUL'S CHILI

Chock-full of flavor, vitamins, minerals, and water-soluble fiber, this recipe makes a lot, so freeze some for an easy meal another day—

1 **pound lean ground beef**
2 **large onions, chopped**
2 **15½-ounce cans red**
   kidney beans
2 **15½-ounce cans dark red**
   kidney beans
1 **28-ounce can peeled Italian-style**
   tomatoes, cut up
1 **14½-ounce can stewed**
   tomatoes
2 **4-ounce cans diced green**
   chili peppers
¼ **cup chili powder**
1 **teaspoon garlic powder**
1 **teaspoon dried oregano,**
   crushed
¼ **teaspoon ground red pepper**
   (optional)
⅛ **teaspoon pepper**

● **In a large Dutch oven cook** the ground beef and chopped onion till meat is brown and onion is tender. Drain off fat.
● **Stir in** the *undrained* beans, the *undrained* tomatoes, and the green chili peppers. Stir in the chili powder; garlic powder; oregano; ground red pepper, if desired; and pepper. Bring to boiling; reduce heat.
● **Simmer,** uncovered, about 1¼ hours or till desired consistency, stirring occasionally. Makes 12 (1-cup) servings.
  Nutrition information per serving: 226 cal., 17 g pro., 32 g carbo., 4 g fat, 27 mg chol., 968 mg sodium, 823 mg potassium, 10 g dietary fiber. U.S. RDA: 75% vit. A, 39% vit. C, 18% thiamine, 14% riboflavin, 18% niacin, 23% iron.

PEA SOUP

There are 15 grams of dietary fiber in only one cup of this soup. That's half of your recommended daily fiber intake—

 2 stalks celery, coarsely chopped (1 cup)
 2 large carrots, coarsely chopped (1 cup)
 1 medium onion, coarsely chopped (½ cup)
 2 tablespoons olive oil
 8 cups water
 1 pound dry green split peas
 1 teaspoon salt
 1 teaspoon dried thyme, crushed
 ½ teaspoon pepper
 ¼ cup snipped parsley *or* 2 tablespoons dried parsley flakes
 4 cups hot cooked brown rice (optional)

● **In a Dutch oven cook** celery, carrots, and onion in olive oil till crisp-tender.
● **Stir in** water, peas, salt, thyme, and pepper. Bring to boiling; reduce heat.
● **Simmer,** covered, for 45 to 60 minutes, or till peas are tender. Add parsley. Simmer, uncovered, for 45 to 60 minutes or till thick. If desired, place ½ *cup* cooked brown rice atop *each* serving. Makes 8 (1-cup) servings.
   Nutrition information per serving: *242 cal., 14 g pro., 39 g carbo., 4 g fat, 0 mg chol., 308 mg sodium, 631 mg potassium, 15 g dietary fiber. U.S. RDA: 105% vit. A, 30% thiamine, 11% riboflavin, 10% niacin, 19% iron.*

THREE-LETTUCE SALAD

A Womack favorite, this colorful combination of lettuces, mandarin orange sections, red grapes, and almonds will become a favorite of yours as well—

 2 tablespoons olive oil
 2 tablespoons red wine vinegar
 1 to 2 cloves garlic, minced
 ⅛ teaspoon salt
 4 cups torn romaine
 3 cups torn butter lettuce
 3 cups torn leaf lettuce
 1 11-ounce can mandarin orange sections, drained
 1 cup seedless red grapes, halved
 ⅓ cup slivered almonds, toasted

● **In a screw-top jar combine** olive oil, vinegar, garlic, and salt. Cover; shake till well combined. Chill.
● **In a large salad bowl combine** the romaine, butter lettuce, leaf lettuce, orange sections, grapes, and almonds.
● **To serve, pour dressing atop salad;** toss to coat. Makes 6 servings.
   Nutrition information per serving: *128 cal., 3 g pro., 13 g carbo., 8 g fat, 0 mg chol., 54 mg sodium, 413 mg potassium, 3 g dietary fiber. U.S. RDA: 47% vit. A and 52% vit. C.*

RHO RHO'S ROLLS

Mix up these easy no-knead whole wheat rolls and refrigerate them overnight before baking—

 4¼ cups unbleached all-purpose flour
 ⅓ cup sugar
 2 envelopes active dry yeast
 2 teaspoons salt
 2 eggs
 2 cups warm water (120° to 130°)
 ¾ cup cooking oil
 2 cups whole wheat flour
Nonstick spray coating *or* shortening

● **In a large mixer bowl mix** *3 cups* of the all-purpose flour, the sugar, yeast, and salt. Stir together the eggs, water, and oil; add to flour mixture.
● **Beat with an electric mixer** on low speed for ½ minute, scraping bowl. Beat 3 minutes on high speed. Using a spoon, stir in remaining all-purpose flour and all of the whole wheat flour.
● **Transfer dough** to a very large greased bowl; turn once. Cover and refrigerate for 2 to 24 hours.
● **Stir dough down.** Let dough rest 10 minutes.
● **Spray** a 13x9x2-inch baking pan and a 9x9x2-inch baking pan with nonstick spray coating, or lightly grease baking pans with shortening.
● **On well-floured surface roll dough** to 1-inch thickness; cut with a 2½-inch round floured cutter. Transfer rolls to pans. Form scraps into a ball. Let rest 10 minutes; reroll and cut. Transfer rolls to pans. Cover; let rise in a warm place till doubled (about 40 minutes).
● **Bake in a 375° oven** about 25 minutes or till golden. Serve warm. *Or,* use the cooled rolls for sandwiches. Makes 21 rolls.
   Nutrition information per roll: *222 cal., 5 g pro., 31 g carbo., 9 g fat, 26 mg chol., 211 mg sodium, 94 mg potassium, 2 g dietary fiber. U.S. RDA: 17% thiamine, 10% riboflavin, 11% niacin, and 10% iron.*

TUNA STEAKS

This delicious entrée is high in omega-3 fatty acids, which some researchers say might protect against heart disease—

 1 pound fresh *or* frozen tuna, swordfish, *or* halibut steaks, cut ½ inch thick
 2 teaspoons olive oil
 2 teaspoons margarine, melted
 2 teaspoons soy sauce
Coarse ground pepper (optional)
Lemon wedges (optional)
Lime wedges (optional)
Fresh cilantro sprigs (optional)

● **Thaw fish,** if frozen. Place fish steaks in a well-greased wire grill basket. Combine oil, melted margarine, and soy sauce; brush some of the soy mixture over fish steaks.
● **Grill fish steaks** over *medium-hot* coals 4 minutes. Turn the grill basket; brush fish again with remaining soy mixture. Grill 3 to 5 minutes more or till fish just flakes with a fork. Season to taste with pepper and serve with lemon and lime wedges, and cilantro sprigs, if desired. Makes 4 servings.
   Broiling instructions: Preheat broiler. Place steaks on the greased, unheated rack of a broiler pan. Combine oil, melted margarine, and soy sauce; brush some of the soy mixture over fish. Broil 4 inches from heat for 4 to 6 minutes (no need to turn) or till fish just flakes with a fork, brushing occasionally with remaining soy mixture. Season to taste with pepper and serve as above.
   Nutrition information per serving: *190 cal., 28 g pro., 0 g carbo., 8 g fat, 64 mg chol., 236 mg sodium, 328 mg potassium. U.S. RDA: 76% niacin.*

VEGETABLES WITH PASTA

A colorful, nutritious, quick-fix vegetable-pasta combination—

- 1 medium yellow summer squash
- 1 medium zucchini
- 1 medium sweet red pepper
- 6 ounces linguine *or* fusilli
- 2 tablespoons olive oil
- 1½ cups sliced fresh mushrooms
- 2 to 3 cloves garlic, minced
- ¼ cup dry white wine
- ¼ teaspoon dried basil, crushed
- ¼ teaspoon dried tarragon, crushed
- ¼ teaspoon crushed red pepper
- ¼ cup grated Parmesan cheese

● **Cut** summer squash and zucchini into ¼-inch-thick slices; cut each slice into thirds. Cut the sweet red pepper into very thin strips. Set aside.
● **Cook linguine** or fusilli according to package directions.
● **Meanwhile, preheat a wok** or large skillet over high heat; add olive oil. Add squash, zucchini, sweet red pepper, mushrooms, and garlic. Stir-fry 2 to 3 minutes or till vegetables are crisp-tender. Combine the white wine, basil, tarragon, crushed red pepper, and ¼ teaspoon *salt*. Drizzle mixture over vegetables; toss to coat. Heat through.
● **Drain pasta** and return to pan. Add the cooked vegetable mixture. Toss to mix. Transfer to a large serving platter. Sprinkle with cheese. Makes 6 to 8 side-dish servings.

Microwave directions: Cook linguine or fusilli according to package directions. Meanwhile, in a 1½-to 2-quart microwave-safe casserole micro-cook summer squash, zucchini, sweet red pepper, mushrooms, and garlic (omit the olive oil), covered, on 100% power (high) for 5 to 7 minutes or till vegetables are crisp-tender, stirring once. (For low-wattage ovens, micro-cook for 7 to 9 minutes.) Drain excess liquid. Stir together wine, salt, basil, tarragon, and crushed red pepper. Drizzle mixture over vegetables; toss to coat. Cook, covered, for 30 to 60 seconds more or till heated through. Continue as directed.

Nutrition information per serving: *192 cal., 6 g pro., 26 g carbo., 6 g fat, 3 mg chol., 171 mg sodium, 289 mg potassium, 2 g dietary fiber. U.S. RDA: 27% vit. A, 50% vit. C, 21% thiamine, 14% riboflavin, 14% niacin.*

ROMAINE SALAD

It's all done in the same bowl! First make the dressing, then add the vegetables, and toss—

- 2 cloves garlic, minced
- ¾ teaspoon dry mustard
- ⅛ teaspoon pepper (or to taste)
- ¼ cup olive oil
- 3 tablespoons red wine vinegar
- 1 bunch romaine, torn (about 8 cups)
- 1½ cups sliced fresh mushrooms
- ½ of a small red onion, sliced and separated into rings

● **In a large salad bowl stir** garlic, mustard, and pepper together with a fork to make a paste. Gradually stir in olive oil and vinegar, mixing well.
● **Add** romaine, mushrooms, and onion. Toss to coat. Makes 6 servings.

Nutrition information per serving: *101 cal., 2 g pro., 4 g carbo., 9 g fat, 0 mg chol., 7 mg sodium, 301 mg potassium, 1 g dietary fiber. U.S. RDA: 38% vit. A and 22% vit. C.*

WHOLE WHEAT BAGUETTES

These great-tasting whole wheat loaves contain virtually no fat or cholesterol—

- 2½ to 3 cups unbleached all-purpose flour
- 2 packages active dry yeast
- 1 tablespoon sugar
- 1½ teaspoons salt
- 2 cups warm water (120° to 130°)
- 2 cups whole wheat flour
- 1 slightly beaten egg white
- 1 tablespoon water

● **In a large mixer bowl mix** *2 cups* of the all-purpose flour, the yeast, sugar, and salt. Add warm water.
● **Beat with an electric mixer** on low speed for ½ minute, scraping sides of bowl constantly. Beat 3 minutes on high speed. Using a spoon, stir in the whole wheat flour and as much of the remaining all-purpose flour as you can.
● **Turn out** onto a lightly floured surface. Knead in enough of the remaining all-purpose flour to make a stiff dough that is smooth and elastic (8 to 10 minutes total). Shape into a ball. Place in a lightly greased bowl; turn once to grease surface.
● **Cover; let rise in a warm place** till double (1 to 1¼ hours).
● ***Or,* to raise dough in a microwave** oven, first test your microwave oven to make sure it is suitable for proofing bread. If 2 tablespoons cold, stick margarine melt completely in less than 4 minutes on oven's lowest setting (10% power), the setting has too much power and will kill the yeast before the bread has a chance to rise.

To raise, place ball of dough in a lightly greased microwave-safe mixing bowl; turn once to grease the surface. Cover dough with waxed paper. Set aside. Pour 3 cups *water* into a 4-cup measure. Micro-cook water, uncovered, on high for 6½ to 8½ minutes or till boiling. Move measure with water to the back of the oven. Place dough in microwave oven. Heat dough and water on 10% power (low) for 13 to 15 minutes or till dough is almost double.
● **Punch dough down;** turn out onto a lightly floured surface. Divide dough into thirds. Cover; let rest 10 minutes.
● **Roll** each third into a 12x10-inch rectangle. Roll up tightly from long side; seal well. Taper ends. Place, seam side down, on a greased baking sheet. Mix together egg white and water. Brush egg-white mixture over loaves.
● **Cover; let rise** till nearly double (30 to 45 minutes). With a sharp knife, make 3 diagonal cuts about ¼ inch deep across tops of loaves.
● **Bake in a 450° oven** for 15 to 20 minutes or till done. Serve same day or freeze. Makes 3 loaves, 24 servings.

Note: If the three loaves do not fit on one large baking sheet in your oven, you can put one of the loaves in the refrigerator while you bake two.

Nutrition information per serving: *86 cal., 3 g pro., 18 g carbo., 0 g fat, 0 mg chol., 137 mg sodium, 67 mg potassium, 2 g dietary fiber.*

POPPY SEED CASSEROLE

Ellen uses low-fat cheeses and yogurt—

- 1½ **pounds ground raw turkey**
- ⅓ **cup chopped onion**
- ⅓ **cup chopped green pepper**
- 1 **15-ounce can tomato sauce**
- ½ **teaspoon salt**
- ¼ **teaspoon pepper**
- 1 **8-ounce package wide noodles**
- 1 **8-ounce package Neufchâtel cheese, cubed**
- 1 **cup low-fat cottage cheese**
- ½ **cup plain low-fat yogurt**
- 1 **tablespoon poppy seed**

● **In a large skillet cook** the ground turkey, the onion, and the green pepper till the meat is no longer pink and the onion and green pepper are tender. Drain off any excess liquid. Stir in the tomato sauce, salt, and pepper.

● **Meanwhile, cook the noodles** according to the package directions, *except* omit the salt; drain.

Poppy Seed Casserole: Kids and adults alike will love it!

● **In a small mixing bowl combine** Neufchâtel cheese, cottage cheese, yogurt, and poppy seed; toss the cheese mixture with the hot noodles.

● **Layer ¾ of the noodle mixture** in a 13x9x2-inch baking dish. Spoon the meat mixture over the center of the noodles, leaving a 1- to 2-inch border of uncovered noodles. Layer the remaining noodle mixture over the center of the meat mixture, leaving a 1- to 2-inch meat border.

● **Bake, covered, in a 375° oven** for 30 minutes. Uncover the casserole. Bake for 10 to 15 minutes more or till the casserole is heated through. Serves 8.

Microwave directions: Cook the noodles according to the package directions, *except* omit the salt; drain.

Meanwhile, in a 2-quart microwave-safe casserole, crumble the ground turkey. Add the onion and the green pepper. Micro-cook, covered, on 100% power (high) for 8 to 10 minutes (low-wattage oven: 10 to 12 minutes) or till no pink remains in the turkey and the onion and green pepper are tender, stirring halfway through the cooking time. Drain off any excess liquid.

Stir in the tomato sauce, the salt, and the pepper. In a small mixing bowl combine the Neufchâtel cheese, cottage cheese, yogurt, and poppy seed; toss the cheese mixture with the hot noodles. Assemble and bake the casserole as directed above.

Nutrition information per serving: *348 cal., 31 g pro., 29 g carbo., 12 g fat, 73 mg chol., 741 mg sodium, 570 mg potassium, 2 g dietary fiber. U.S. RDA: 18% vit. A, 18% vit. C, 24% thiamine, 23% riboflavin, 30% niacin, 12% calcium, 15% iron.*

ADAM'S FETTUCCINE

You'll need only one pan to cook in—

- 8 **ounces fettuccine** *or* **linguine**
- 1 **tablespoon olive oil**
- ¾ **cup evaporated skim milk**
- ⅓ **cup grated Parmesan cheese (1½ ounces)**
- ¼ **cup sliced green onion**
- 2 **tablespoons snipped fresh basil** *or* **½ teaspoon dried basil, crushed**
- ¼ **teaspoon finely shredded lemon peel**
- ¼ **teaspoon garlic powder**
- ⅛ **teaspoon pepper**
- **Grated Parmesan cheese (optional)**
- **Fresh basil sprig (optional)**
- **Quartered lemon slices (optional)**

● **Cook pasta** according to package directions. Drain; immediately return pasta to pan. Add olive oil; toss to coat.

● **Add** the milk, the ⅓ cup Parmesan cheese, green onion, basil, lemon peel, garlic powder, and pepper.

● **Cook** over medium-high heat till bubbly, stirring constantly. Season to taste. Top with additional Parmesan cheese and fresh basil, if desired. Serve with lemon, if desired. Makes 6 side-dish servings.

Nutrition information per serving: *213 cal., 10 g pro., 33 g carbo., 4 g fat, 6 mg chol., 141 mg sodium, 205 mg potassium, 1 g dietary fiber. U.S. RDA: 24% thiamine, 15% riboflavin, 12% niacin, 18% calcium.*

Adam's Fettuccine: A delectable and low-fat version of Fettuccine Alfredo—and wonderfully easy to make.

HOT, HEARTY SANDWICH
IT'S HEALTHFUL AND KIDS LOVE IT!

By Joy Taylor

On a chilly day, warm your family with Super Sloppy Joshes. Kids love these sandwiches because they're simple to fix and fun to eat.

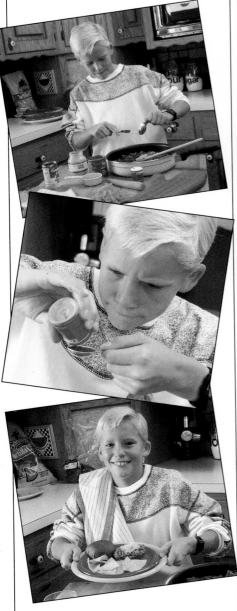

Josh did such a super job of preparing this recipe that we named it after him!

For an easy lunch or dinner, try Super Sloppy Joshes.

SUPER SLOPPY JOSHES

Bulgur wheat and carrot give this classic sandwich a fiber boost—

- 1 pound lean ground meat (beef, pork, lamb, *or* turkey)
- ½ cup chopped onion
- 1 tablespoon prepared mustard
- 2 to 3 teaspoons chili powder
- ¼ teaspoon salt
- 1 8-ounce can tomato sauce
- 1 6-ounce can tomato juice
- ½ cup shredded carrot
- ⅓ cup bulgur wheat

• • •

- 6 whole wheat hamburger buns, split
- 2 ounces shredded cheddar cheese (½ cup)

● **In a 10-inch skillet cook** meat and onion till meat is brown and onion is tender. Drain off any excess fat. Stir in the prepared mustard, chili powder, and salt. Cook and stir for 1 minute.

● **Add** tomato sauce, tomato juice, shredded carrot, and bulgur wheat. Bring mixture to boiling; reduce heat. Simmer meat mixture, uncovered, for 10 minutes, stirring occasionally. Meanwhile, toast hamburger buns, if desired.

● **To serve,** spoon the meat mixture onto toasted buns; sprinkle each sandwich with shredded cheese. Makes 6 servings.

Nutrition information per serving: 342 cal., 23 g pro., 35 g carbo., 12 g fat, 66 mg chol., 763 mg sodium, 522 mg potassium, and 4 g dietary fiber. U.S. RDA: 15% vit. C, 20% thiamine, 19% riboflavin, 29% niacin, 12% calcium, and 24% iron.

Menu suggestion: Serve Super Sloppy Joshes with a handful of tortilla chips, pickles, crisp vegetable sticks, and a glass of milk.

BETTER-THAN-EVER
GOOD HOME COOKING

"Whether it's Grandma's meat loaf or Mom's fruit pie, some foods just make you feel all cozy inside . . ."

By Lisa Holderness

Some of my best memories as a child come from the special foods that were traditions at our house. On Sundays the aroma of simmering pot roast and vegetables wafted through the house. Nowhere could my rumbling tummy get relief from that wonderful smell!

In spring, when Mom made rhubarb pie, I'd rush through dinner to get right to dessert. Years later when I begged Mom for her recipe, she revealed that it came from *Better Homes and Gardens®* magazine!

Now that I'm the resident cook, I love to reinvent those treasured foods. I start with tried-and-true recipes and add my own personal touches here and there. Now, Mom asks me for recipes!

Try these new classic dishes in your kitchen, and someday your children may say they're "just like my folks used to make!"

MACARONI AND LOTS OF CHEESE

SOUR CREAM MEATLOAF

STRAWBERRY LEMON SHORTCAKE

Photographs: Jim Krantz. Food stylist: Janet Herwig

DEEP-DISH CHICKEN PIE

The crust is so golden and flaky that no one will guess you used a ready-made piecrust.

DEBONE
● When the chicken is cool enough, go ahead and use your fingers to pull the chicken meat from the bones.

FLUTE EDGE
● Crimping the edge of the piecrust finishes your chicken pie with style. It also prevents the crust from shrinking.

"Food from the heart warms the soul . . ."

▼

MACARONI AND LOTS OF CHEESE

Colorful pasta spirals and three cheeses brighten up an old childhood favorite.

MAKE A ROUX
● For a lump-free sauce stir flour into margarine mixture to make a roux. This allows the fat to coat the flour, preventing lumps when you add the milk.

ADD CHEESES
● Slowly stirring cheeses into the white sauce till blended makes a smooth and silky cheese sauce.

MARINATED POT ROAST WITH VEGETABLES

Fill your home with the tantalizing aroma of simmering pot roast and assorted vegetables.

MARINATE
● An easy way to marinate meat is to put it in a plastic bag placed in a bowl. Pour marinade over meat; close bag and chill.

BROWN FOR FLAVOR
● Quickly cooking meat on both sides in hot oil adds lots of flavor, gives a rich appearance, and seals in the juices for a moist roast.

"*In this ever-changing world, hurrah for meat and potatoes!*"

▼

SOUR CREAM MEAT LOAF WITH MASHED POTATOES

Turn meat loaf into a hearty meal with home-made mashed potatoes and savory gravy.

MIX GENTLY

● Dig in! Mix the meat and seasonings with your hands. But don't get carried away. Too much handling makes a compact meat loaf.

MISH, MASH

● Whether you use an electric mixer or a masher, mash potatoes till smooth, then add milk and butter.

59

RHUBARB RASPBERRY CUSTARD PIE

*Garden rhubarb and plump raspberries—
one forkful of this pie and you'll be hooked!*

ADD CUSTARD

● Blend custard well using a wire whisk or rotary beater; pour it evenly over fruit. These steps help create a perfectly set custard.

COVER CRUST

● For a lightly browned pastry, cover edge with foil: Fold 12-inch piece of foil in quarters; cut circle from center. Unfold; place over pie.

"Hot dessert fresh from the oven makes everything all better . . ."

▼

DOUBLE CHOCOLATE BREAD PUDDING

A soothing dessert dedicated to all chocolate lovers.

CUT STRIPS
● Use a bread knife to cut French bread into strips (about 2 inches long). When measuring, pack bread loosely into measuring cup.

CHECK DONENESS
● When done, knife inserted near center comes out clean. Knife may be wet but egg mixture won't cling.

"Blushing strawberries— a true gift of spring . . ."

▼

STRAWBERRY LEMON SHORTCAKE

Lemon butter adds a fresh new taste to this springtime tradition.

BLEND DOUGH

● For flaky shortcake, cut margarine into flour mixture with a pastry cutter till the mixture resembles coarse crumbs.

SHAPE BISCUITS

● Roll each piece of dough into a ball and flatten with your fingers till ¾ inch thick.

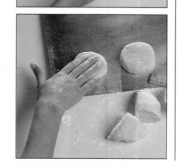

RECIPES FOR HOME COOKING

STRAWBERRY LEMON SHORTCAKE

Decorate each portion of this luscious shortcake with edible flowers such as bachelor's buttons—

   3 cups sliced fresh strawberries
 ¼ cup sugar
   1 cup all-purpose flour
   1 tablespoon sugar
 1½ teaspoons baking powder
 ¼ teaspoon salt
 ¼ cup margarine *or* butter
   1 beaten egg yolk
 ¼ cup milk
 1½ teaspoons finely shredded lemon peel
   2 tablespoons margarine *or* butter, softened
 ¼ teaspoon sugar
   1 cup whipping cream, well chilled
   1 tablespoon sugar
Lemon peel strips (optional)

● **Combine strawberries** and the ¼ cup sugar. This allows berries to juice out and create a thin syrup; set aside.

● **In a medium bowl** thoroughly stir together flour, the 1 tablespoon sugar, baking powder, and salt. Using a pastry blender, cut in the ¼ cup margarine or butter till mixture resembles coarse crumbs. (Do not overblend or the mixture will be like a dough; this will result in a mealy-textured pie-crust instead of a flaky one.) Combine egg yolk, milk, and *1 teaspoon* of the shredded lemon peel; add all at once to flour mixture and stir just till moistened.

● **On a lightly floured surface** knead dough gently. For easy kneading, pull dough toward you, then push it down and away from you with the heel of your hand. Give dough a quarter turn; fold toward you, push down. Repeat for 12 strokes. Pat dough into a circle.

● **Cut dough** into 4 pieces. Roll into balls by hand. On an ungreased baking sheet flatten each till ¾ inch thick.

● **Bake in a 450° oven** 8 to 10 minutes or till golden. Remove from baking sheet and cool slightly on a wire rack.

● **Meanwhile, stir together** the remaining shredded lemon peel, the 2 tablespoons softened margarine or butter, and the ¼ teaspoon sugar. Split warm biscuits; spread bottom layers with lemon butter mixture.

● **Immediately beat well-chilled cream** and the 1 tablespoon sugar with an electric mixer on high speed till soft peaks form. (For best results, chill bowl and beaters before using.) Be careful not to overbeat cream. The peaks should mound slightly when beaters are removed. Fill and top shortcakes with strawberries and whipped cream. Top with lemon peel strips. Serve immediately. Makes 4 servings.

Nutrition information per serving: 627 cal., 7 g pro., 59 g carbo., 42 g fat, 151 mg chol., 482 mg sodium, 432 mg potassium, and 6 g dietary fiber. U.S. RDA: 35% vit. A, 183% vit. C, 18% thiamine, 11% niacin, 17% calcium.

DEEP-DISH CHICKEN PIE

Freeze any leftover chicken broth and use it for soups or sauces—

- 1 2½- to 3-pound broiler-fryer chicken
- 5 cups water
- 3 stalks celery with leaves, cut up
- 1 small onion, quartered
- 1 bay leaf
- 1 teaspoon salt
- ¼ teaspoon pepper
- ½ of a 15-ounce package folded refrigerated unbaked piecrusts (1 crust)
- ¼ cup margarine *or* butter
- 1 cup sliced fresh mushrooms
- 1 large leek *or* onion, chopped
- ½ cup sliced celery
- ½ cup sweet red *or* green pepper cut into ½-inch pieces
- ⅓ cup all-purpose flour
- 1 teaspoon poultry seasoning
- ½ teaspoon salt
- ¼ teaspoon pepper
- 1 cup light cream *or* milk
- ½ cup loose-pack frozen peas
- 1 beaten egg

● **Rinse chicken.** Place in large kettle. Add water, celery with leaves, quartered onion, bay leaf, 1 teaspoon salt, and ¼ teaspoon pepper. Bring to boiling; reduce heat. Cover and simmer 45 to 60 minutes or till chicken is tender.

● **Remove chicken and set aside.** To strain broth, line a sieve with several layers of 100% cotton cheesecloth. Then, set sieve over a large bowl; pour broth through sieve. Discard cheesecloth, vegetables, and bay leaf. Use a metal spoon to skim fat that rises to the surface of the broth. Measure *1½ cups* of the broth. Reserve any remaining broth for another use. When chicken is cool enough to handle, pull the chicken meat from the bones (see photo, *page 56*) and cut the meat into ½-inch cubes. Discard skin and bones.

● **Let piecrust stand** at room temperature according to package directions.

● **In large saucepan melt** margarine or butter over medium heat. Add mushrooms, leek, sliced celery, and red pepper. Cook about 3 minutes or till tender. Stir in flour, poultry seasoning, ½ teaspoon salt, and ¼ teaspoon pepper. Add the 1½ cups broth and cream

all at once; cook and stir till thickened and bubbly. Stir in chicken and peas; pour into a round 1½-quart casserole.

● **Unfold piecrust.** Cut into a circle 2 inches larger in diameter than top of casserole. Brush edge of casserole with some of the beaten egg. Place crust atop casserole; turn edge under and flute to top edge of casserole (see photo, *page 56*). Cut a small hole in center of crust to allow steam to escape. Cut pastry scraps into decorative strips; brush top of crust with egg and lay on the strips. Brush again with egg.

● **Bake in a 400° oven** for 30 to 40 minutes or till the crust is golden brown. Serve immediately. Makes 6 servings.

Microwave directions: Prepare chicken and broth as directed. In a 1½-quart microwave-safe casserole microcook margarine or butter, mushrooms, leek, sliced celery, and red pepper, covered, on 100% power (high) for 3 to 5 minutes (low-wattage oven: 5 to 7 minutes) or till tender, stirring once. Stir in flour, poultry seasoning, ½ teaspoon salt, and ¼ teaspoon pepper. Stir in the 1½ cups broth and cream all at once.

Cook, uncovered, on high for 7 to 9 minutes (low-wattage oven: 10 to 12 minutes) or till thickened and bubbly, stirring after every minute till sauce starts to thicken, then stirring every 30 seconds. Stir in chicken and peas. Top with piecrust; bake as directed.

Nutrition information per serving: *558 cal., 33 g pro., 30 g carbo., 33 g fat, 157 mg chol., 656 mg sodium, and 489 mg potassium. U.S. RDA: 31% vit. A, 36% vit. C, 14% thiamine, 22% riboflavin, 50% niacin, 17% iron.*

MACARONI AND LOTS OF CHEESE

- 3 cups tricolored corkscrew macaroni *or* regular corkscrew macaroni (8 ounces)
- ¼ cup finely chopped green onion
- 2 tablespoons margarine *or* butter
- 2 tablespoons all-purpose flour
- ⅛ teaspoon pepper
- 2 cups milk
- 1½ cups shredded sharp cheddar cheese (6 ounces)
- 1 3-ounce package cream cheese, cubed and softened
- ⅓ cup grated Parmesan cheese
- 1 medium tomato, cut into wedges (optional)

Green onions (optional)

● **In a large kettle or Dutch oven cook** corkscrew macaroni according to package directions; drain.

● **Meanwhile, in a large saucepan** cook the chopped green onion in margarine or butter till tender. Stir in flour and pepper till blended (see photo, *page 57*). Add milk all at once. Cook and stir over medium heat till thickened and bubbly. Gradually add cheddar cheese and cream cheese, stirring till melted (see photo, *page 57*). Gently stir macaroni into cheese mixture. Transfer to a greased 1½-quart casserole. Sprinkle with Parmesan cheese.

● **Bake in a 350° oven** for 20 to 25 minutes or till heated through. Serve with tomato wedges and green onion, if desired. Makes 4 main-dish servings.

Microwave directions: Cook and drain macaroni as directed.

Meanwhile, in a 2-quart microwave-safe casserole micro-cook margarine or butter and the chopped green onion, covered, on 100% power (high) for 1½ to 2½ minutes or till tender. Stir in flour and pepper till blended. Add milk all at once. Stir to combine.

Cook, uncovered, on high for 6 to 8 minutes (low-wattage oven: 9 to 12 minutes) or till thickened and bubbly, stirring after every minute till the sauce starts to thicken, then stirring every 30 seconds. Gradually add cheddar cheese and cream cheese, stirring till nearly melted. Gently stir macaroni into cheese mixture.

Cook, uncovered, on high for 3 minutes; stir. Sprinkle with Parmesan cheese. Cook, uncovered, on high for 2 to 4 minutes more or till heated through. Serve as directed.

Nutrition information per serving: *626 cal., 27 g pro., 53 g carbo., 33 g fat, 84 mg chol., 617 mg sodium, 399 mg potassium. U.S. RDA: 32% vit. A, 40% thiamine, 39% riboflavin, 19% niacin, 61% calcium, 15% iron.*

MARINATED POT ROAST WITH VEGETABLES

    1   2½- to 3-pound boneless beef
        chuck pot roast
    1   cup dry red wine
    1   teaspoon finely shredded
        orange peel
    ¼   cup orange juice
    2   tablespoons olive *or* cooking oil
    1   teaspoon dried basil, crushed
    ¼   teaspoon pepper
All-purpose flour
    2   tablespoons olive *or* cooking oil
    2   teaspoons instant beef bouillon
        granules
    1   pound whole tiny new potatoes,
        quartered
    1   10-ounce package frozen tiny
        whole carrots
    1   9-ounce package frozen
        Italian-style green beans
    1   cup peeled fresh pearl onions
        or small frozen whole onions
    2   tablespoons cornstarch

● **Trim fat from meat.** Place meat in a plastic bag; set in a bowl. Combine wine, orange peel and juice, 2 tablespoons oil, basil, and pepper. Pour mixture over meat and close bag (see photo, *page 58*). Chill several hours or overnight, turning bag occasionally.
● **Remove meat from marinade,** reserving marinade. Pat meat dry. Coat all sides with flour. In a 5-quart Dutch oven heat 2 tablespoons oil. Carefully add meat to hot oil (see photo, *page 58*). Slowly brown meat on both sides. Drain off fat. Add marinade, bouillon granules, and 1 cup *water*.
● **Cook, covered, in a 325° oven** for 1 hour. Add potatoes; cook, covered, 30 minutes more. Add carrots, green beans, and onions; spoon juices over. Cover and return to oven. Cook about 45 minutes more or till meat and vegetables are tender. Transfer to a warm platter, reserving juices. Cover meat and vegetables with foil to keep warm.
● **For gravy, strain** pan juices through a sieve into a large measuring cup; use a metal spoon to skim off fat that rises to the surface. Measure *2 cups* of the juices; discard remaining juices. Return juices to Dutch oven. In a small bowl combine cornstarch and 2 tablespoons *cold water;* stir into the 2 cups juices. Cook and stir till thickened and bubbly; cook and stir 2 minutes more. Serve with meat and vegetables. Serves 8.

Microwave directions: Marinate meat as directed. Omit coating meat with flour and browning. In a 3-quart microwave-safe casserole combine meat, reserved marinade, and bouillon granules. Turn meat to coat all sides.

Micro-cook meat, covered, on 100% power (high) for 5 minutes or till liquid is boiling. Cook, covered, on 50% power (medium) for 40 minutes. Turn meat over. Add potatoes; cook, covered, on medium for 15 minutes. Turn meat over. Add carrots, green beans, and onions; spoon juices over. Cook, covered, on medium for 25 to 30 minutes more or till meat and vegetables are tender. Transfer meat and vegetables to warm platter, reserving juices. Keep warm.

For gravy, strain pan juices through a sieve into a 4-cup glass measure; use a metal spoon to skim off fat that rises to the surface. Measure *2 cups* of juices; discard remaining juices.

In a small bowl combine cornstarch and 2 tablespoons *cold water;* stir into reserved juices. Cook, uncovered, on 100% power (high) for 2½ to 3 minutes or till thickened and bubbly, stirring after every minute till slightly thickened, then every 30 seconds. Cook, uncovered, on 50% power (medium) for 30 seconds more. Serve as directed.

Note: *Not recommended for low-wattage microwave ovens.*

Nutrition information per serving: *356 cal., 27 g pro., 23 g carbo., 15 g fat, 77 mg chol., 199 mg sodium, 616 mg potassium, and 3 g dietary fiber. U.S. RDA: 154% vit. A, 19% vit. C, 16% riboflavin, 21% niacin, 22% iron.*

SOUR CREAM MEAT LOAF WITH MASHED POTATOES

    2   beaten eggs
    1   8-ounce carton dairy sour cream
    ¼   cup milk
    ½   cup fine dry bread crumbs
    ¼   cup finely chopped onion
    2   tablespoons snipped parsley
    1   tablespoon Worcestershire
        sauce
    1   tablespoon Dijon-style mustard
    ¼   teaspoon salt
    ¼   teaspoon pepper
1½   pounds lean ground beef
    1   0.75-ounce package brown
        gravy mix
Mashed Potatoes

● **In a large bowl combine** eggs, *½ cup* of the sour cream, and milk; stir in bread crumbs, onion, parsley, Worcestershire sauce, mustard, salt, and pepper. Add beef; mix well (see photo, *page 59*). Pat into a 9x5x3-inch loaf pan or shape into loaf of the same size and place in a 12x7½x2-inch baking dish.
● **Bake, uncovered, in a 350° oven** about 1¼ hours or till a meat thermometer inserted in the center of the meat loaf registers 170°. Let cool 10 minutes; remove from pan.
● **Meanwhile, for gravy,** in medium saucepan stir together the remaining sour cream and the dry gravy mix. Add water as called for on package. Cook according to package directions.
● **Slice meat loaf** and serve with Mashed Potatoes and gravy. Serves 6.

Microwave directions: Mix meat loaf ingredients as directed.

In a microwave-safe 9-inch pie plate shape the meat mixture into an 8-inch ring, 2½ inches wide. Cover with waxed paper. Micro-cook, covered, on 100% power (high) for 10 to 12 minutes (low-wattage: 16 to 18 minutes) or till a meat thermometer inserted in the center of the loaf registers 170°, giving the dish a quarter turn every 3 minutes. Let cool 10 minutes.

Meanwhile, for gravy, in a microwave-safe 1-quart casserole stir together remaining sour cream and dry gravy mix. Stir in water as directed on package. Micro-cook, uncovered, on high for 3 to 5 minutes (low-wattage: 5 to 7 minutes), or till thickened and bubbly, stirring twice (low-wattage: stir 3 times). Slice meat loaf and serve as directed.

Mashed Potatoes: Peel and quarter 4 medium *potatoes* (1 pound, 6 ounces). In a large saucepan cook potatoes in boiling water, covered, for 20 to 25 minutes or till tender; drain. Beat with an electric mixer (see photo, *page 59*) or mash with a potato masher till smooth. Add 2 tablespoons *margarine or butter,* ¼ teaspoon *salt,* and dash *pepper.* Gradually add enough *milk* (2 to 3 tablespoons) and continue beating till potatoes are light and fluffy.

Nutrition information per serving: *478 cal., 31 g pro., 33 g carbo., 24 g fat, 190 mg chol., 672 mg sodium, 801 mg potassium, and 2 g dietary fiber. U.S. RDA: 13% vit. A, 19% vit. C, 18% thiamine, 23% riboflavin, 36% niacin, 11% calcium, 23% iron.*

RHUBARB RASPBERRY CUSTARD PIE

For a delicious topping, beat 1 cup whipping cream and 1 tablespoon raspberry liqueur to soft peaks; spoon onto each slice of pie—

1¼ cups sugar
 1 tablespoon all-purpose flour
 ¼ teaspoon ground nutmeg
 4 beaten eggs
Pastry for Single-Crust Pie
 1 pound rhubarb cut into 1-inch pieces (3 cups)
 1 cup fresh *or* frozen unsweetened raspberries
 ¼ cup all-purpose flour
 ¼ cup sugar
 ¼ cup chopped almonds
 ½ teaspoon ground cinnamon
 ½ teaspoon ground nutmeg
 2 tablespoons margarine *or* butter

● **In a small mixing bowl combine** the 1¼ cups sugar, the 1 tablespoon flour, and the ¼ teaspoon nutmeg. Add eggs. Beat till well mixed using a wire whisk or rotary beater.
● **Prepare Pastry** for Single-Crust Pie as directed. Combine rhubarb and raspberries. Spoon fruit into the pastry. Pour the egg mixture over fruit (see photo, *page 60*).
● **To prevent overbrowning** of the pastry, cover the edge with foil (see photo, *below*). Bake in a 375° oven for 25 minutes. Remove the foil from the pie. Bake about 15 minutes more or till the custard is set.

● **Meanwhile,** for topping, in a medium mixing bowl combine the ¼ cup flour, the ¼ cup sugar, almonds, cinnamon, and the ½ teaspoon nutmeg. With a pastry blender, cut in margarine or butter till the pieces are the size of small peas.
● **Remove pie** from the oven. Sprinkle topping mixture around outer edge of fruit and custard, leaving a 5-inch circle in the center uncovered. Return to oven and bake for 5 minutes more. Cool on a wire rack. Cover and chill any leftover pie. Makes 8 servings.

Pastry for Single-Crust Pie: In a medium mixing bowl stir together 1¼ cups *all-purpose flour* and ½ teaspoon *salt*. With a pastry blender, cut in ⅓ cup *shortening* or *lard* till pieces are the size of small peas.

Sprinkle 1 tablespoon *water* over part of the mixture; gently toss with a fork. Push to side of bowl. Repeat with 2 to 3 tablespoons more *water* till all is moistened. Form dough into a ball.

On a lightly floured surface, slightly flatten dough with hands. Roll the dough from center to edge, forming a circle about 12 inches in diameter.

Loosely wrap the pastry around a rolling pin. Unroll pastry onto a 9-inch pie plate. Ease pastry into pie plate, being careful not to stretch pastry. Trim to ½ inch beyond edge of pie plate; fold under extra pastry. Make a fluted edge. *Do not* prick the pastry.

Nutrition information per serving: *416 cal., 7 g pro., 61 g carbo., 17 g fat, 137 mg chol., 207 mg sodium, 246 mg potassium, and 2 g dietary fiber. U.S. RDA: 13% vit. C, 14% thiamine, 14% riboflavin, 11% iron.*

DOUBLE CHOCOLATE BREAD PUDDING

A chocolaty version of a favorite dessert that's easy to make and impressive to serve—

2½ cups French bread strips, about 2 inches long (see photo, page 61)
 1 cup (5 ounces) white baking pieces with cocoa butter
 ½ cup light raisins
 3 eggs
 2 cups milk
 ⅓ cup sugar
 1 teaspoon vanilla
 ¼ cup miniature semisweet chocolate pieces

● **In a greased 12x8½-inch tart pan** or shallow 1½-quart oval baking dish combine bread strips, white baking pieces, and raisins.
● **In a large mixing bowl beat** eggs, milk, sugar, and vanilla till well mixed. Pour over bread mixture; let stand for 15 minutes so bread will absorb liquid.
● **Bake in a 375° oven** for 40 to 45 minutes or till a knife inserted near the center comes out clean (see photo, *below*). Remove the pudding to a wire rack. Sprinkle semisweet chocolate pieces atop. Let the pudding cool for 30 minutes. Serve warm, spooned into dessert dishes. Makes 6 to 8 servings.

Nutrition information per serving: *384 cal., 10 g pro., 54 g carbo., 15 g fat, 149 mg chol., 214 mg sodium, 361 mg potassium, and 1 g dietary fiber. U.S. RDA: 21% riboflavin, 18% calcium.*

Cover crust with foil.

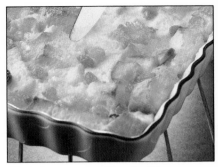
Test doneness with a knife.

THE MAGAZINE FOR AMERICAN FAMILIES

YUMMY FAMILY BREAKFASTS Page 137

Better Homes and Gardens

MAY 1989 $1.50

IN THIS ISSUE
AMERICA'S BEST FAMILY VACATION RESORTS

GARDENER'S ALMANAC
• SPRINGTIME TIPS

PLUS

PERENNIALS
WHAT TO PLANT WITH WHAT

NEW HOUSE OF THE YEAR!

AFFORDABLE STYLE
REDECORATING ON A SHOESTRING

FOR KIDS

HAPPY BIRTHDAY PARTIES
EASY-ON-PARENTS IDEAS

A.M. CUISINE

FABULOUS WEEKEND BREAKFAST AND BRUNCH

BY BARBARA GOLDMAN

Weekend mornings— the best times of the week! You can sleep late, read the paper in your pajamas, or be up at the crack of dawn—it's your choice. And you can enjoy breakfast in ways you just can't during the week. Sometimes it's a family affair and everyone pitches in to fix their favorites. Or what better time for a casual brunch with friends? Put together a couple of easy dishes the night before, add the final touches next day, and you'll find that brunch will be a breeze.

FAMILY BREAKFAST
Strawberry Pancake Stacks: a terrific pancake variation.

BRUNCH FOR EIGHT
A giant cinnamon roll: an elegant brunch bread.

Photographs: Perry Struse. Food stylist: Judy Tills

STRAWBERRY PANCAKE STACKS
Sensational! Personalized pancakes with strawberries.

SIGNATURE PANCAKES
What's in a name? Eating pleasure just for you.

WEEKEND FAMILY BREAKFAST

● *Let the kids join in the fixing of this easy family breakfast. They can set the table, mix up the orange juice, do the microwave cocoa, and choose a favorite variation of our healthful, great-tasting pancake recipe. Then, while you work the griddle, watch the kids create pancake letters and names, come up with individualized fruit and nut variations, or build luscious Strawberry Pancake Stacks.*

MENU
Personalized Pancakes
·
Quick Pineapple Combo
·
Choose Your Cocoa

◀ **A.M. REWARD**
Breakfast making is fun;
eating it is even better!

▲ **KITCHEN CAPERS**
Cooking is a romp when
everyone gets into the act.

▲ **JUST FOR MOM**
"Designer" pancakes, with help
from a plastic squeeze bottle.

QUICK PINEAPPLE COMBO
*Kiwi fruit, grapes, and yogurt
top canned pineapple quarters.*

CHOOSE YOUR COCOA
*Caramel- or mocha-flavored cocoa
in minutes from the microwave.*

SPRINGTIME BRUNCH FOR EIGHT

● *Want to know what leisurely entertaining feels like? Put together a stylish, comfy brunch with just a few terrific foods—most prepared the day before. Come morning, bake the pre-shaped refrigerated bread ring. While that cools, slip the Turkey-Asparagus Brunch Bake into the oven. Then drizzle the fruit platter with raspberry puree, set out drink mixings for the fabulous Peach Slush, and enjoy!*

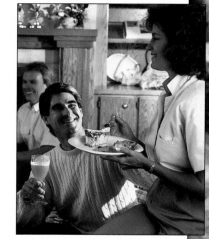

▲ EASY DOES IT!
When guests arrive, all you have left to do is relax.

▲ HAPPY LISTENING
An informal brunch is a great way to catch up with friends.

▼ BRUNCH STRATEGY
Flexible eating arrangements allow guests to mingle freely.

MENU

**Turkey-Asparagus
Brunch Bake**

•

**Super-Colossal
Cinnamon-Pecan Ring**

•

**Painter's Palette
Fruit Plate**

•

Peach Slush

PERSONALIZED PANCAKES

1⅓ cups all-purpose flour
⅔ cup oat bran *or* whole wheat flour
3 tablespoons brown sugar
1 tablespoon baking powder
½ teaspoon baking soda
2 beaten eggs
1¾ cups buttermilk
2 tablespoons cooking oil
Maple syrup *or* fruit topping (optional)

● **In a medium mixing bowl stir** together flour, oat bran or whole wheat flour, brown sugar, baking powder, and baking soda. In a small mixing bowl combine eggs, buttermilk, and cooking oil; add all at once to flour mixture, stirring till blended but still slightly lumpy.
● **Pour** about ¼ *cup* of the batter onto a hot, lightly greased griddle or heavy skillet. Continue as directed for desired variations.
● **Cook** over medium-high heat till golden brown, turning to cook other side when pancakes have a bubbly surface and slightly dry edges. If desired, serve pancakes with syrup or fruit topping. Makes twelve 4-inch pancakes.
Strawberry Pancake Stacks: Prepare pancakes as directed. Place on a baking sheet, cover with foil, and keep warm at lowest oven setting till ready to assemble and serve. To assemble, place about ¼ cup sliced *sweetened strawberries** over 1 pancake; repeat with two more pancakes, topping *each* stack with an additional ¼ cup *strawberries*. Add a large dollop of *whipped dessert topping* or *vanilla yogurt*. Top with a whole *fresh strawberry*.
***Note:* For sweetened strawberries stir ⅓ cup *sugar* into 3 cups sliced *strawberries*. Let stand at least 20 minutes to allow berries to juice out.
At-Your-Whim Pancakes: Prepare pancakes as directed, *except* when undersides of cakes are nicely brown, lightly sprinkle about 1 tablespoon *mixed dried fruit bits, raisins, coarsely chopped pecans*, or *drained blueberries* evenly over top of *each* pancake. Turn; brown other side.
Signature Pancakes: Prepare pancake batter as directed, *except* thin batter with enough *water* (about 3 tablespoons) to make of proper consistency to squirt through a plastic squeeze-top bottle** or to pour from a

small pitcher. Squeeze or pour batter onto greased griddle to form letters for names or slogan.
***Note:* Clean, empty plastic squeeze-top bottles that once contained ice-cream topping work well for squeezing batter into the letter shapes.
It's important to write each letter *backward* on the griddle so that when the pancake letters are flipped they will be read correctly.
Nutrition information per 4-inch pancake: 123 cal., 5 g pro., 19 g carbo., 4 g fat, 47 mg chol., 172 mg sodium, 120 mg potassium, 1 g dietary fiber. U.S. RDA: 11% thiamine, 10% calcium.

CHOOSE YOUR COCOA

1½ cups milk
2 tablespoons presweetened cocoa powder
2 tablespoons caramel topping *or* 1 tablespoon instant coffee crystals
Marshmallow creme *or* tiny marshmallows (optional)
Caramel topping *or* ground cinnamon (optional)

● **In a 4-cup** microwave-safe measure combine milk, presweetened cocoa powder, and the 2 tablespoons caramel topping or 1 tablespoon instant coffee crystals. Stir till mixture is blended.
● **Micro-cook,** uncovered, on 100% power (high) for 3 to 4 minutes or till hot, stirring once. Serve in 2 small mugs. If desired, top each serving with marshmallow creme or tiny marshmallows and drizzle with caramel topping or sprinkle with ground cinnamon. Makes two 6-ounce servings.
For 4 servings: Prepare as directed, using a 4-cup microwave-safe measure, *except* double amounts of milk, presweetened cocoa powder, caramel topping or instant coffee crystals. Micro-cook, uncovered, on 100% power (high) for 6 to 8 minutes, stirring twice. Continue as directed.
Nutrition information per serving: 169 cal., 7 g pro., 26 g carbo., 4 g fat, 14 mg chol., 155 mg sodium. U.S. RDA: 21% riboflavin, 27% calcium.

SUPER-COLOSSAL CINNAMON-PECAN RING

If you prefer, shape and chill overnight. Bake the next day and serve warm—

2 1-pound loaves frozen bread dough, thawed
⅓ cup margarine *or* butter, melted
⅓ cup sugar
⅓ cup packed brown sugar
2 teaspoons ground cinnamon
½ cup chopped pecans
1¼ cups sifted powdered sugar
½ teaspoon vanilla
Milk (about 4 teaspoons)
Cinnamon sticks (optional)
Pecan halves (optional)

● **Grease a 12-inch pizza pan;** set aside. On a lightly floured surface, flatten thawed dough slightly. Cut each loaf into 4 pieces (8 pieces total). Form each piece into a rope about 18 inches long. Brush each rope on all sides with melted margarine or butter.
● **Stir together** the sugar, brown sugar, and ground cinnamon. Place mixture in shallow pan or on large sheet of foil.
● **Roll one rope** in sugar mixture to coat evenly. Shape rope into coil in center of the prepared 12-inch pizza pan. Roll another rope in sugar mixture. Attach securely to end of first rope and coil around first coil. Continue coating remaining ropes with sugar mixture and attaching them to form a 10- to 11-inch circle. Sprinkle any of the remaining sugar mixture over cake ring. Sprinkle ½ cup chopped pecans on top.
● **Cover and let rise** in a warm place for 30 to 40 minutes or till nearly doubled. (*Or,* cover with plastic wrap and let rise overnight in the refrigerator. Before baking, remove from the refrigerator and let stand 15 to 20 minutes.)
● **Bake** in a 350° oven for 30 to 35 minutes or till done. Cover with foil the last 10 minutes, if necessary, to prevent overbrowning. Cool about 15 minutes.
● **Stir together** powdered sugar, vanilla, and enough milk to make a thick glaze. Spoon over cake ring. If desired, decorate with cinnamon sticks and pecan halves. Serve warm. Serves 16.
Nutrition information per serving: 275 cal., 5 g pro., 44 g carbo., 9 g fat, 3 mg chol., 320 mg sodium, 88 mg potassium, 1 g dietary fiber. U.S. RDA: 15% thiamine, 10% iron.

TURKEY-ASPARAGUS BRUNCH BAKE

To save time, assemble this dish ahead and chill overnight before baking—

 1 pound fresh asparagus *or* one 10-ounce package frozen cut asparagus *or* one 10-ounce package frozen cut broccoli
 1 pound ground raw turkey
 1 cup chopped onion
 ½ cup chopped sweet red pepper
Nonstick spray coating
 8 eggs
 2 cups milk
 1 cup all-purpose flour
 ¼ cup grated Parmesan cheese
 1 teaspoon lemon pepper
 ¾ teaspoon salt
 ¾ teaspoon dried tarragon, crushed
 1 cup shredded Swiss cheese (4 ounces)
Steamed asparagus spears (optional)
Lemon slices (optional)
Sweet red pepper cutouts (optional)

● **To cook fresh asparagus,** wash and scrape off scales. Break off woody bases where spears snap easily. Reserve a few spears for garnish, if desired. Cut remaining asparagus into 1½-inch pieces; cook, covered, in a small amount of boiling water for 7 to 9 minutes or till crisp-tender. (For frozen asparagus or broccoli, cook according to package directions. Then drain and set aside.)
● **In a large skillet cook** turkey, onion, and chopped red pepper till vegetables are just tender and no pink remains in turkey. Remove from heat; drain. Set aside. Spray bottom and sides of a 13x9x2-inch baking dish with nonstick spray coating. Arrange meat mixture in dish; top with cooked cut asparagus.
● **In a large mixing bowl combine** eggs, milk, flour, Parmesan cheese, lemon pepper, salt, and tarragon; beat smooth with rotary beater. (Or, combine all in blender container; cover and blend for 20 seconds.)* Pour egg mixture evenly over layers in baking dish.
● **Bake in a 425° oven** for 20 minutes or till a knife inserted near the center comes out clean. Sprinkle with the Swiss cheese; bake 3 to 5 minutes more or till the cheese is melted. If desired, garnish with reserved asparagus spears, lemon slices, and red pepper cutouts. Serve immediately. Serves 10.

To make ahead: Prepare as directed to the *. Pour egg mixture into a bowl or pitcher; cover and chill. Cover and chill turkey and asparagus in baking dish. To bake, stir egg mixture well and pour over turkey mixture. Bake, uncovered, in 425° oven 30 minutes or till a knife inserted near center comes out clean. Continue as directed.

Nutrition information per serving: 263 cal., 23 g pro., 16 g carbo., 11 g fat, 268 mg chol., 403 mg sodium, 1 g dietary fiber. U.S. RDA: 16% vit. A, 24% vit. C, 14% thiamine, 25% riboflavin, 15% niacin, 25% calcium, 14% iron.

PAINTER'S PALETTE FRUIT PLATE

You'll find the ornamental ruscus leaves at your florist—

 2 cups fresh *or* frozen raspberries *or* strawberries
Sugar (optional)
 4 pink *or* white grapefruit, peeled and sectioned
 4 oranges, peeled and sectioned
Fresh raspberries and blueberries *or* other fresh fruit (optional)
Ruscus *or* mint leaves (optional)

● **Thaw berries, if frozen.** Place the 2 cups berries in a blender container or food processor bowl. Cover and blend or process till smooth. Strain. If desired, stir in enough sugar to taste. Cover and chill till serving.
● **On a large plate or platter arrange** grapefruit and orange sections in rows. Drizzle berry mixture over fruit. Sprinkle with fresh berries or with other fresh fruit. If desired, garnish with ruscus or mint leaves. Serves 8.

Note: Use any remaining fruit puree as topping for pancakes, waffles, cake, or ice cream.

Nutrition information per serving: 84 cal., 2 g pro., 21 g carbo., 0 g fat, 0 mg chol., 0 mg sodium, 332 mg potassium, 5 g dietary fiber. U.S. RDA: 140% vit. C.

QUICK PINEAPPLE COMBO

 1 20-ounce can peeled, cored, whole pineapple, chilled
 1 cup red *or* green seedless grapes
 2 kiwi fruit, peeled and sliced, *or* 1 cup fresh strawberries *or* raspberries
 1 8-ounce carton low-fat piña colada yogurt
 ¼ cup toasted coconut

● **Cut the whole pineapple** lengthwise into quarters. Arrange pineapple quarters on a serving plate, or place *each* quarter on a small plate.
● **In a medium mixing bowl** combine grapes and kiwi fruit or berries. Carefully fold yogurt into fruit. Spoon ¼ of mixture over *each* pineapple quarter. Sprinkle *each* with toasted coconut. Serve immediately. Makes 4 servings.

Nutrition information per serving: 184 cal., 4 g pro., 38 g carbo., 3 g fat, 2 mg chol., 39 mg sodium, 518 mg potassium, 2 g dietary fiber. U.S. RDA: 88% vit. C, 13% thiamine, 11% riboflavin, 12% calcium.

PEACH SLUSH

 1 16-ounce package frozen unsweetened peaches, thawed slightly
 1 12-ounce can peach *or* apricot nectar
 1 6-ounce can frozen orange juice concentrate
Peach wine cooler, chilled, *or* lemon-lime carbonated beverage, chilled

● **In blender container combine** *undrained* peaches, nectar, and orange juice concentrate. Cover; blend till smooth. Pour into ice-cube trays. Cover; freeze for 3 to 4 hours or till firm.
● **To serve,** remove frozen cubes from the freezer trays. Place the cubes into a large ice bucket or bowl. Let stand 20 to 30 minutes to thaw slightly. Place *two or three* cubes into each goblet. Add ¾ cup wine cooler or carbonated beverage; stir gently to make a slush. Makes 28 cubes (10 servings).

Nutrition information per serving: 180 cal., 1 g pro., 34 g carbo., 0 g fat, 7 mg sodium. U.S. RDA: 57% vit. C.

GOOD FOOD, GOOD HEALTH

BY BARBARA GOLDMAN

SALAD SMARTS!

How to keep calories and fat in line

You choose a salad when you want to eat something light, right? Crisp greens, vegetables, and fruits are refreshing and, best of all, low calorie. Plus, they're full of vitamins and fiber.

HEALTHFUL CHOICES

Before tossing your greens with dressing, or mounding them high with other goodies, check your options. The amounts and types of dressing and toppers often determine your salad's healthfulness. When you fix a dinner salad at home or at a restaurant salad bar, you can go mighty (salad A) or light (salad B). Compare:

● **Salad A** includes one cup of mixed greens topped with diced tomato, shredded cheddar cheese, crumbled bacon, sunflower nuts, and a generous two tablespoons of Thousand Island Dressing. *Salad total:* about 300 calories and 23 grams of fat!

● **Salad B** also starts with a cup of mixed greens and diced tomato. But it's topped with low-fat fixings including sliced cucumber, alfalfa sprouts, and diced green pepper. The salad is then lightly dressed with one tablespoon of reduced-calorie Thousand Island dressing. *Salad total:* fewer than 70 calories and just 2 grams of fat!

APRICOT-SESAME DRESSING

Apricot nectar replaces most of the oil in this low-fat dressing—
- 1 **teaspoon cornstarch**
- ⅛ **teaspoon garlic powder**
- ⅛ **teaspoon ground ginger**
- 1 **5½-ounce can apricot nectar**
- ¼ **cup red wine vinegar**
- 1 **tablespoon honey**
- 1 **teaspoon sesame oil**
- 1 **teaspoon toasted sesame seed (optional)**

In a small saucepan combine cornstarch, garlic powder, and ginger. Stir in apricot nectar, vinegar, honey, and oil. Cook, stirring constantly, till thickened and bubbly. Cook and stir 2 minutes more. Chill, covered. Stir before serving. If desired, sprinkle sesame seed over salad greens. Makes ⅔ cup.

Nutrition information per tablespoon: 22 cal., 0 g pro., 5 g carbo., 0 g fat, 0 mg chol., 1 mg sodium, 27 mg potassium. U.S. RDA: 10% vit. C.

Do yourself a favor! Pour on a low-fat dressing.

DRESSING-UP TIPS

● *Read labels!* Many bottled dressings average 60 to 80 calories per tablespoon; reduced-calorie versions just one-fourth to one-half that amount.

● *Before serving creamy dressings,* dilute fat and calories by stirring in some low-fat plain yogurt.

● *Create tasty, low-fat dressings* in your own kitchen. You can replace one-half or more of the oil in most recipes with fruit juice or broth. For creamy dressings, replace part of the mayonnaise with low-fat yogurt, cottage cheese, buttermilk, or tofu.

● *Use one part oil to one part vinegar* rather than the typical three to one ratio whenever possible. A mild vinegar (such as balsamic) reduces tartness.

APPROXIMATE CALORIES AND FAT IN 1 TABLESPOON DRESSING

Dressing	Calories	Fat (g)
Blue cheese	60–80	6–8
Blue cheese, reduced calorie	10–40	1–4
Buttermilk based	60–80	6–8
Buttermilk, reduced calorie	30–40	3–4
French	60–70	6–7
French, reduced calorie	20–30	1–2
Italian	45–80	4–8
Italian, reduced calorie	15–35	2–3
Italian, oil free	4–6	0–1
Mayonnaise	100	11–12
Mayonnaise, reduced calorie	40–50	4–5
Oil and vinegar	70–100	7–9
Salad dressing	70	7
Salad dressing, reduced calorie	35–45	3–4

BY
BARBARA JOHNSON

HAPPY BIRTHDAY PARTIES

FUN FOR KIDS; EASY ON PARENTS

Birthday memories last a lifetime. And, a party in your own home makes those memories extra special. A birthday bash can be a blast for the kids, yet easy on you. To help out, we've gathered dozens of nifty hints, inside tips (from experienced parents, no less!), and doable ideas for birthday celebrations at home. We bet *you'll* have fun, too!

BLOCKBUSTER BIRTHDAY CAKE

Spell out a wish for your young one by placing colorful lettered blocks on a frosted sheet cake. Decorate the top and sides with candies, and, of course, candles! Even after the party, the blocks are a happy reminder of the special day.

Photographs: Scott Little and Perry Struse. Food stylist: Janet Herwig

BIRTHDAY BALLOONS!

Center your party around balloons—for color, whimsy, and pure fun!

Dress the whole room with helium-filled balloons! Tie a bright cluster to each chair. Scatter more balloons around the room, weighted with blocks or bricks. At the party's end, pass out the balloons for kids to carry home.

BALLOON PLACE SETTINGS

Create colorful place settings and party favors by tying a personalized balloon to the chair of each party guest. Write the child's name on a small card and attach the card to a balloon. Then tie the balloons to chairs. Each child will then have a balloon to take home. You might even put small party favors in the balloons and let the kids pop them as part of the games you play at the party.

BALLOON INVITATIONS

Get the kids thinking balloons from the moment they're invited! Your child can help you attach the ribbon-tied balloons to paper clouds telling who, what, when, and where.

HOT-AIR BALLOON CAKES

These sprightly sprinkled balloon cupcakes do double duty: Use them to decorate the center of your party table, then serve them to the kids for party treats. Let the birthday boy or girl blow out candles that you placed on several extra frosted cupcakes.

DYNAMITE DINOSAURS!

A perfect party for kids who are crazy about dinosaurs!

Dinosaurs are everywhere, and kids love 'em! If your child is one who does, throw him or her a dinosaur-themed party that includes a dinosaur cake, two prehistoric snack mixes, clever hats to make, and dinosaur favors to take home.

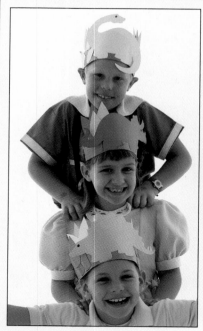

DINOSAUR HATS

Whether it's stegosaurus, brontosaurus, or triceratops, everyone seems to have a favorite creature. Set out the supplies and start the party by letting the guests make their own creations to wear.

PREHISTORIC CAKE

Kids flip over this edible "re-creation" of prehistoric times! Pebbles, rocks, boulders, plants . . . and, yes, even dinosaurs are here. Purchase ready-made cookies at your grocery store, or make your own dinosaur cookies. (Give extra cookies to kids who don't get one off the cake.)

PARTY SNACKS

Hungry "monsters" will gobble up *Dinosaur Trail Mix* (a savory collection of fish crackers, peanuts, pretzels, and popcorn) and *Prehistoric Party Chow* (a sweet mix of dinosaur-shaped cereal, fruit bits, coconut, and sunflower nuts).

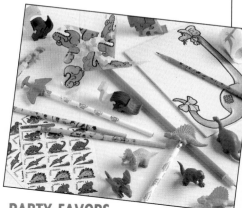

PARTY FAVORS

Give the kids inexpensive dinosaur "relics" to take home. Shown here are dinosaur puzzles, pencils, stickers, and notepads.

DINOSAUR GRAHAM COOKIES

FRESH MINT SPRIG SHRUBS AND TREES

PEACH-HALF BOULDERS

GUMDROP ROCKS

PEANUT PEBBLES

MALTED-MILK-BALL BORDER

MORE PARTY IDEAS

A collage of treats, themes, activities—

BIRTHDAY PARTY THEMES

● **ytraP drawkcaB:** That's a backward party! Do everything backward. Print the invitations backward. Ask the partygoers to wear their clothes backward. Run the party in reverse: blow out candles, eat cake and ice cream, open presents, and end up with games. For kicks, run a slapstick comedy film backward.

● **Breakfast Party:** Hold an a.m. party—even have the kids come in their pj's! Stage a mattress jump or pillow fight. Show cartoons.

BIRTHDAY PARTY ACTIVITIES

T-SHIRT COLORING

Give the kids white T-shirts and heat-set fabric crayons, then turn them loose as fashion designers. While they're enjoying treats, quickly set the designs by running a hot iron over each (see package directions). The shirt doubles as a party favor.

MUSICAL RUGS

The same game as musical chairs, but played with rugs! Pull out your old rugs, or ask each child to bring one. Either way, the scrambling is great fun!

COOKIE BAKING

Kids love making cookies! Let them shape dough you've made ahead. Bake their cookies while they're playing games. Send some cookies home with each child.

CANDY NECKLACES

The best jewelry is the kind kids can eat! Thread fruit-flavored circle candies or tubular licorice bits onto shoestring licorice. Tie the ends together to finish the "priceless jewels."

CONE-HEAD TREATS

Great spill-proof treats for kids to tote to school or day care! Fill ice-cream cones with kids' favorite snacks: trail mix, granola, gumdrops, or other candy.

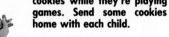

For unique party keepsakes, take instant photos of the gang wearing their T-shirt creations. Send a photo home with each child.

DIRECTIONS AND RECIPES
BIRTHDAY BALLOONS!
(Pictured on pages 76–77.)

Hot-Air Balloon Cakes: a high-flying treat!

HOT-AIR BALLOON CAKES
If you make your own cupcakes, bake them in foil baking cups, frost with white frosting, and sprinkle with colored sugar as we did for the photo—
7-inch round balloons
Cellophane tape
Plastic drinking straws
Crinkle *or* thin metallic gift wrap ribbon
Frosted cupcakes *or* muffins
● **Blow up the balloons** so that they're about 5 inches in diameter (they won't be full). Tie balloons and then tape each one to the end of a straw. Depending on the size of your straws, you may want to trim a little off the length of the straws.
● **Next, for decoration, tie** some ribbon around the straw at the balloon's base. Shred and curl the ribbon, if you like. Insert other end of straw into middle of cupcake or muffin so straw and attached balloon stand upright as shown, *above*.
● **Cut three long pieces of ribbon.** (The length you'll need depends on how tall your balloon is. Cut a length that goes around the balloon and the base of the cupcake about 1½ times. That way, you'll have plenty of ribbon left to tie on top.)
● **Arrange the pieces of ribbon** spoke-fashion on a table, crossing the ribbons in the center; tape the ribbons together in the center. Turn the whole ribbon arrangement over. Set one cupcake on the tape in the center of the ribbons, taping ribbon to baking cup. Bring the ribbons up over the balloon, tying or taping to the top of the balloon. Curl the ends of the ribbons, if you like. Have a happy birthday flight!

RENTING A HELIUM TANK FOR BLOWING UP BALLOONS
Look in the Yellow Pages of your local phone directory under "Helium" or "Rental Service Stores" for businesses that rent helium tanks. Cost can run from approximately $15 to $35. Most places will require a deposit of $50 to $100.

MORE BALLOON PARTY FUN: MAKE AN AUTOGRAPH CLOUD!
Create a lasting record of the party guests—have all the kids sign an autograph cloud as they arrive at the party.

To make one, draw a large cloud (about 24×12 inches) on a piece of sturdy white paper. Write "Happy Birthday!" and attach a star cut out of colored construction paper. Provide different-colored pens for the kids to use as they add their birthday greetings.

MORE BALLOON PARTY FUN: STAR STRAW FAVORS
Let the kids play with these favors during treat time—

Trace star shapes on different colors of construction paper. (Use a magic marker and draw freehand, *or* trace around a star-shaped cookie cutter.) Draw eyes and mouth on the star, then make a slit where the nose would be.

Tape *or* glue the open end of a balloon to one end of a straw. Press the other end of the balloon through the slit in the star, forming the nose. Secure the balloon and straw with tape on the back of the star.

If you like, tape some curled crinkle ribbon or a construction paper "tail" to the edge of the star on the back. (To create a "tail," cut out a slightly curved 3×½-inch piece of construction paper.) For a special touch, write each child's name on one of the tails!

Kids at your party will giggle with delight over Star Straw Favors.

DYNAMITE DINOSAURS
(Pictured on page 78.)

DINOSAUR HATS
Kids will have a blast creating their own versions of these whimsical hats!

To begin, cut 12×5-inch rectangles from different colors of construction paper. Fold up 1 inch along one of the long sides of the rectangle. Tape or glue a 4-foot-long piece of ribbon inside this fold. (The kids will tie this ribbon around their heads to hold the hats on.)

Next, trace dinosaur shapes onto construction paper. (Look for pictures to trace. *Or,* trace around dinosaur-shape cookie cutters.) Cut out the dinosaurs and add eyes or other facial features. Glue or tape the dinosaurs onto the hats.

If you like, cut rectangular stems and teardrop-shape petals out of construction paper. Assemble the petals on top of the stems to form trees and shrubs next to the dinosaur.

Prehistoric Cake: the center attraction!

PREHISTORIC CAKE
Easy! Start with purchased cake and cookies. If you can't find dinosaur graham cookies, make Whole Wheat Dinosaur Cookies (see recipe, page 81)—
2 *or* 3 dinosaur graham cookies *or* Whole Wheat Dinosaur Cookies
Decorating gel (optional)
1 frosted round 2-layer chocolate cake
1 can chocolate frosting
1 small fresh peach, nectarine, *or* apricot, halved
Small gumdrops
Chopped peanuts
Malted milk balls
Fresh mint sprigs

● **If desired, outline** features such as mouth and nose on dinosaur cookies with decorating gel.

● **A few hours before party time,** on top of the cake place 2 or 3 mounds of frosting (about 1 tablespoon each). Press the cookies into the mounds so the cookies stand up. Arrange peach halves, cut side down, to one side of the cookies for boulders. Place gumdrops in clusters around cake top for rocks. Sprinkle nuts on cake top for pebbles. Attach the malted milk balls around the bottom edge of the cake, using more of the frosting, if necessary. Cover any remaining frosting and chill in the refrigerator for another use.

● **Just before serving,** add fresh mint sprigs for shrubs and trees. Makes 12 servings.

Nutrition information per serving: 573 cal., 6 g pro., 87 g carbo., 26 g fat, 51 mg chol., 341 mg sodium, 299 mg potassium, and 2 g dietary fiber. U.S. RDA: 12% iron.

WHOLE WHEAT DINOSAUR COOKIES
Many grocery stores and gourmet shops carry dinosaur cookie cutters.

- 1½ **cups whole wheat flour**
- 1 **teaspoon baking powder**
- ¼ **teaspoon salt**
- ½ **cup margarine *or* butter**
- ½ **cup packed brown sugar**
- 1 **egg**
- 1 **teaspoon vanilla**

● **In a small mixing bowl combine** flour, baking powder, and salt.

● **In a large mixer bowl beat** margarine or butter with an electric mixer on medium speed for 30 seconds. Add brown sugar; beat till fluffy. Add egg and vanilla; beat well. Add flour mixture; beat till well blended. Cover and chill for 2 hours or till easy to handle.

● **On a lightly floured surface roll** dough ⅛ inch thick. Cut with 4-inch dinosaur cookie cutters. Place on an ungreased cookie sheet.

● **Bake in a 375° oven** for 10 to 12 minutes or till very light brown around the edges. Cool on a wire rack. To store, place in an airtight container. Makes 15 to 20 cookies.

Nutrition information per cookie: 127 cal., 2 g pro., 16 g carbo., 7 g fat, 18 mg chol., 134 mg sodium, 77 mg potassium.

DINOSAUR TRAIL MIX
You can make this mix up to several days ahead of party time—

- 2 **cups bite-size fish-shape crackers**
- 1½ **cups bite-size twisted pretzels**
- 1 **cup peanuts**
  ● ● ●
- ¼ **cup margarine *or* butter, melted**
- 1 **teaspoon Worcestershire sauce**
- 3 **cups popped popcorn**

HELPFUL HINTS ON PARTY PLANNING

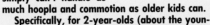

● *Whom to invite:* Try to invite children who are all about the same age. That way, they'll have the same interests, skills, and attention spans. Also, if you invite kids who know each other, it'll be easier for them to play together.

● *How many to invite:* The old adage, "limit the number of guests to your child's age" is good advice. Young kids simply can't handle as much hoopla and commotion as older kids can.

Specifically, for 2-year-olds (about the youngest age at which a child really knows what's going on), keep parties low key. No outside guests is probably best—one or two would be plenty. By age 3, invite a maximum of two guests.

● *Activities:* The activities you plan will depend on the age and maturity of the kids involved. For 2- and 3-year-olds, avoid (or minimize) activities that cause excitement, such as races. And, avoid competitive activities altogether. If you give prizes, make sure every child gets one. Ideally, the prizes you give should all be the same. Different prizes can cause competition, too.

By age 5 or 6, children should be able to participate in competitive games in which only some children receive prizes.

Make plans for several more games and other activities than you think the kids will have time to do. They will go through things faster than you would ever think or believe!

● *Invitations:* Be sure to include date, time, place, who the party is for, your phone number, and RSVP, if you want one. Also mention any special information, such as something to bring or wear to the party, or that you'll be taking the kids home.

● *Party length:* As Mom always said, it's better to leave while you're having a good time. So, plan on short parties. An hour is plenty long for preschoolers, while two hours is a good guide for older kids.

● *Party helpers:* Have at least one other adult help you with the party. (If you have more than a dozen kids at the party, you might want to consider having a couple of adults help you!) If you can't find another adult, perhaps hire a neighborhood teen or one of your baby-sitters to lend a hand with the festivities.

● *Cartoon break:* A video cartoon break sometime during the middle of the birthday party can really settle the kids down—and give you a much-needed breather! Have a couple of flicks handy.

● **In a bowl combine** crackers, pretzels, and peanuts. Combine margarine or butter and Worcestershire sauce; pour over cracker mixture; stir to coat. Add popcorn; toss to mix. Spread evenly in a 15x10x1-inch baking pan.

● **Bake in a 325° oven** about 20 minutes or till brown and crispy, stirring once or twice. Transfer to another pan or a large piece of foil. Cool. Store in an airtight container. Makes about 8 cups.

Microwave directions: In a 3-quart microwave-safe casserole combine the crackers, pretzels, and peanuts. Set mixture aside.

In a 1-cup glass measure micro-cook *unmelted* margarine or butter, uncovered, on 100% power (high) for 45 to 60 seconds or till melted. Stir in Worcestershire sauce. Pour over cracker mixture; stir till coated. Add popcorn; toss to mix. Cook, uncovered, on high for 5 minutes or till hot (low-wattage ovens: 6 minutes), stirring 3 times. Cool. (Mix will crisp during standing.)

Nutrition information per ½-cup serving: 148 cal., 4 g pro., 13 g carbo., 9 g fat, 0 mg chol., 245 mg sodium, 86 mg potassium, 1 g dietary fiber.

PREHISTORIC PARTY CHOW
All the vivid colors and sweet flavors kids love!

- 2½ **cups fruit-flavored dinosaur-shape cereal**
- ¾ **cup peanuts**
- ½ **cup coconut**
- ½ **cup sunflower nuts**
  ● ● ●
- ½ **cup honey**
- ¼ **cup orange juice**
- 2 **tablespoons margarine *or* butter, melted**
- ½ **cup raisins *or* mixed dried fruit bits**

● **In a bowl combine** cereal, peanuts, coconut, and sunflower nuts. In another small bowl stir together honey, orange juice, and margarine or butter; pour over cereal mixture. Stir till coated. Spread evenly in a buttered 15x10x1-inch baking pan.

● **Bake in a 300° oven** for 40 to 45 minutes or till brown, stirring every 15 minutes, then several times during the last 15 minutes. Remove from oven. Stir in raisins or fruit bits. Transfer to another pan or a large piece of foil; cool. Break into chunks. Store in an airtight container. Makes about 6 cups.

Nutrition information per ½-cup serving: 191 cal., 4 g pro., 26 g carbo., 9 g fat, 0 mg chol., 40 mg sodium, 168 mg potassium, and 2 g dietary fiber. U.S. RDA: 14% niacin.

THE MAGAZINE FOR AMERICAN FAMILIES

OUR READERS TALK ABOUT CHILD CARE Page 20

Better Homes and Gardens

JUNE 1989 •$1.50

TRAVEL AMERICA'S FABULOUS NORTHWEST

SUMMER BARBECUES
NEW RECIPES FOR GREAT GRILLING

OUTDOOR LIVING
A POOL AND GARDEN PLAN FOR BACKYARD FAMILY FUN

HOW TO BUILD THAT VACATION HOUSE YOU WANT

GOOD FOOD, GOOD HEALTH Page 45

PARENTING
TEACHING KIDS RESPONSIBILITY

GIANT BURGER
FOR 4

SMOKED TURKEY
FOR 6

GRILLED SALMON
FOR 8

Great Grilling! 3 Easy Menus for Summer

BARBECUES

BY BARBARA JOHNSON

Summertime — your chance to enjoy the outdoors
*with your family and friends. And, that usually
includes plenty of backyard grilling. Whether you're
cooking over the coals for a weeknight supper or a
weekend party, try these easy, stylish menus. They're
perfect for all your laid-back days of summer.*

FUN FAMILY BARBECUE FOR 4

Give your family barbecue for dinner any night of the week! Grill the hearty summer foods they all love: burgers, corn, and potatoes. With this simple menu, you can dig in just 60 minutes after lighting the coals.

MENU

Giant Stuffed Burger with
Texas Toast
·
Cheese and Peas Potatoes
·
Corn on the cob
·
Lemonade
·
Strawberries, Peaches,
and Cream

STRAWBERRIES, PEACHES, AND CREAM: A fresh dessert your kids will love.

SMOKED TURKE DINNER FOR 6

Come the weekend, relax with family and friends. This leisurely menu lets you do that—the turkey smokes unattended in a smoker or covered grill. For fun, take turns cranking ice cream!

MENU
▼

Raclette-Style Cheese
·
Smoked Turkey with
Orange Glaze
·
Honey Mustard Slaw
·
Iced Lime Tea
·
Chocolate 'n' White-Chocolate
Chunk Ice Cream

CHOCOLATE
'N' WHITE-
CHOCOLATE
CHUNK ICE
CREAM: Yum!

BACKYARD COOKOUT FOR 8

Whenever the whim strikes, invite some folks over for a stylish barbecue. It's easy to serve these recipes—you can put most of them together ahead so they're ready to grill. While they sizzle, you're free to join in yard games.

MENU

Caramelized Onion and Cheese Bites

·

Salmon Roast with Marinated Vegetables

·

Spinach Couscous Salad

·

Nectarine Sunrise

·

Custard Fruit Tart

CUSTARD FRUIT TART: An incredible fruit and yogurt masterpiece.

Fun Family Barbecue Menu
(Pictured on pages 84–85.)

Giant Stuffed Burger with
Texas Toast*
Cheese and Peas Potatoes*
Corn on the cob
Lemonade
Strawberries, Peaches, and Cream*
*Recipe included

Place the second meat circle over the stuffing.

GIANT STUFFED BURGER WITH TEXAS TOAST

If you don't have a grill basket to cook the giant burger in, shape the meat mixture into individual burgers and cook as directed at right. Serve either version with all of your favorite burger accompaniments: pickle slices, lettuce leaves, tomato slices, pickle relish, mustard, or catsup—

    1 beaten egg
    ¼ cup quick-cooking rolled oats
    2 tablespoons bottled barbecue
       sauce
    1 pound ground beef, pork, *or* lamb
    ¼ cup coarsely shredded carrot
    ¼ cup finely chopped celery
    2 green onions, thinly sliced
       (3 tablespoons)
    1 2-ounce can mushroom stems
       and pieces, drained
    Bottled barbecue sauce
    4 slices Texas toast, toasted and
       halved diagonally

● **In a medium bowl stir together** egg, oats, the 2 tablespoons barbecue sauce, ¼ teaspoon *salt*, and ⅛ teaspoon *pepper*. Add meat; mix well. Divide mixture in half. On waxed paper, pat *each* half into a 7-inch circle.

● **For stuffing,** in a small bowl combine carrot, celery, green onions, and mushrooms. Spoon over *one* circle of meat to within 1 inch of the edge. Top with second circle of meat; peel off top sheet of waxed paper and seal edges of meat together (see photo, *top right*).

● **Invert meat patty** onto a well-greased wire grill basket; peel off re-

maining waxed paper. Grill directly over *medium* coals (4-second count, see tip box, *page 94*) for 10 minutes. Turn and grill for 9 to 12 minutes more or till done. Brush with additional barbecue sauce before serving. Cut into wedges and serve with Texas toast. Makes 4 servings.

Individual Stuffed Burgers: Prepare meat mixture as directed, *except* shape into eight 3½-inch-wide patties each ¼ inch thick. Evenly divide stuffing atop *four* of the patties, spreading to within ½ inch of edge. Top with remaining patties. Seal edges well.

Grill directly over *medium-hot* coals (3-second count, see tip box, *page 94*) for 13 to 14 minutes or till done, turning once.

Nutrition information per serving: *360 cal., 25 g pro., 20 g carbo., 19 g fat, 146 mg chol., 515 mg sodium, 380 mg potassium, 2 g dietary fiber. U.S. RDA: 48% vit. A, 16% thiamine, 17% riboflavin, 29% niacin, 23% iron.*

CHEESE AND PEAS POTATOES

Put the potatoes on the grill just a few minutes before you start cooking the Giant Stuffed Burger—

    1 4-ounce container cheese
       spread with mild Mexican flavor
       (½ cup)
    ½ of a 16-ounce package (2 cups)
       loose-pack frozen hash brown
       potatoes with onion and peppers
    ¾ cup loose-pack frozen peas
    ¼ cup chopped salami

● **Spoon cheese spread** into a saucepan; stir over low heat till melted. (*Or,* spoon cheese spread into a microwave-safe mixing bowl; micro-cook, uncovered, on 100% power (high) for 30 to 60 seconds or till spread is melted, stirring once.) Stir in the potatoes, the peas, and the salami.

● **Cut** a 22x18-inch piece of heavy foil. Place the potato mixture in the center of the foil. Bring up the long edges of the foil and, leaving a little space for expansion of steam, seal tightly with a double fold (see photo, *below*). Fold in the short ends to seal.

Seal the foil packet tightly with a double fold.

● **Grill foil packet,** on an uncovered grill, directly over *medium* coals (4-second count, see the tip box, *page 94*) for 20 to 25 minutes (or over *medium-hot* coals [3-second count, see tip box, *page 94*] for 17 to 20 minutes), turning frequently. Makes 4 servings.

Nutrition information per serving: *172 cal., 9 g pro., 16 g carbo., 8 g fat, 21 mg chol., 524 mg sodium, 290 mg potassium, 2 g dietary fiber. U.S. RDA: 13% vit. C, 10% thiamine, 11% riboflavin, 17% calcium.*

Indirect Grilling

Indirect grilling means barbecuing the food over a drip pan, rather than directly over the heat.

Charcoal

For indirect cooking with charcoal, mound and light the coals as you normally would. When the coals are ready, arrange them around a drip pan.

Hot coals provide *medium-hot* heat over the drip pan. *Medium-hot* coals provide *medium* heat, *medium* coals provide *medium-slow* heat, and so on.

Gas

To cook indirectly with a gas grill, light the burner on just one side and place the food over a drip pan on the other side.

Or, place the drip pan on the grate over the center of the burner. Then, cook the food on the grill rack directly over the drip pan. The same temperature test applies as for indirect cooking with charcoal.

STRAWBERRIES, PEACHES, AND CREAM

So simple and quick to make, yet so good. To save time cleaning and cutting up fruit, you can use frozen unsweetened strawberries and peaches, thawed—

½ of an 8-ounce container soft-style sweetened cream cheese *or* soft-style cream cheese with pineapple
¼ teaspoon finely shredded orange peel
3 to 4 tablespoons orange juice
½ of a 4-ounce container (about 1 cup) frozen whipped dessert topping, thawed
1 pint strawberries, sliced
2 peaches, pitted and sliced

● **In a small mixer bowl beat** cream cheese, orange peel, and orange juice. Fold in whipped dessert topping.
● **Divide the strawberries and the** peaches among 4 individual dessert dishes. Dollop *each* fruit serving with a *fourth* of the cream cheese mixture. Serve immediately. Makes 4 servings.
Nutrition information per serving: 189 cal., 3 g pro., 16 g carbo., 14 g fat, 0 mg chol., 76 mg sodium, 272 mg potassium, 3 g dietary fiber. U.S. RDA: 19% vit. A, 87% vit. C.

Smoked Turkey Dinner Menu
(Pictured on pages 86–87.)

Raclette-Style Cheese*
Smoked Turkey with Orange Glaze*
Honey Mustard Slaw*
Iced Lime Tea*
Chocolate 'n' White-Chocolate Chunk Ice Cream*
***Recipe included**

RACLETTE-STYLE CHEESE

Add this piquant cheese round to your smoker or grill anytime while the turkey is smoking. Then, enjoy it to stave off hunger pangs from the enticing aroma of the mesquite—

1½ cups shredded process Gruyère *or* process Swiss cheese (6 ounces)*
1 cup shredded Gouda cheese (4 ounces)
1 tablespoon snipped fresh basil *or* oregano (*or* 1 teaspoon dried basil *or* oregano, crushed)
2 teaspoons Dijon-style mustard
1 teaspoon white wine Worcestershire sauce
Several dashes bottled hot pepper sauce
Pimiento slices (optional)
Fresh thyme, rosemary, *and/or* savory sprigs (optional)
Blanched cauliflower *and/or* broccoli flowerets, boiled halved tiny new potatoes, pita bread wedges**

● **In a small mixer bowl** or food processor bowl combine cheeses; let stand to soften. Add basil or oregano, mustard, Worcestershire sauce, and hot pepper sauce; beat with an electric mixer on low speed, or cover and process till well combined. (Mixture will be crumbly.) Form into a ball. Shape into a 4½-inch round about 1 inch high. Wrap in clear plastic wrap; chill several hours or overnight.

● **Unwrap cheese round; place** in a 6-inch cast-iron skillet or heavy pan. Cut into 6 wedges; separate wedges slightly. Place skillet or pan on the rack of a smoker or grill over *slow* coals (6-second count, see tip box, *page 94*). Cover and smoke for 5 to 7 minutes or till softened and heated through, checking often to make sure the cheese doesn't overmelt. (The cheese shouldn't lose its shape or start to run.) Top each wedge with a pimiento slice and herb sprig, if desired. Serve with warm vegetables and bread. Makes 6 appetizer servings.

***Recipe note:** It's important to use process cheese rather than natural cheese. Process cheese melts smoothly, giving an acceptable texture.

****Tip:** To blanch cauliflower and broccoli flowerets, cook in boiling water, uncovered, for 2 minutes. Drain. For tiny new potatoes, cook in boiling water, uncovered, for 10 to 15 minutes or till tender.

If you like, blanch or boil the vegetables ahead of time; cover and chill. Wrap in foil and reheat on the grill while the cheese smokes. *Or,* place in a microwave-safe dish and reheat in your microwave oven.

Nutrition information per serving with ¼ cup vegetables and 2 pita bread wedges: 247 cal., 15 g pro., 13 g carbo., 15 g fat, 53 mg chol., 311 mg sodium, 163 mg potassium, and 1 g dietary fiber. U.S. RDA: 10% vit. A, 12% vit. C, 10% riboflavin, 44% calcium.

A Note About Barbecue Smokers

In our testing, we found that smokers vary. Some restrict airflow so the coals don't burn as hot. If your smoker is like this, some foods may take longer to cook than the recipe suggests. For example, the cooking time for Smoked Turkey with Orange Glaze (see recipe, *page 92*) holds true for most smokers. But, the turkey needs to reach 160° in 3 hours. If after 3 hours the turkey is less than 160°, remove it from the smoker; place turkey in a 325° oven till it reaches 170°.

SMOKED TURKEY WITH ORANGE GLAZE

Smoke the turkey in a smoker or covered grill. If you use a smoker, see the tip box on page 91. Pictured on page 82—

    1 10-ounce jar orange marmalade
       (about 1 cup)
    2 tablespoons lemon juice
    1 teaspoon prepared mustard
       Dash ground cloves
    4 cups mesquite chunks (for
       smoker method) *or* mesquite
       chips (for covered-grill method)
    1 3- to 3½-pound fresh breast
       half of turkey with bone
  Kale leaves (optional)
  Shredded cabbage (optional)
  Orange slices, halved (optional)

● **For glaze,** in a small saucepan cook and stir marmalade, lemon juice, mustard, and cloves over low heat till melted. Set glaze aside.

Smoker method:

● **About 1 hour before grilling,** soak mesquite chunks in enough water to cover. For large smokers, fill coal pan ¾ full with coals; place the pan in the smoker. (For small smokers, use a full pan of coals.) Ignite the coals. When the coals are ready (hot and ash covered), drain the mesquite chunks; sprinkle over coals. Fill the smoker water pan with water; set the pan in place.

● **Insert a thermometer** into thickest part of turkey breast, making certain thermometer bulb doesn't touch bone. Place turkey on rack over water pan. Cover and smoke for 2 to 2½ hours. (Don't peek for the first 1¾ hours; opening the smoker will cool it off too much.) When the thermometer registers 170°, brush the turkey generously with glaze; smoke for 5 minutes more. Brush again. Smoke for 5 minutes more. Serve on a kale- and cabbage-lined platter with orange slices, if desired. Pass any remaining glaze.

Covered-grill method:

● **About 1 hour before grilling,** soak mesquite chips in enough water to cover. In a covered grill, arrange *medium* coals (4-second count, see tip box, *page 94*) around a 12x10-inch foil drip pan in firebox. Fill pan with 2 cups *water*. Drain chips; sprinkle *half* on charcoal.

● **Insert thermometer** into the thickest part of turkey, making sure bulb doesn't touch bone. Place turkey on rack over drip pan. Lower grill hood; smoke for 45 minutes. Add remaining chips and more briquettes. Lower hood; smoke ¾ to 1¼ hours or till thermometer registers 170°, adding briquettes every 45 minutes. Brush turkey generously with glaze. Cover; smoke for 5 minutes more. Brush again. Cover and smoke for 5 minutes more. Serve on a kale- and cabbage-lined platter with orange slices, if desired. Pass any remaining glaze. Makes 6 servings.

Nutrition information per serving: *304 cal., 41 g pro., 34 g carbo., 1 g fat, 111 mg chol., 87 mg sodium, 414 mg potassium. U.S. RDA: 11% riboflavin, 50% niacin, 13% iron.*

HONEY MUSTARD SLAW

To save time, use 3 cups of the preshredded cabbage that's available in the produce section of your grocery store—

    ½ cup mayonnaise *or* salad
       dressing
    ½ cup dairy sour cream
    2 tablespoons honey
    1 to 2 tablespoons Dijon-style *or*
       coarse-grain brown mustard
    3 cups coarsely shredded cabbage
       (about ½ of a medium head)*
    2 cups coarsely shredded
       romaine*
    1 small jicama, peeled and
       shredded (2 cups)
    ¼ cup sliced green onion
  Romaine leaves (optional)
    ½ cup toasted broken pecans

● **For dressing,** in a small bowl stir together mayonnaise, sour cream, honey, and mustard. Cover and chill.

● **In a large salad bowl combine** cabbage, shredded romaine, jicama, and green onion; cover and chill.

● **To serve,** add dressing to cabbage mixture; toss to coat. If desired, serve in a romaine-lined bowl. Sprinkle with pecans. Makes 6 servings.

Use a knife to cut the cabbage into long, coarse shreds.

*To coarsely shred greens: For cabbage, hold a quarter-head of cabbage firmly against the cutting board. Use a chef's knife to slice the cabbage into long, coarse shreds (see photo *above*). For romaine, stack leaves and use a chef's knife to slice crosswise into long, coarse shreds.

Nutrition information per serving: *299 cal., 3 g pro., 17 g carbo., 26 g fat, 20 mg chol., 197 mg sodium, 230 mg potassium, 3 g dietary fiber. U.S. RDA: 19% vit. A, 56% vit. C, 10% thiamine.*

ICED LIME TEA

To make strong tea for this smooth, sweet-tart drink, our Test Kitchen brewed six tea bags in 5 cups boiling water. Try the unique sake (Japanese wine made from rice) version for a pleasant flavor surprise—

    5 cups cold strong tea
    1 6-ounce can (¾ cup) frozen
       limeade concentrate, thawed
  Ice
  Halved lime slices (optional)
  Sake (optional)

● **In a pitcher combine** the cold tea and the limeade. Pour into individual ice-filled glasses. If desired, add lime slices to each glass. If desired, add *2 tablespoons* sake to *each* serving. Makes 6 (9-ounce) servings.

Nutrition information per serving: *70 cal., 0 g pro., 18 g carbo., 0 g fat, 0 mg chol., 0 mg sodium, 71 mg potassium.*

CHOCOLATE 'N' WHITE-CHOCOLATE CHUNK ICE CREAM

A creamy smooth treat with a flavor reminiscent of frosted malts sold at the ballpark—

```
1    cup sugar
⅓    cup unsweetened cocoa powder
2    cups light cream
3    cups whipping cream
4    1¼-ounce white baking bars
     with cocoa butter and almonds,
     coarsely chopped
¼    cup light corn syrup
2    teaspoons vanilla
White baking bar with cocoa
     butter and almonds, coarsely
     chopped (optional)
```

● **In a large saucepan combine** the sugar and the cocoa powder. Stir in the light cream. Heat mixture till cocoa is dissolved. Cool. Stir in whipping cream, the 4 chopped baking bars, corn syrup, and vanilla.

● **Freeze the mixture** in a 4- or 5-quart ice-cream freezer according to the manufacturer's directions.

● **To serve,** scoop ice cream from the freezer and sprinkle each serving with additional chopped white baking bar, if desired. Makes 2 quarts, 16 (½-cup) servings.

Nutrition information per serving: 330 cal., 3 g pro., 25 g carbo., 25 g fat, 83 mg chol., 53 mg sodium, 110 mg potassium, 1 g dietary fiber. U.S. RDA: 18% vit. A.

Backyard Cookout Menu
(Pictured on pages 88–89.)

Caramelized Onion and Cheese Bites*
Salmon Roast with Marinated Vegetables*
Spinach Couscous Salad*
Nectarine Sunrise*
Custard Fruit Tart*
***Recipe included**

CARAMELIZED ONION AND CHEESE BITES

Grill these sweet golden nibbles alongside the salmon roast—

```
1    large onion, halved and
     thinly sliced
1    tablespoon olive or cooking oil
⅓    cup coarsely chopped walnuts
1    teaspoon sugar
1    tablespoon herb mustard or
     Dijon-style mustard
16   ¼-inch-thick slices baguette
     French bread or other long,
     thin firm bread
½    cup freshly grated Parmesan
     or Romano cheese
```

● **In a large skillet cook** onion in hot oil about 3 minutes or just till tender. Add walnuts and sugar. Cook and stir about 5 minutes or till onion is slightly caramelized and walnuts are lightly toasted. Stir in mustard.

● **Spoon onion mixture** atop each of the bread slices. Sprinkle with the cheese. If desired, cover bread slices and let stand at room temperature up to 1 hour.

● **To serve,** place bread slices, onion side up, directly over *medium-hot* coals (3-second count, see tip box, *page 94*) about 2 minutes or just till bottoms are toasted and slices are heated through. Watch carefully the last ½ minute to avoid overbrowning. Makes 8 appetizer servings.

Nutrition information per serving: 138 cal., 5 g pro., 13 g carbo., 7 g fat, 5 mg chol., 274 mg sodium, 83 mg potassium, and 1 g dietary fiber. U.S. RDA: 10% calcium.

Controlling Flare-Ups

Fat and meat juices dripping onto hot coals can cause sudden bursts of flame (flare-ups), which char your food. To control flare-ups:

Charcoal grills
● raise the grill rack
● cover the grill
● space the hot coals farther apart
● remove a few hot coals
● take the food off the grill and mist the fire with water

Gas grills
● lower the burner's heat setting
● take the food off the grill

SALMON ROAST WITH MARINATED VEGETABLES

A salmon roast is a thick center portion cut from a large fish. You may need to special order it from a fish market. Ask for a roast similar to the one on page 88. Have the store bone it for you, too—

```
⅓    cup dry white wine
¼    cup cooking oil
1    tablespoon white wine
     Worcestershire sauce
1    tablespoon snipped fresh
     sage or 1 teaspoon dried
     sage, crushed
1    medium sweet red pepper
1    medium sweet yellow pepper
1    medium zucchini
6    green onions
1    4-pound salmon roast (about 8
     inches long and 2¼ inches
     thick), boned or one 5- to
     6-pound whole dressed salmon
Fresh herb sprigs (optional)
```

● **For marinade,** combine the wine, oil, white wine Worcestershire sauce, sage, ½ teaspoon *salt*, and ¼ teaspoon cracked *black pepper*. Cut peppers and zucchini into thin 2-inch strips. Cut green onions into 2-inch pieces; sliver pieces. Add vegetables to marinade. Cover; chill 6 hours or overnight.

● **To grill,** shape a piece of heavy foil larger than the fish into a pan; grease or spray with nonstick spray coating.

● **Drain vegetable mixture,** reserving marinade. Place fish in foil pan. Spoon as much of the pepper mixture as you can into fish cavity. Set aside remaining vegetable mixture. Brush fish lightly with reserved marinade.

● **Arrange** *medium-hot* coals (3-second count, see tip box, *page 94*) around drip pan in grill. Test for *medium* heat (4-second count, see tip box, *page 94*) above pan. Place fish in foil pan on rack over center of drip pan. Cover; grill 40 minutes, adding coals if necessary to maintain heat. Add any remaining vegetable mixture to foil pan; brush fish with reserved marinade. Cover; grill 10 to 20 minutes longer or till fish just flakes with a fork. Garnish with fresh herb sprigs, if desired. Serves 8.

Nutrition information per serving: 316 cal., 37 g pro., 3 g carbo., 16 g fat, 106 mg chol., 121 mg sodium, 796 mg potassium, 1 g dietary fiber. U.S. RDA: 37% vit. A, 90% vit. C, 26% thiamine, 17% riboflavin, 50% niacin.

Grilling Helps

TESTING FIRE TEMPERATURE FOR DIRECT GRILLING

Here's how to determine the temperature of the lighted coals in your grill box or the heat of the flame from the burner of your gas grill. Hold your hand, palm down, above the coals or the burner flame at the height your food will be cooked. Then count the seconds, "one thousand one, one thousand two. . . ." If you need to remove your hand after two seconds, the fire is *hot;* after three seconds, the fire is *medium-hot;* after four seconds, the fire is *medium;* after five seconds, the fire is *medium-slow;* and, after six seconds, the fire is *slow.*

ADJUSTING THE HEAT OF COALS

When your coals aren't the right temperature, adjust the heat in one of the following ways:

Coals too hot
- raise the grill rack
- spread the coals apart
- close the air vents halfway to restrict the airflow
- remove some of the hot briquettes

Coals too cold
- use tongs to tap the ashes off the burning coals
- move the coals closer together
- add more briquettes
- lower the grill rack
- open the vents to allow more air to circulate

SPINACH COUSCOUS SALAD

This colorful salad has a wonderful flavor our tasters raved about. With just six ingredients, it's a snap to make. Pictured on page 82—

- 1 **cup chicken broth**
- ¾ **cup couscous**
- ½ **cup golden Caesar** *or* **Italian salad dressing**
- 2 **cups shredded fresh spinach**
- 12 **cherry tomatoes, halved**
- ½ **of an 8-ounce can sliced water chestnuts**

Spinach leaves

- In a saucepan bring chicken broth to boiling; stir in couscous. Remove from heat. Cover and let stand for 5 minutes. Transfer to a bowl; add salad dressing. Cover and chill for 2 to 4 hours or till completely chilled.
- Before serving, toss couscous mixture with shredded spinach, tomatoes, and water chestnuts. Serve on spinach leaves. Makes 8 servings.

Nutrition information per serving: 135 cal., 3 g pro., 14 g carbo., 8 g fat, 0 mg chol., 235 mg sodium, 251 mg potassium, 2 g dietary fiber. U.S. RDA: 36% vit. A, 17% vit. C.

NECTARINE SUNRISE

The beautiful golds and reds in this fruity sipper look like the colors of a sunrise. To re-create the swirled effect shown in the photo on page 82, simply use a swizzle stick or straw to stir the drink ever so slightly in a circular motion after pouring the nectarine mixture atop the grenadine—

- 4 **nectarines**
- 1 **6-ounce can frozen orange juice concentrate**
- ⅔ **cup tequila**

Crushed ice
- ½ **cup grenadine syrup**

Fresh mint sprigs

- Pit and slice *one* of the nectarines; set aside for garnish. Halve, pit, and coarsely chop remaining nectarines.
- In a blender container combine the chopped nectarines, orange juice concentrate, and tequila; cover and puree till smooth. Gradually add crushed ice, blending till slushy and mixture measures 5 cups.
- Place *1 tablespoon* of the grenadine syrup in *each* of 8 stemmed glasses. Add nectarine mixture. Top each with a mint sprig and hang a nectarine slice on the side of each glass. Serve at once. Makes 8 (5-ounce) servings.

Nutrition information per serving: 184 cal., 1 g pro., 34 g carbo., 0 g fat, 0 mg chol., 15 mg sodium, 325 mg potassium, 1 g dietary fiber. U.S. RDA: 11% vit. A, 67% vit. C.

CUSTARD FRUIT TART

If you like, strain the marmalade-water mixture to create a shiny glaze as we did for the photos on page 82—

- 1 **cup all-purpose flour**
- ¼ **cup cold margarine** *or* **butter**
- 1 **tablespoon shortening**
- 1 **egg yolk**
- 1 **8-ounce package cream cheese, softened**
- ½ **of an 8-ounce carton vanilla yogurt (scant ½ cup)**
- ¼ **cup sugar**
- 2 **tablespoons orange liqueur** *or* **orange juice**
- ½ **of a small papaya, peeled, seeded, and thinly sliced**
- ½ **of a kiwi fruit, peeled and thinly sliced**
- ½ **cup blueberries**
- ½ **cup raspberries**
- ½ **cup seedless green grapes**
- ¼ **cup sliced strawberries**
- ½ **cup orange marmalade**
- 1 **tablespoon hot water**

- For crust, in a mixing bowl combine flour and ¼ teaspoon *salt.* Cut in cold margarine or butter and shortening till the mixture resembles coarse crumbs. Make a well in the center. Beat together egg yolk and 3 tablespoons *cold water.* Add egg mixture to flour mixture. Using fork, stir till dough forms a ball. Wrap in clear plastic wrap and chill 20 minutes in the freezer or 1½ hours in the refrigerator or till easy to handle.
- On a lightly floured surface roll dough into a 12- to 13-inch circle. Fit into 10- to 11-inch flan pan with removable bottom. Turn overhanging dough inside and press against pan sides.
- Bake in a 375° oven for 25 minutes or till golden. Cool.
- For filling, in a small mixer bowl beat cream cheese, yogurt, sugar, and orange liqueur till smooth. Spread mixture evenly over the cooled crust. Cover and chill at least 1 hour or till set.
- Just before serving, arrange fruit on top of filling. For glaze, combine marmalade and hot water. If desired, strain through a sieve. Spoon over fruit. Chill till serving time. Serves 8.

Nutrition information per serving: 354 cal., 5 g pro., 44 g carbo., 18 g fat, 66 mg chol., 233 mg sodium, 191 mg potassium, 2 g dietary fiber. U.S. RDA: 20% vit. A, 36% vit. C, 10% thiamine, 11% riboflavin.

EASY BRUNCH BREADS
DELECTABLE HOMEMADE GOODNESS!

Highlight summer brunches with eye-catching breads you can make in 15 minutes or less!

SAVORY BRUNCH PULL-APART

It's perfectly simple. Assemble this zesty bread a day ahead and bake the next morning, or micro-raise and bake the same day—

- ¼ **cup grated Parmesan cheese**
- 3 **tablespoons sesame seed**
- ½ **teaspoon dried basil, crushed**
- 1 **30-ounce package (24) frozen unbaked rolls**
- ¼ **cup margarine *or* butter, melted**
- 2 **tablespoons real bacon bits (optional)**

Thoroughly grease a 10-inch fluted tube pan. In a small bowl combine Parmesan cheese, sesame seed, and basil. Add about *one-third* of the mixture to greased pan; lift and turn pan to coat the sides and bottom.

Place *10* of the frozen rolls in the pan; drizzle with *half* of the margarine or

Savory Brunch Pull-Apart: Easy to serve and a delicious way to greet the day.

PHOTOGRAPHS: SCOTT LITTLE

butter. Sprinkle *half* of the remaining cheese mixture atop. If desired, sprinkle with bacon bits. Add remaining rolls. Drizzle with remaining margarine or butter and sprinkle with remaining cheese mixture.

Cover; let rolls thaw and rise overnight (12 to 24 hours) in refrigerator.

The next day let stand at room temperature for 30 minutes. Bake, uncovered, in a 350° oven for 20 minutes. Cover with foil and bake 10 to 15 minutes more or till golden. Remove bread from pan onto a wire rack. Serve warm. Makes 12 servings.

To micro-raise and serve the same day: Prepare bread as directed, using a 12-inch fluted tube pan that is safe in both microwave and conventional ovens. Instead of thawing and raising rolls overnight in refrigerator, pour 3 cups water into a 4-cup glass measure. Micro-cook, uncovered, on 100% power (high) 6½ to 8½ minutes or till boiling. Move water to back of oven. Place tube pan in microwave oven; cover with waxed paper. Heat bread and water on 10% power 10 minutes. Let rest 5 minutes. Repeat this step 3 times till dough is nearly doubled. Bake as directed.

Nutrition information per serving: *255 cal., 7 g pro., 34 g carbo., 10 g fat, 5 mg chol., 426 mg sodium, 73 mg potassium, 2 g dietary fiber.*

DOUBLE LADDER LOAF

Press two jam-filled loaves together for a delicious, innovative coffee cake—

- 3 **cups packaged biscuit mix**
- 1 **8-ounce carton dairy sour cream**
- 3 **tablespoons milk**
- ¾ **cup strawberry *or* raspberry all-fruit spread *or* jam**

Confectioners' Icing

In a large mixing bowl stir together biscuit mix, sour cream, and milk. Turn onto a lightly floured surface; knead 8 to 10 strokes. Divide in half.

Double Ladder Loaf: It takes just half an hour to bring this luscious, strawberry-filled coffee cake to the table.

Roll *each* dough half into a 10x6-inch rectangle. Place one slightly off-center on a greased baking sheet. Spread *half* of the fruit lengthwise down center. Make 2-inch cuts at 1-inch intervals on long sides. Alternately fold opposite strips of dough across filling, overlapping slightly in center. Place second dough rectangle onto same baking sheet so 10-inch sides touch. Repeat spreading fruit and shaping. Gently press loaves toward each other till they almost touch.

Bake in a 450° oven 12 to 15 minutes or till top is golden. Transfer loaf to wire rack. Drizzle warm loaf with Confectioners' Icing. Makes 1 (16 servings).

Confectioners' Icing: Combine 1 cup *sifted powdered sugar*, ¼ teaspoon *vanilla*, and enough *milk* (about 4 teaspoons) to make drizzling consistency.

Nutrition information per serving: *187 cal., 2 g pro., 31 g carbo., 6 g fat, 7 mg chol., 280 mg sodium.*

JULY

BY LISA HOLDERNESS

SUMMER FUN

10 FUN-FOR-ALL SUMMER RECIPES

- **BACKYARD SNACKS**
- **PICNIC TOTABLES**
- **CAMPERS' CUISINE**
- **RAINY-DAY TREATS**

Three cheers for summer, good times, and good food! Whether your family is relaxing at home or heading out for sport and adventure, one or more of our 10 super-easy-to-fix recipes is sure to be perfect for the occasion. What's more, each one—from main-dish to sweet treat—is finger-lickin' scrumptious.

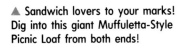

▲ Sandwich lovers to your marks! Dig into this giant Muffuletta-Style Picnic Loaf from both ends!

▶ Wow! These patriotic candy-filled cookies are so crunchy every bite bursts with flavor!

Photographs: Jay Graham, Scott Little
Food stylists: Stevie Bass, Janet Herwig
Regional editor: Helen Heitkamp

BACKYARD SNACKS
3 Tasty Ways to Eat Up Summer!

WACKY WAFFLE CONES

Make building gooey frozen yogurt sundaes an event for the whole family!

● First, put a *malted-milk ball* in the bottom of a *waffle ice-cream cone* to keep the cone from leaking. (Look for these cones in your supermarket or local ice-cream shop.) Add large scoops of *blueberry* and *strawberry frozen yogurt,* then top with fresh *berries, yogurt-covered raisins, Grape Nuts cereal,* and *pressurized whipped dessert topping.* Eat quickly and enjoy!

SNAPPY HOT
MUSTARD SAUCE

EASY-WAY-OUT
BARBECUE SAUCE

SWEET AND SOUR
DIPPING SAUCE

THREE-WAY CHICKEN WINGS

Paint appetizer wings with 3 quick-fix sauces.

● Prepare three sauces: Snappy Hot Mustard Sauce, Easy-Way-Out Barbecue Sauce, and Sweet and Sour Dipping Sauce (**see recipes, *page 105***). Grill 24 *chicken wings* directly over *medium* coals for 15 minutes or till almost cooked through. Brush wings with the 3 sauces (8 per sauce). Grill chicken about 5 minutes more or till tender and no longer pink, turning as needed. Serve with bowls of sauces for dipping. Makes 8 appetizer servings.

SLUSHY CANTALOUPE SIPPERS

Hollow out sun-ripened melons, fill with fruit slush, and enjoy!

● Slice tops off 4 small *cantaloupes;* reserve tops. Scoop out seeds and pulp. Discard seeds. Cover melons and tops; chill till needed. Measure *4 cups* pulp and combine in a blender container or food processor bowl with 1 cup *water*. Cover and blend or process till smooth. Stir in one 6-ounce can frozen *orange juice concentrate*, thawed. Pour fruit mixture into a 9x9x2-inch pan. Cover and freeze 6 hours or till you're ready to eat.

● At sipping time, let frozen fruit mixture soften about 10 minutes. Meanwhile, cut a thin slice off melon bottoms to avoid tipping. With an apple corer, punch straw holes in melon tops. Spoon fruit mixture into melons. Fill with chilled *lemon-lime carbonated beverage* or *flavored seltzer* (one or two 12-ounce cans total). Stir till slushy. Put the tops on the melons, poke in a straw, and sip away! Makes 4 servings.

PICNIC TOTABLES
Easy Treats to Pack

QUICK-ENERGY HIKERS' BARS

Mix these bars together in minutes for a healthful snack.

● In a large saucepan stir together ¾ cup packed *brown sugar* and ½ cup *honey*. Bring to boiling, stirring constantly. Remove from heat.

● Stir in 1½ cups *peanut butter* till smooth. Stir in 5 cups *whole grain cereal flakes*. Set aside ⅓ cup *mixed dried fruit* bits from one 6-ounce package and stir the rest into honey mixture till well coated. Spread mixture into a greased 12x7½x2-inch baking pan. Press reserved fruit bits into top. Cool. Cut into bars and wrap each in plastic wrap. Perfect for families on the go! Makes 24 bars.

DIPPITY FRUIT

Easy-to-store fruit kabobs and sauces make an instant picnic dessert.

● Prepare Mint Chocolate Fudge Sauce and Creamy Orange Praline Sauce (**see recipes, *page 105***). Chill in nonbreakable storage containers.

● For fruit kabobs, slice or cut up 5 to 6 cups *fresh fruit* such as *strawberries, bananas, kiwi fruit,* and *peaches.* (If using bananas, dip first in *lemon juice* to keep them from turning brown.) Thread fruit onto 6-inch skewers. Place kabobs in a large storage container; pack kabob and sauce containers in a cooler with ice to keep cold. Serve fruit kabobs with the sauces. Dip to eat! Makes about 20 kabobs.

MINT CHOCOLATE
FUDGE SAUCE

CREAMY ORANGE
PRALINE SAUCE

MUFFULETTA-STYLE PICNIC LOAF

This giant sandwich is styled after the New Orleans muffuletta, traditionally loaded with meats, cheeses, and marinated vegetables.

● Slice one 16-inch loaf *French bread* in half horizontally. Hollow out bottom half; brush both cut halves with *Italian salad dressing.* In a bowl toss 2 cups thinly sliced *zucchini or yellow summer squash* with ⅓ cup *Italian salad dressing.* Cut 8 ounces sliced *turkey salami* into strips.

● To build sandwich, layer salami on bottom half of loaf. Follow with slices of *provolone or mozzarella cheese* (about 6 ounces), the zucchini, sliced *pitted ripe olives, alfalfa sprouts,* and thinly sliced *tomatoes.* Drizzle any remaining dressing from zucchini on top half of loaf and add top half to rest of sandwich. Wrap loaf with plastic wrap and chill in a cooler for up to three hours. Slice to serve. Makes 6 servings.

CAMPERS' CUISINE
Easy Dishes for the Campfire

QUICK-TO-FIX QUESADILLA

All you need are 5 ingredients and 10 minutes for this Mexican specialty.

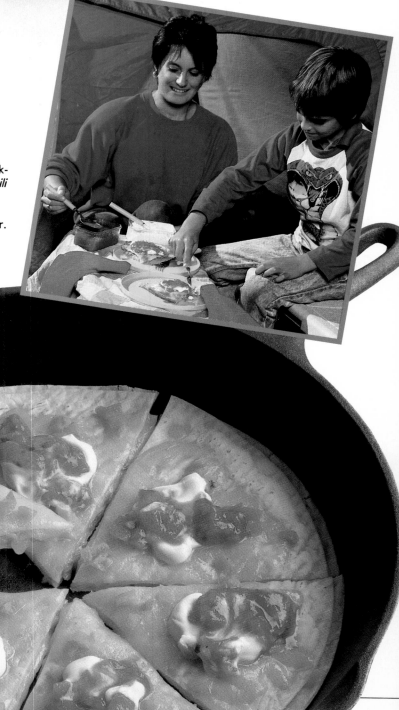

● Start with: three 10-inch *flour tortillas*, one 8-ounce package *shredded cheddar cheese*, one 4-ounce can *diced green chili peppers*, one jar *salsa*, and one can or carton *sour cream*.

● In a cast-iron skillet stack tortillas with cheese and peppers in between, ending with cheese and peppers on top; cover. Place on embers of campfire or on grill rack above *medium* coals. Cook about 5 minutes or till cheese is melted. Cut into 6 to 8 wedges. Serve with salsa and sour cream.

Note: If using a grill, you can substitute heavy foil for the skillet. Seal foil around quesadilla and place on grill rack.

To serve, transfer to a plate.

BREAKFAST ON A STICK

Grab a stick and roast breakfast over the morning fire!

● Before breakfast, hunt for four long sticks; scrape off bark. Or, use skewers. In a small bowl cover *half* of one 8-ounce package *mixed dried fruit* with water; let stand 10 minutes. Drain and set aside.

● Meanwhile, in a small bowl combine ½ cup *sugar* and 2 teaspoons *ground cinnamon.* Dip 4 quartered *brown-and-serve rolls* into ⅓ cup melted *margarine* or *butter* and then roll in cinnamon-sugar mixture.

● Starting with 1 pound thinly sliced *Canadian-style bacon,* fold one slice into quarters. Thread onto one of the sticks. Continue threading bacon alternately with dried fruit, rolls, and *spiced crab apples* (use one 16-ounce jar, drained) onto the four sticks.

● Hold and turn sticks over *low* coals of grill or over campfire, avoiding direct flame, for 10 to 12 minutes or till heated through. Breakfast's on! Makes 4 servings.

HOT FRUIT KNAPSACKS

Cook and eat this hobo-style dessert all in the same foil pouch.

● On four large pieces of heavy foil, evenly divide 2 *bananas,* cut into chunks; 2 *plums* and 2 *peaches,* cut into wedges; and one 8-ounce can *pineapple chunks,* drained. Add 1 tablespoon *brown sugar,* 1 tablespoon *margarine* or *butter,* and 1 teaspoon *lemon juice* to each fruit packet.

● Fold up edges of foil and wrap each pouch tightly around a stick or skewer, like a knapsack. Hold over *medium* coals of grill or campfire, avoiding large flames, for 8 to 10 minutes or till fruit is heated through. Makes 4 knapsacks.

103

RAINY-DAY TREATS
Celebrate Independence Day with Style!

4TH OF JULY COOKIES

Cookies that crackle—a fun indoor project for a rainy day, and a great way to celebrate the 4th!

         2   cups all-purpose flour
      1½   teaspoons baking powder
        ¼   teaspoon salt
        ¾   cup sugar
        ⅔   cup shortening
         1   egg
         1   tablespoon milk
      1½   teaspoons vanilla
        ¼   teaspoon yellow food coloring
        ¼   teaspoon red food coloring
         1   can vanilla frosting
         1   cup finely crushed candy pieces
              (red cinnamon candies, almond brickle
              pieces, fruit-flavored circles *or*
              any crunchy candies)

Red decorator gel

**Assorted candies such as red cinnamon candies,
     fruit-flavored circles, and red licorice *or* red-
     or blue-colored sugar**

Red shoestring licorice

   ● **In a bowl stir together** flour, baking powder, and salt. In a large mixer bowl beat sugar and shortening till fluffy. Add egg, milk, and vanilla; beat well. Add flour mixture, beating till well combined.

SUMMER RECIPES
Fun-For-All

TIPS FOR ROLLING OUT COOKIES

● Work with one portion of dough at a time, keeping remaining portions covered and chilled.

● Roll out your dough to an even thickness (⅛ inch), starting from the center and rolling toward the edges. Use a ruler to measure the thickness of the dough.

● Using cookie cutters, cut out shapes as close to each other as possible so very little dough will need to be rerolled. Too much rerolling of the dough scraps may make your cookies dry and tough.

● If you do quite a bit of rerolling, try rolling your dough on a surface dusted with a mixture of equal parts all-purpose flour and powdered sugar. Your cookies won't be as tough as those made with the dough rerolled on flour alone.

● Transfer your cutouts to a cookie sheet with a pancake turner or wide metal spatula.

SPECIALTY EQUIPMENT

● An electric waffle cone maker
● Barbecue utensils
● A 5-piece star cookie cutter set

MICROWAVE NOTE

All microwave recipes are thoroughly tested in a variety of microwave ovens to determine cooking times. Recipes are tested in both high-wattage (600 to 700 watts) and low-wattage (400 to 500 watts) ovens. If low-wattage cooking times differ from high-wattage, they appear in parentheses.

4TH OF JULY COOKIES
(recipe continued from page 104)

● **Divide dough into thirds.** For stars, tint a *third* of the dough with yellow food coloring. For firecrackers, tint a *third* of the dough with red food coloring, and leave remaining *third* plain. Wrap doughs separately and chill till firm (about 1 hour).

● **On a lightly floured surface roll** *yellow* portion of dough ⅛ inch thick. Using a 3-inch floured star-shaped cutter, cut out star cookies. Roll *red* portion of dough ⅛ inch thick. Using a ruler and a knife, cut 3x1½-inch rectangles for firecrackers. Roll remaining plain dough ⅛ inch thick; cut into firecrackers or stars. (Make sure you have an even number of each cookie shape since you will be stacking 2 together to make sandwich cookies.)

● **Place cookies** on ungreased cookie sheets. Bake in a 375° oven for 7 to 8 minutes or till light brown around the edges. Remove and cool on a wire rack.

● **Frost the bottoms** of *half* of the cookies with vanilla frosting. Top *each* with about ½ *teaspoon* of the finely crushed candy. Frost the bottoms of the remaining cookies and place, frosted side down, on the candy-topped cookies.

● **To decorate cookies,** tint some of the extra frosting with red and/or blue food coloring. Decorate cookies with frosting, decorator gels, assorted candies, and sugars. For firecracker cookies, attach a piece of licorice between 2 cookies for the wick. Store cookies in a single layer in a covered container. Makes 32 to 34 sandwich cookies.

SNAPPY HOT MUSTARD SAUCE
Dedicated to those who like their chicken on the spicy side—
- ⅔ **cup chicken broth**
- ¼ **cup hot-style mustard**
- 2 **teaspoons cornstarch**
- 1 **teaspoon soy sauce**

● **In a 2-cup glass measure combine** broth, mustard, cornstarch, and soy sauce. Micro-cook, uncovered, on 100% power (high) for 2 to 3 minutes or till mixture is thickened and bubbly, stirring after every minute. Cook on high 30 seconds more. Makes about ¾ cup.

EASY-WAY-OUT BARBECUE SAUCE
Just dump these ingredients together and stir for a sweet, yet zesty, sauce—
- 1 **cup chili sauce**
- ½ **cup currant jelly**
- 2 **tablespoons snipped chives**
- 2 **teaspoons prepared mustard**

● **In a small bowl stir together** chili sauce, currant jelly, chives, and mustard. Makes about 1½ cups.

SWEET AND SOUR DIPPING SAUCE
Microwave your own sweet-sour sauce! Chill any extra sauce to serve with egg rolls and Oriental foods—
- ⅓ **cup packed brown sugar**
- ⅓ **cup unsweetened pineapple juice**
- ⅓ **cup red wine vinegar**
- 1 **tablespoon cornstarch**
- 1 **tablespoon soy sauce**
- ⅛ **teaspoon ground ginger**

● **In a 2-cup glass measure combine** brown sugar, pineapple juice, vinegar, cornstarch, soy sauce, and ginger. Micro-cook, uncovered, on 100% power (high) for 2 to 3 minutes (low-wattage oven: 3 to 4 minutes) or till mixture is thickened and bubbly, stirring after every minute. Makes about 1 cup.

MINT CHOCOLATE FUDGE SAUCE
It takes just three ingredients and a couple of minutes to make this refreshing dessert sauce—
- 1 **12-ounce jar fudge ice-cream topping**
- 10 **layered chocolate-mint candies, finely chopped (about ⅓ cup)**
- 1 **tablespoon milk**

● **In a small storage container mix** ice-cream topping, chocolate-mint candies, and enough of the milk to make a sauce of dipping consistency. If toting along on a picnic, store in a cooler packed with ice. Makes about 1 cup.

CREAMY ORANGE PRALINE SAUCE
Serve this nutty caramel sauce with fresh fruit for a simple dessert—
- 2 **3-ounce packages cream cheese, softened**
- ½ **cup packed brown sugar**
- 1 **teaspoon finely shredded orange peel**
- 1 **teaspoon vanilla**
- ⅓ **cup chopped pecans**

● **In a small storage container stir** together cream cheese, brown sugar, orange peel, and vanilla till smooth. Stir in pecans. Serve immediately or, for a picnic, store in a cooler packed with ice. Makes about 1⅔ cups.

SUMMER RECIPES
Nutrition Information

WACKY WAFFLE CONES

Nutrition information per cone filled with 2 scoops frozen yogurt, 2 tablespoons strawberries, 1 tablespoon blueberries, 1 tablespoon pressurized whipped dessert topping, and 1 teaspoon Grape Nuts cereal: 347 cal., 8 g pro., 55 g carbo., 11 g fat, 15 mg chol., 199 mg sodium, 384 mg potassium, 1 g dietary fiber. U.S. RDA: 11% vit. A, 32% vit. C, 22% riboflavin, 22% calcium.

THREE-WAY CHICKEN WINGS

Nutrition information per 3-wing serving with 1 tablespoon of each sauce: 273 cal., 21 g pro., 35 g carbo., 6 g fat, 54 mg chol., 865 mg sodium, 369 mg potassium, and 1 g dietary fiber. U.S. RDA: 11% vit. A, 28% niacin, 11% iron.

SLUSHY CANTALOUPE SIPPERS

Nutrition information per serving: 226 cal., 3 g pro., 56 g carbo., 1 g fat, 0 mg chol., 16 mg sodium, 853 mg potassium, and 2 g dietary fiber. U.S. RDA: 106% vit. A, 235% vit. C, 14% thiamine.

QUICK-ENERGY HIKERS' BARS

Nutrition information per bar: 185 cal., 6 g pro., 25 g carbo., 8 g fat, 0 mg chol., 135 mg sodium, 221 mg potassium, and 2 g dietary fiber. U.S. RDA: 17% niacin, 10% iron.

DIPPITY FRUIT
(with sauces)

Nutrition information per 1 fruit skewer (banana, kiwi, strawberry, and peach) with 1 tablespoon of each dessert sauce: 149 cal., 2 g pro., 22 g carbo., 7 g fat, 10 mg chol., 45 mg sodium, 199 mg potassium, and 2 g dietary fiber. U.S. RDA: 27% vit. C.

MUFFULETTA-STYLE PICNIC LOAF

Nutrition information per serving: 460 cal., 20 g pro., 37 g carbo., 26 g fat, 52 mg chol., 1,210 mg sodium, 365 mg potassium, and 3 g dietary fiber. U.S. RDA: 15% vit. A, 16% vit. C, 21% thiamine, 20% riboflavin, 18% niacin, 27% calcium, 16% iron.

QUICK-TO-FIX QUESADILLA

Nutrition information per wedge: 226 cal., 11 g pro., 10 g carbo., 16 g fat, 46 mg chol., 565 mg sodium, 127 mg potassium, and 1 g dietary fiber. U.S. RDA: 56% vit. A, 16% vit. C, 33% calcium.

BREAKFAST ON A STICK

Nutrition information per serving: 615 cal., 27 g pro., 72 g carbo., 25 g fat, 59 mg chol., 1,931 mg sodium, 795 mg potassium, and 4 g dietary fiber. U.S. RDA: 20% vit. A, 51% vit. C, 65% thiamine, 18% riboflavin, 40% niacin, 15% iron.

HOT FRUIT KNAPSACKS

Nutrition information per knapsack: 265 cal., 2 g pro., 42 g carbo., 12 g fat, 0 mg chol., 140 mg sodium, 510 mg potassium, and 3 g dietary fiber. U.S. RDA: 17% vit. A, 30% vit. C.

4TH OF JULY COOKIES

Nutrition information per cookie: 159 cal., 1 g pro., 24 g carbo., 7 g fat, 9 mg chol., 62 mg sodium, 14 mg potassium.

A REGAL RIB-EYE ROAST

Beef rib-eye roast shines on its own. Season with herbs and serve with au jus. It's an easy, succulent, and special entrée.

ROYAL RIB-EYE ROAST

- ¾ teaspoon fines herbes, crushed
- ½ teaspoon lemon pepper
- 1 4- to 4½-pound beef rib-eye roast
- Horseradish Mushrooms (optional)
- 1 teaspoon instant beef bouillon granules

Combine ½ *teaspoon* fines herbes and pepper. Moisten roast with *water;* rub with herb mixture. Place roast, fat side up, on rack in 13x9x2-inch roasting pan. Insert meat thermometer in thickest portion. *Do not* add water or cover. Roast in a 325° oven till thermometer

MEAL EXTRAORDINAIRE: tender and juicy beef rib-eye roast.

registers 140° for rare (1¼ to 1¾ hours), 160° for medium (1½ to 2 hours), or 170° for well done (1¾ to 2 hours). If desired, prepare Horseradish Mushrooms. Transfer roast to platter; let stand, covered, 5 to 10 minutes before carving. For au jus, skim fat from

juices in pan. Stir in remaining fines herbes, bouillon granules, and ⅔ cup *water.* Cook, stirring up any brown bits in pan, till mixture boils; strain through a cheesecloth-lined sieve. Serve with beef. Serves 10 to 12.

Horseradish Mushrooms: Remove stems from 24 large fresh *mushrooms.* Lightly cover and chill stems for another use. Combine ½ cup *dairy sour cream,* 2 tablespoons *prepared horseradish,* and 2 tablespoons *Dijon-style mustard;* spoon into mushroom caps. Place in a 12x7½x2-inch baking pan. Bake, uncovered, in a 325° oven 15 minutes. Serve with roast.

Nutrition information per serving with 2 mushrooms: 186 cal., 22 g pro., 10 g fat, 70 mg chol., 87 mg sodium. U.S. RDA: 26% niacin, 16% iron, 12% riboflavin, 18% phosphorus.

BY BARBARA GOLDMAN

GOOD FOOD, GOOD HEALTH

PASS THE FRUITS AND VEGETABLES, PLEASE!

Take one simple step toward a more healthful diet: Try to eat five servings of fruits and vegetables each day.

5 A DAY FOR BETTER HEALTH

A recent survey in health-conscious California suggests that as many as a third of Californians eat no vegetables at all on a given day, and that only one out of two eats a piece of fruit. Across America, our fruit and vegetable habits are no different, according to statistics.

As a result, the California Department of Health Services and the National Cancer Institute suggest we eat "5 a Day for Better Health." The U.S. Department of Agriculture backs that recommendation.

WHAT ARE THE BENEFITS?

● Eating plenty of low-fat, high-fiber fruits and vegetables may reduce the risk of cancer, heart disease, high blood pressure, and diabetes.

● Fruits and vegetables are rich sources of vitamin A and vitamin C. These vitamins are linked to reduced cancer risk.

● Fruits and vegetables contain no cholesterol.

● They are naturally low in calories and sodium.

● Some fruits and vegetables are good sources of minerals, including potassium, folacin, and calcium.

WHAT'S ONE SERVING OF A FRUIT OR VEGETABLE?

One serving equals ½ cup of fruit, ½ cup fruit or vegetable juice, ½ cup cooked vegetable, *1 cup* leafy vegetable, or ¼ cup dried fruit. If you pile the

BROCCOLI WITH ORANGE AND SWEET RED PEPPER

This low-fat combo is loaded with vitamins A and C—and tastes terrific!

- **1 large orange**
- **½ pound broccoli spears**
- **1 large sweet red pepper, cut into thin strips**
- **2 tablespoons water**
- **1 teaspoon sesame oil**

● **Finely shred** ¼ *teaspoon* peel from orange. Peel and section orange over a 1-cup glass measure to catch juice. Stir orange peel into juice. Set juice mixture and orange sections aside.

● **In a 1½-quart microwave-safe** casserole combine broccoli, red pepper, and water. Micro-cook, covered, on 100% power (high) for 6 to 8 minutes (low-wattage ovens: 9 to 11 minutes) or till broccoli is crisp-tender, stirring once. Drain; return to dish. Set aside.

● **For sauce,** add sesame oil to the reserved juice mixture. Cook, uncovered, on high for 20 to 30 seconds or till bubbly; set aside.

● **Gently stir** reserved orange sections into broccoli-pepper mixture. Cook, uncovered, on high 30 seconds (low-wattage ovens: 1 minute) or till heated through. To serve, drizzle the sauce over broccoli mixture. Serves 4.

Nutrition information per serving: 54 cal., 2 g pro., 10 g carbo., 2 g fat, 0 mg chol., 17 mg sodium, 333 mg potassium, 3 g dietary fiber. U.S. RDA: 66% vit. A, 176% vit. C.

Three of nature's most nutritious foods in one dish: broccoli, sweet pepper, orange.

CHOOSE A VARIETY

1. Eat at least one vitamin-A-rich selection a day (greens, carrots).
2. Eat at least one vitamin-C-rich selection each day (citrus fruit, broccoli, Brussels sprouts, green pepper).
3. Eat at least one high-fiber selection a day (prunes, dried peas, dried beans).
4. Eat a cruciferous vegetable several times each week (broccoli, cauliflower, cabbage, mustard greens, kale, turnips).

PESTICIDE RESIDUE CONCERNS?

Sampling and testing conducted by the U.S. Food and Drug Administration show that pesticide residues in fruits and vegetables do not pose a health hazard. Nevertheless, should you wish to go a step further toward reducing dietary exposure to pesticides, you can follow this advice issued by the Environmental Protection Agency:

Thoroughly rinse and scrub fruits and vegetables—with a brush, when possible. Rinse with *plain* water. Washing foods with soap is not recommended because soap residues may be difficult to remove. Furthermore, soap is not intended for consumption.

Peel produce, if appropriate, though some nutrients will be peeled away.

Discard outer leaves of leafy vegetables such as lettuce and cabbage.

vegetables onto your dinner plate, that may actually be two servings. And don't forget to count the raisins in your cereal bowl.

AUGUST

MICROWAVE COOKBOOK FOR SUMMER-FRESH VEGETABLES

20 EASY, ELEGANT RECIPES

PHOTOGRAPHS: TIM SCHULTZ. FOOD STYLIST: PAT GODSTED

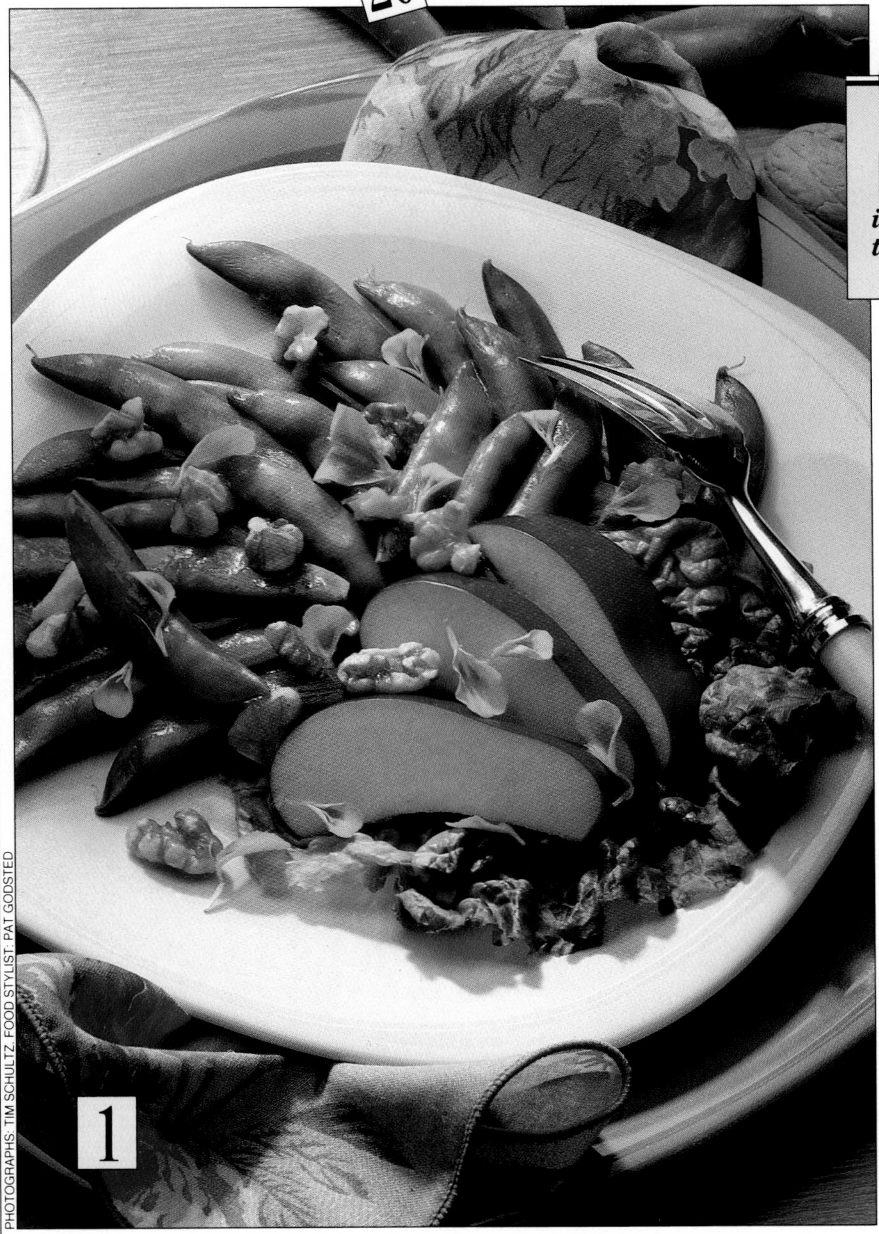

BY BARBARA GOLDMAN

SNAP PEAS

The peas everyone wants in their garden these days. Eat them pod and all!

1 SNAP PEAS WITH WALNUTS

A savory, sophisticated side dish—in less than 10 minutes!

8 oz. snap peas, cleaned
2 Tbsp. water
¼ cup apple juice
2 tsp. walnut oil
1 tsp. cornstarch
¼ tsp. salt
2 Tbsp. broken walnuts
Red leaf lettuce (optional)
Apple wedges (optional)
Edible marigold petals (optional)

In a 1-quart microwave-safe casserole combine peas and water. Micro-cook, covered, on 100% power (high) 3½ to 5 minutes (low-wattage ovens: 5 to 6 minutes) or till crisp-tender. Stir once. Cover; set aside.

In a 2-cup glass measure combine juice, oil, cornstarch, and salt. Cook, uncovered, on high 1½ minutes (low-wattage ovens: 1½ to 2 minutes) or till thickened and bubbly, stirring every 30 seconds. Stir in nuts. Cook on high 30 seconds more to heat through. Drain peas; return to casserole. Add nut mixture; stir to coat. Serve with lettuce and apples. Sprinkle with edible marigold petals, if desired. Makes 4 servings.

Nutrition information per serving: *78 cal., 2 g pro., 7 g carbo., 5 g fat, 0 mg chol., 137 mg sodium, 2 g dietary fiber. U.S. RDA: 40% vit. C.*

TOMATOES

Bright, juicy, and luscious—a cook's and gardener's joy. And now America's most popular meal mate comes in a variety of colors and sizes.

2 BABY PEAR TOMATOES AND BRIE

Sure to wow guests—

Fresh herb sprigs
- **1   4½-ounce round Brie cheese**
Coarsely cracked black pepper
- **7   ounces baby pear tomatoes (red and yellow)**
- **1   to 2 tablespoons snipped fresh herbs (choose from basil, oregano, marjoram, savory, dill, *or* a combination of them)**
Sliced French bread

Generously line a 9-inch microwave-safe pie plate or quiche dish with fresh herb sprigs. Place cheese over herbs in dish. Using the tip of a paring knife, score top of the cheese in a diamond pattern. Generously top cheese with black pepper. Micro-cook, uncovered, on 100% power (high) 1½ to 2 minutes or till cheese just starts to melt. Arrange tomatoes around cheese. Sprinkle cheese and tomatoes with snipped herbs. Cook on high 1 minute more or till tomatoes are warm. Cut cheese into wedges; serve with tomatoes and bread. Makes 4 to 6 appetizer servings.

Nutrition information per serving (without bread): *117 cal., 7 g pro., 3 g carbo., 9 g fat, 32 mg chol., 206 mg sodium, 164 mg potassium, 1 g dietary fiber. U.S. RDA: 16% vit. A, 10% vit. C, and 11% riboflavin.*

3 FRESH TOMATO SCALLOP

A home-style favorite with a yummy pecan topping—

- **2   tablespoons sliced green onion**
- **1   tablespoon margarine *or* butter**
- **⅓   cup fine dry bread crumbs**
- **2   tablespoons grated Parmesan cheese**
- **2   tablespoons chopped toasted pecans**
- **5   medium tomatoes**
- **1   tablespoon white wine Worcestershire sauce**

In a 2-cup glass measure micro-cook onion and margarine or butter, uncovered, on 100% power (high) 1 minute or

till crisp-tender. Add crumbs, cheese, and pecans; toss to mix. Set aside.

Peel tomatoes, if desired; cut into ½-inch slices. In an 8-inch microwave-safe quiche dish arrange tomatoes in spiral. Sprinkle with Worcestershire sauce.

Cover loosely with waxed paper. Micro-cook on 100% power (high) for 2 to 3 minutes (low-wattage ovens: 2½ to 3½ minutes) or till almost heated through, giving plate a half-turn once.

Sprinkle crumb mixture over tomatoes. Cook, uncovered, on high 30 to 60 seconds (low-wattage ovens: 1 to 2 minutes) or till heated through. Makes 4 to 6 side-dish servings.

Nutrition information per serving: *122 cal., 4 g pro., 13 g carbo., 7 g fat, 3 mg chol., 203 mg sodium, 275 mg potassium, 3 g dietary fiber. U.S. RDA: 32% vit. A, 25% vit. C.*

4 PLUM TOMATOES WITH SESAME SAUCE

Micro-cook in 5 minutes, then savor the flavor and crunch of this saucy tomato-sprout combo—

- **6   plum (Italian) tomatoes (12 ounces)**
- **¼   cup sliced green onion**
- **1   tablespoon water**
- **1   clove garlic, minced**
- **1½   teaspoons cornstarch**

- **½   cup chicken broth**
- **1   tablespoon soy sauce**
- **½   teaspoon sesame oil**
- **1   cup bean sprouts**
- **1   teaspoon sesame seed, toasted**
Red oak leaf lettuce (optional)

Halve tomatoes lengthwise; place around edge of a 9-inch microwave-safe pie plate, leaving center open. Cover with vented microwave-safe plastic wrap; set aside.

For sesame sauce, in a 2-cup glass measure combine green onion, water, and garlic. Micro-cook, uncovered, on 100% power (high) 1 minute or till onion is just tender. Stir cornstarch into broth and soy sauce. Add to onion mixture. Cook, uncovered, on high 2 to 3 minutes or till thickened and bubbly, stirring twice. Stir in oil.

Cook tomatoes on high 1 to 2 minutes or till heated through, rotating once.

Line platter with bean sprouts. Place tomato halves atop. Drizzle with sesame sauce. Sprinkle with sesame seed. Garnish with lettuce, if desired. Serve at once. Makes 4 side-dish servings.

Nutrition information per serving: *51 cal., 3 g pro., 8 g carbo., 2 g fat, 0 mg chol., 362 mg sodium, 281 mg potassium, 2 g dietary fiber. U.S. RDA: 25% vit. A, 25% vit. C.*

GREENS

Once the poor relatives of the vegetable family, greens have become trendsetters! Heap your plate high with these nutritious vegetables.

5 WILTED SORREL SALAD

The greens are wilted, but the salad will lift appetites—

- **2   slices bacon, cut up**
- **½   of a small red onion, sliced**
- **1   tablespoon dry sherry**
- **1   tablespoon honey**
- **4   cups torn sorrel *and/or* spinach**
Edible flowers (such as nasturtium, violet, *or* pansy) (optional)

Place bacon in 1½-quart microwave-safe casserole. Micro-cook, covered, on 100% power (high) about 3 minutes (low-wattage ovens: 4 to 5 minutes) or till crisp; stir once. Drain; return *1 ta-*

blespoon fat to casserole. Stir in onion, sherry, and honey; cook, covered, on high 30 to 60 seconds. Add greens; toss to wilt. Garnish with flowers, if desired. Serves 2.

Nutrition information per serving: *175 cal., 6 g pro., 14 g carbo., 11 g fat, 13 mg chol., 208 mg sodium, 683 mg potassium, 3 g dietary fiber. U.S. RDA: 148% vit. A, 58% vit. C, 10% thiamine, 14% riboflavin, 11% calcium, 18% iron.*

once. Serve hot corn with *2 teaspoons* honey-butter mixture per ear. Store any remaining mixture, covered, in the refrigerator. Makes 4 servings.

Nutrition information per serving (1 ear corn, 2 teaspoons honey-butter): 143 cal., 3 g pro., 17 g carbo., 9 g fat, 0 mg chol., 261 mg sodium, 215 mg potassium, 2 g dietary fiber. U.S. RDA: 11% vit. A.

7 BABY CORN AND PEPPERS

A fresh, zesty side dish—with tiny, tender ears of corn—

- ½ **of a small onion, sliced and separated into rings**
- 1 **small fresh hot red chili pepper *or* jalapeño pepper, halved lengthwise, seeded, and sliced***
- 1½ **teaspoons cooking oil**
- 1 **small clove garlic, minced**
- ½ **of a small sweet red pepper, cut into strips**
- ½ **of a small green pepper, cut into strips**
- 2 **cups fresh *or* one 8-ounce package frozen baby cob corn (*or:* 2 cups whole kernel corn cut from regular-size cobs)**
- ¼ **cup chicken broth**
- 1 **tablespoon soy sauce**
- 1½ **teaspoons cornstarch**
- ⅛ **teaspoon ground ginger**

In a 1½-quart microwave-safe casserole micro-cook onion, hot red chili or jalapeño pepper, oil, and garlic, covered, on 100% power (high) for 1 minute. Stir to mix well.

Stir in red and green peppers. Cook, covered, on high 2 minutes. Stir in fresh or frozen baby cob corn. Cook, covered, on high 2 to 3 minutes more or till crisp-tender, stirring once. *Or,* if using fresh kernel corn, cook on high 4 to 5 minutes or till crisp-tender. Drain; turn into serving bowl. Cover; keep warm.

In a 1-cup measure stir together broth, soy sauce, cornstarch, and ginger. Cook, uncovered, on high about 1 to 2 minutes or till thickened and bubbly, stirring once. Pour over vegetables and stir to coat. Serves 4.

*Note: Chili peppers contain volatile oils that can burn skin and eyes, so avoid direct contact as much as possible. Wear plastic or rubber gloves or work under cold running water. If your bare hands touch the peppers, wash well with soap and water.

Nutrition information per serving: 102 cal., 4 g pro., 19 g carbo., 3 g fat, 0 mg chol., 318 mg sodium, 308 mg potassium, 3 g dietary fiber. U.S. RDA: 26% vit. A, 55% vit. C, 12% thiamine.

CORN

Mayans, Aztecs, and Incas grew this New World vegetable more than 3,000 years ago. Later, native Americans shared their corn-growing secrets with the Pilgrims. Now you can choose from countless varieties. Many new types of corn retain just-picked flavor long after harvest.

6 HONEY-BUTTERED CORN

No need to boil water. Simply wrap the ears of corn in waxed paper and micro-cook—

- ⅓ **cup margarine *or* butter, softened**
- 1 **tablespoon honey**
- ¾ **teaspoon lemon-pepper seasoning**
- ½ **teaspoon seasoned salt**
- 4 **medium fresh ears of corn**

Mix margarine or butter, honey, lemon-pepper, and seasoned salt. Remove husks from corn. Scrub corn with a stiff brush to remove silks. Rinse.

Wrap each ear in waxed paper. Micro-cook on 100% power (high) for 9 to 11 minutes or till tender, turning over

BEANS

A favorite on the plate! Today, most varieties are stringless and a snap to prepare. But happily, their "string bean" image persists. One cup of green (or yellow or purple) beans, for instance, contains only about 35 calories. Beans micro-cook well by themselves—or in vegetable combos.

8 GREEN BEANS WITH BASIL TOPPING

Micro-cook the beans in less than 15 minutes, then accent with an elegant basil topping—

- **12 ounces whole green beans *or* Italian green beans, cleaned**
- **2 tablespoons water**
- **2 teaspoons snipped fresh basil *or* ½ teaspoon dried basil, crushed**
- **1 teaspoon water**
- **¼ teaspoon finely shredded orange peel**
- **2 tablespoons mayonnaise *or* salad dressing**
- **2 tablespoons plain low-fat yogurt**

Halved orange slices (optional)
Purple basil sprig (optional)

In a 1½-quart microwave-safe casserole combine beans and the 2 tablespoons water. Micro-cook, covered, on 100% power (high) for 12 to 15 minutes (low-wattage ovens: 16 to 18 minutes) or till tender, stirring once. Sprinkle lightly with *salt* and *pepper*. Set aside.

In a 1-cup glass measure combine snipped fresh or dried basil, the 1 teaspoon water, and orange peel. Cook, uncovered, on high for 30 seconds; using a fork or whisk, blend into mayonnaise and yogurt till smooth.

Drain beans; transfer to a platter. Garnish with orange slices and basil sprig, if desired. Serve with the mayonnaise-yogurt mixture. Serves 4.

Nutrition information per serving: *81 cal., 2 g pro., 7 g carbo., 6 g fat, 5 mg chol., 50 mg sodium, 204 mg potassium, 2 g dietary fiber. U.S. RDA: 12% vit. A, 17% vit. C.*

9 GARDEN BOUNTY CASSEROLE

Great-tasting, nutritious, and microwave-easy—

- **½ pound green, yellow wax, *and/or* purple beans**
- **2 medium carrots**
- **2 medium fresh ears of corn**
- **¼ cup water**
- **¾ cup shredded Monterey Jack cheese (3 ounces)**
- **½ cup couscous**
- **¼ cup milk**
- **⅛ teaspoon salt**
- **⅛ teaspoon pepper**
- **¼ cup shredded Monterey Jack cheese (1 ounce)**

Clean beans and bias-cut into 1-inch pieces. Thinly bias-slice carrots. Cut corn from cob.

In a 1½-quart microwave-safe casserole combine beans and water. Micro-cook, covered, on 100% power (high) for 4 minutes (low-wattage ovens: 6 minutes); stir once. Stir in carrots and corn. Cook, covered, on high for 5 minutes more (low-wattage ovens: 7 minutes); stir once.

Stir in the ¾ cup cheese, couscous, milk, salt, and pepper. Cook, covered, on high for 3 to 4 minutes (low-wattage ovens: 4 to 5 minutes) or till heated through and all vegetables are crisp-tender, stirring once. Sprinkle the ¼ cup cheese atop. Makes 6 servings.

Nutrition information per serving: *158 cal., 8 g pro., 19 g carbo., 6 g fat, 18 mg chol., 166 mg sodium, 260 mg potassium, 3 g dietary fiber. U.S. RDA: 146% vit. A, 12% vit. C, 18% calcium.*

10

11 **STUFFED WHITE EGGPLANT**
Eggplant goes gourmet with pine nuts, feta cheese, and sun-dried tomatoes in this sophisticated vegetable side dish—

- 2 **small white eggplants (10 to 11 ounces each)**
- 2 **tablespoons water**
- 1 **tablespoon margarine** *or* **butter**
- 3 **tablespoons fine dry seasoned bread crumbs**
- 1 **tablespoon pine nuts** *or* **chopped almonds, toasted**
- 1 **tablespoon snipped parsley**
- ½ **cup chopped onion**
- 1 **to 2 tablespoons snipped fresh basil** *or* **1½ teaspoons dried basil, crushed**
- ½ **cup finely crumbled feta cheese**
- ¼ **cup chopped sun-dried tomatoes**
- 2 **tablespoons snipped parsley**
- ¼ **teaspoon salt**
- ⅛ **teaspoon pepper**

Fresh fennel and basil sprigs (optional)
Baby plum tomatoes (optional)

Halve the eggplants lengthwise. Scoop out the center and reserve the pulp, leaving a ¼-inch shell. Chop the pulp; set aside. Place the shells, cut side down, on a microwave-safe plate; sprinkle with the water. Cover with vented microwave-safe plastic wrap. Microcook on 100% power (high) for 4 to 6 minutes or till tender, rotating the shells once. Set aside.

In a small microwave-safe bowl cook the margarine or butter on high for 45 to 60 seconds or till melted. Stir in the bread crumbs, the toasted nuts, and the 1 tablespoon parsley. Set aside the crumb mixture.

In a 1-quart microwave-safe casserole cook chopped eggplant, onion, and snipped basil, covered, on high 3 to 5 minutes or till tender, stirring once. Stir in feta cheese, sun-dried tomatoes, the 2 tablespoons parsley, salt, and pepper. Spoon eggplant mixture into shells. Sprinkle crumb mixture atop.

Place on the microwave-safe plate. Cook, uncovered, on high for 4 to 5 minutes or till heated through, rotating plate once. Serve with fennel and basil sprigs plus baby plum tomatoes, if desired. Makes 4 servings.

Nutrition information per serving: 126 cal., 5 g pro., 10 g carbo., 8 g fat, 13 mg chol., 359 mg sodium, 240 mg potassium, 2 g dietary fiber. U.S. RDA: 11% vit. A, 10% riboflavin, 11% calcium.

BEETS
Enjoy their sweet flavor and rich red tone. Beet greens are great, too!

10 **BABY BEETS IN CURRANT SYRUP**
Substitute cubed beets for baby beets, if you prefer—

- 1 **pound baby beets** *or* **1 pound beets**
- 2 **tablespoons orange juice**
- ⅛ **teaspoon ground nutmeg**
- ½ **cup currant jelly**

Dairy sour cream *or* **plain yogurt (optional)**
Mint sprig (optional)

Remove tops and roots from beets. Scrub well. For baby beets, use a zester to make lengthwise cuts from stem to root of beet. Using crinkle cutter, halve beets lengthwise. For large beets, peel and cut into ¾-inch cubes.

In 2-quart microwave-safe casserole combine beets and ½ cup *water*. Microcook, covered, on 100% power (high) 6 minutes, stirring once. Drain. Add juice and nutmeg. Cook, covered, on high 5 to 8 minutes or till tender; stir once.

Place jelly in a 1-cup glass measure. Cook, uncovered, on high 1 to 2 minutes or till melted. Pour over beets. Cook, uncovered, on high 1 to 2 minutes or till heated through. Transfer beets and syrup to 4 individual plates. If desired, dollop sour cream around beets; draw knife or toothpick through sour cream into syrup, forming a circle of hearts. Serve with mint, if desired. Makes 4 side-dish servings.

Nutrition information per serving: 156 cal., 2 g pro., 39 g carbo., 0 g fat, 0 mg chol., 88 mg sodium, 411 mg potassium, 2 g dietary fiber. U.S. RDA: 20% vit. C.

11

EGGPLANT
This glossy-skinned vegetable has found a niche in American kitchens. Its meaty taste makes it a great meat substitute. Choose from a variety of sizes and colors. Go small for stuffed individual servings. And bear in mind that oriental miniatures have fewer seeds and thinner skins.

Rinse the eggplant and cut off the top. Peel, if desired, and cut crosswise into ½-inch slices. Place eggplant in a 12x7½x2-inch microwave-safe baking dish, overlapping the slices as needed; add 2 tablespoons *water*. Cover with vented microwave-safe plastic wrap. Micro-cook on 100% power (high) for 5 to 7 minutes or till the eggplant is tender, rotating the dish once; drain.

In a small bowl combine tomatoes, chili peppers, oregano, cumin, salt, and pepper. Top eggplant with the tomato mixture. Cook, uncovered, on high for 1 to 2 minutes or till heated through. Sprinkle cheese over all. Let stand, covered, for 2 to 3 minutes or till cheese is melted. Sprinkle with cilantro, if desired. Makes 6 side-dish servings.

Note: This recipe is not recommended for low-wattage ovens.

Nutrition information per serving: 61 cal., 3 g pro., 6 g carbo., 3 g fat, 8 mg chol., 268 mg sodium, 235 mg potassium, 1 g dietary fiber. U.S. RDA: 44% vit. A, 19% vit. C, 10% calcium.

12 EGGPLANT OLÉ

Enjoy the zippy southwestern flavor—

- 1 medium eggplant (about 1 pound)
- 2 medium tomatoes, seeded and chopped (2 cups)
- 1 4-ounce can diced green chili peppers, drained
- ½ teaspoon dried oregano, crushed
- ¼ teaspoon ground cumin
- ⅛ teaspoon salt
- ⅛ teaspoon pepper
- ½ cup shredded Monterey Jack cheese (2 ounces)
- Snipped cilantro *or* parsley (optional)

GREEN TOMATOES

Red tomatoes may be the favorite, but green tomatoes hold their own in a cook's heart. Green tomatoes are fantastic fried, and great in relishes.

13 HOT GREEN TOMATOES

Enjoy green tomatoes in this spicy side dish—

- ½ cup bias-sliced celery
- 3 green onions, bias-sliced into 1-inch pieces
- 2 tablespoons olive *or* cooking oil
- 1 clove garlic, minced
- ⅛ teaspoon crushed red pepper
- 3 medium green tomatoes, each cut into 6 wedges
- 1 tablespoon snipped cilantro *or* parsley
- Fresh *or* pickled red hot pepper (optional)

In a small microwave-safe bowl combine celery, green onion, oil, garlic, and crushed red pepper. Micro-cook, covered, on 100% power (high) for 1½ minutes. Meanwhile, arrange green tomato wedges in a shallow 1- to 1½-quart microwave-safe dish. Spoon the onion mixture over the tomatoes. Sprinkle cilantro over all. Cook, covered, on high for 2½ to 4 minutes (low-wattage ovens: 6 minutes) or till the tomatoes are fork-tender and heated through, rotating dish once halfway through cooking. Season to taste with *salt* and *cracked black pepper*. Garnish with a fresh or pickled red hot pepper, if desired. Makes 4 side-dish servings.

Nutrition information per serving: 83 cal., 1 g pro., 5 g carbo., 7 g fat, 0 mg chol., 23 mg sodium, 220 mg potassium, 1 g dietary fiber. U.S. RDA: 22% vit. A, 27% vit. C.

14

ELEPHANT GARLIC

Elephant garlic is milder than its better-known cousin and mellows during cooking. Give this gentle giant a try.

14 GLAZED ELEPHANT GARLIC

A mild garlic dish that's guaranteed to win friends. Serve with roast lamb, beef, or pork. Cooked sliced onion in place of garlic is excellent, too—

- **4 bulbs elephant garlic**
- **1 tablespoon water**
- **2 tablespoons brown sugar**
- **2 tablespoons honey**
- **1 tablespoon margarine *or* butter**

Clean garlic; divide into cloves. (You should have about 20 cloves.) Remove and discard the skins and stems. Slice any large cloves. Arrange the garlic in a 9-inch microwave-safe pie plate. Add water. Cover with vented microwave-safe plastic wrap. Micro-cook on 100% power (high) for 5 to 7 minutes (low-wattage ovens: 7½ to 10½ minutes) or till the garlic is tender, stirring once. Set aside.

In a 1-cup glass measure combine the brown sugar, honey, and margarine or butter. Cook, uncovered, on high for 1½ to 2½ minutes (low-wattage ovens: 2 to 3 minutes) or till the honey mixture is thickened and syrupy, stirring after every minute. Drain garlic, if necessary. Drizzle the honey mixture evenly over the garlic. Cook, uncovered, on high for 1 to 2 minutes more or till heated through. Serve spooned over meat. Makes 4 servings.

Nutrition information per serving: 113 cal., 1 g pro., 22 g carbo., 3 g fat, 0 mg chol., 39 mg sodium, 111 mg potassium. U.S. RDA: 11% vit. C.

CABBAGE

The cabbage family is large—green, red, savoy, and Chinese, to name a few. But the best maxim for their cooking time remains "less is more."

15 SAVOY WEDGES WITH HAVARTI SAUCE

Savoy cabbage is a loose-leaf, crinkly cabbage with a delicate flavor—

- **1 small head savoy cabbage *or* regular cabbage (1¼ pounds)**
- **2 teaspoons cornstarch**
- **¼ teaspoon paprika**
- **⅛ teaspoon garlic salt**
- **⅛ teaspoon ground white pepper**
- **¾ cup milk**
- **½ cup shredded Havarti *or* Swiss cheese (2 ounces)**
- **1 tablespoon snipped fresh dillweed *or* ½ teaspoon dried dillweed**
- **Fresh dill sprigs (optional)**

Remove outer leaves from cabbage; discard. Cut cabbage into 6 wedges.

Place wedges and 2 tablespoons *water* in a 12x7½x2-inch microwave-safe baking dish; sprinkle lightly with *salt*. Cover with vented microwave-safe plastic wrap. Micro-cook on 100% power (high) for 9 to 12 minutes or till cabbage is tender, giving dish a half-turn and turning wedges over once during cooking. Drain well. Set aside; keep warm.

For sauce, in a 2-cup glass measure combine the cornstarch, paprika, garlic salt, and white pepper. Add the milk. Cook, uncovered, on high for 3 to 4 minutes or till thickened and bubbly, stirring after every minute till the sauce starts to thicken, then stirring every 30 seconds. Stir in the shredded Havarti cheese till melted. Serve over the hot cabbage wedges. Sprinkle with snipped fresh dill or dried dillweed. Garnish with fresh dill sprigs, if desired. Makes 6 side-dish servings.

Note: This recipe is not recommended for low-wattage ovens.

Nutrition information per serving: 75 cal., 5 g pro., 7 g carbo., 3 g fat, 11 mg chol., 116 mg sodium, 272 mg potassium, 2 g dietary fiber. U.S. RDA: 48% vit. C, 17% calcium.

16 CABBAGE-MUSTARD DIP

A hollowed-out cabbage, cooked to perfection in the microwave oven, makes a handsome serving dish for a hot, piquant dip—

- **¼ cup dairy sour cream**
- **¼ cup plain yogurt**
- **¼ cup Dijon-style mustard**
- **2 tablespoons cornstarch**
- **¾ cup chicken broth**
- **1 2-ounce jar sliced pimiento, drained**
- **1 medium head green *or* red cabbage (about 1½ pounds)**
- **Red *or* green cabbage leaves (optional)**
- **Assorted fresh vegetables for dipping**

For dip, in a small microwave-safe bowl combine the sour cream, the yogurt, the Dijon-style mustard, and the cornstarch. Blend in the chicken broth. Micro-cook, uncovered, on 100% power (high) for 4 to 6 minutes (low-wattage ovens: 6 to 8 minutes) or till the mixture is thickened and bubbly, stirring after every minute. Stir in the pimiento. Cover and set aside.

Rinse the head of cabbage thoroughly. At the cabbage end opposite the core end, slice off about one-fourth of the cabbage. Cut out the center of the cabbage, leaving about ½ inch of cabbage on the sides and 1 inch on the bottom. (Save the cabbage that has been removed to use in coleslaw.) Place the hollowed cabbage head on a microwave-safe pie plate. Cover loosely with vented microwave-safe plastic wrap. Cook on high for 5 to 8 minutes (low-wattage ovens: 8 to 10 minutes) or till barely tender.

To serve, if desired, carefully transfer cabbage to a basket lined with cabbage leaves. Spoon in about *half* of the warm mustard dip. (Cover any remaining dip; let stand at room temperature up to 1 hour.) Serve dip with assorted fresh vegetables for dipping. Refill cabbage with remaining dip as necessary. To reheat mustard dip, cook on high for 1 to 2 minutes or till just hot, stirring once. Makes about 1⅔ cups dip.

Nutrition information per tablespoon: 13 cal., 0 g pro., 1 g carbo., 1 g fat, 1 mg chol., 93 mg sodium, 19 mg potassium.

PEPPERS

Peter Piper is picking more than green peppers these days. Red, yellow, orange, and even purple sweet peppers brighten our culinary world.

17 SALAD-"STUFFED" PEPPERS
No fussing and no stuffing; how easy—

- **4 medium green, sweet yellow, *and/or* red peppers (about 5 ounces each)**
- **1 medium carrot, cut into thin strips (¾ cup)**
- **1 stalk celery, thinly sliced (½ cup)**
- **½ cup thinly sliced green onion**
- **½ cup chicken broth**
- **½ cup quick-cooking rice**
- **6 ounces cooked, peeled, and deveined shrimp**
- **1 5½- *or* 6-ounce can crabmeat, drained, flaked, and cartilage removed, *or* 6 ounces frozen, crab-flavored, salad-style fish, finely chopped**
- **⅓ cup snipped chutney**
- **¼ cup reduced-calorie mayonnaise *or* salad dressing**
- **1 tablespoon lemon juice**
- **Bibb lettuce leaves**
- **Lemon slices (optional)**

Quarter peppers; remove seeds and membranes. Place peppers and 2 tablespoons *water* in a 12x7½x2-inch microwave-safe baking dish. Cover with vented microwave-safe plastic wrap. Micro-cook on 100% power (high) for 5 to 7 minutes or till crisp-tender, rearranging peppers once. Immerse peppers in cold water for a few minutes to cool quickly. Drain; cover and chill.

In a 1½-quart microwave-safe casserole or bowl combine carrot, celery, green onion, and chicken broth. Cook, covered, on high for 3 to 4 minutes or till boiling. Add rice; cover and let stand 5 minutes or till rice has absorbed liquid, stirring once. Cool. Stir in shrimp and crabmeat.

In a small bowl stir together chutney, mayonnaise or salad dressing, and lemon juice. Add to the seafood mixture; toss to coat well. Cover and chill about 3 hours.

To serve, arrange 4 pepper quarters and some lettuce leaves on 4 individual plates. Spoon on the seafood mixture. Garnish with lemon slices, if desired. Makes 4 main-dish servings.

Note: This recipe is not recommended for low-wattage ovens.

Nutrition information per serving: 266 cal., 19 g pro., 34 g carbo., 6 g fat, 117 mg chol., 450 mg sodium, 675 mg potassium, 3 g dietary fiber. U.S. RDA: 130% vit. A, 190% vit. C, 14% thiamine, 16% niacin, 23% iron.

18 PEPPERS IN PARCHMENT
Discover a unique pepper treat— bundles of tangy-sauced peppers. Test for doneness by carefully pricking a pepper through the paper with a fork—

- **6 12x8-inch rectangles of baking parchment**
- **3 green, sweet red, yellow, *and/or* orange peppers, cut into strips**
- **2 tablespoons sliced green onion**
- **1 tablespoon margarine *or* butter**
- **¼ teaspoon curry powder**
- **⅛ teaspoon ground red pepper**
- **2 tablespoons peanut butter**
- **2 tablespoons chopped peanuts**

Fold each parchment sheet in half, forming an 8x6-inch rectangle; crease. Unfold parchment. Place a *sixth* of the peppers to one side of the crease on *each* parchment sheet.

In a 2-cup glass measure combine green onion, margarine or butter, curry powder, and red pepper. Micro-cook, covered with vented microwave-safe plastic wrap, on 100% power (high) for 1 minute or till onion is just tender. Stir in peanut butter and 3 tablespoons *water*. Cook, uncovered, on high 30 seconds more; stir till combined (mixture may look a little curdled). Drizzle *1 tablespoon* of the peanut butter mixture atop each pepper mound. Sprinkle *each* with peanuts. Fold other half of parchment over peppers; seal closed. Fold under ends and seal.

Place bundles on a 12-inch round microwave-safe pizza plate. Cook on high for 5 to 6 minutes or till peppers are tender, rotating dish a half-turn once. To serve, slit papers diagonally and fold back slits. Makes 6 side-dish servings.

Note: This recipe is not recommended for low-wattage ovens.

Nutrition information per serving: 82 cal., 3 g pro., 5 g carbo., 6 g fat, 0 mg chol., 50 mg sodium, 182 mg potassium, 2 g dietary fiber. U.S. RDA: 10% vit. A, 90% vit. C.

SUMMER SQUASH

Yes, we have our zucchini! But try yellow summer squash and the baby varieties, too.

19 SUMMER SQUASH IN WINE-MUSTARD SAUCE

You'll have six servings in practically no time. Micro-cook the tender summer squash in about five minutes, the zesty mustard sauce in two. Then toss the squash and the sauce together, and enjoy.

- **12 baby zucchini *or* 3 medium zucchini (18 ounces)**
- **1 medium yellow summer squash *or* 5 baby yellow summer squash (6 ounces)**
- **2 tablespoons water**
- **½ cup chicken broth**
- **2 tablespoons dry white wine**
- **1 shallot, finely chopped**
- **1 tablespoon cornstarch**
- **1½ teaspoons snipped fresh tarragon *or* ½ teaspoon dried tarragon, crushed**
- **1 teaspoon Dijon-style mustard**
- **⅛ teaspoon pepper**
- **1 tablespoon margarine *or* butter, softened**

If using baby zucchini and baby summer squash in this recipe, keep the squash whole. If using medium zucchini and summer squash, bias-slice the squash into ¼-inch slices. If the squash slices are large in diameter, then halve the slices crosswise. Place the zucchini and the summer squash in a 2-quart microwave-safe casserole. Add the water. Micro-cook the squash, covered, on 100% power (high) for 5 to 7 minutes or till the squash is crisp-tender, stirring once. Drain the squash. Cover the squash to keep warm.

In a 2-cup glass measure combine the chicken broth; the dry white wine; the finely chopped shallot; the cornstarch; the snipped fresh or dried, crushed tarragon; the Dijon-style mustard; and the pepper. Cook the mixture, uncovered, on high for 2 to 3 minutes or till thickened and bubbly, stirring after every minute. Stir in the margarine or butter. To serve, pour *some* of the wine-mustard sauce over the squash and toss together gently. Serve the squash at once with the remaining sauce. Makes 6 side-dish servings.

Note: This recipe is not recommended for low-wattage ovens.

Nutrition information per serving: 49 cal., 2 g pro., 5 g carbo., 2 g fat, 0 mg chol., 114 mg sodium, 306 mg potassium, 1 g dietary fiber. U.S. RDA: 12% vit. A, 13% vit. C.

20 ZUCCHINI WITH ALMONDS

Watch out—zucchini can really grow! Choose small squash; they're sweeter and more tender—

- **½ cup chopped onion**
- **1 tablespoon water**
- **⅛ teaspoon salt**
- **2 cups zucchini sliced ¼ inch thick (about 8 ounces)**
- **2 tablespoons toasted sliced almonds**
- **2 teaspoons margarine *or* butter**
- **½ teaspoon dried marjoram, crushed**
- **½ teaspoon lemon juice**
- **⅛ teaspoon pepper**
- **2 tablespoons grated Parmesan cheese**

In a 1½-quart microwave-safe casserole micro-cook onion, water, and salt, covered, on 100% power (high) for 2 minutes (low-wattage ovens: 3 minutes). Stir in zucchini. Cook, covered, on high for 3 to 5 minutes (low-wattage ovens: 5 to 7 minutes) or till zucchini is crisp-tender, stirring once. Drain.

Stir in the toasted sliced almonds; the margarine or butter; the dried, crushed marjoram; the lemon juice; and the pepper. Cook, covered, on high for 30 to 60 seconds more or till the mixture is heated through. Sprinkle with the grated Parmesan cheese. Makes 4 side-dish servings.

Nutrition information per serving: 64 cal., 3 g pro., 4 g carbo., 5 g fat, 2 mg chol., 150 mg sodium, 202 mg potassium, 1 g dietary fiber.

SEPTEMBER

THE MAGAZINE FOR AMERICAN FAMILIES

Better Homes and Gardens®

SEPTEMBER 1989
$1.50

BACK-TO-SCHOOL ALMANAC
Page 23

25 MAKE-AHEAD GIFTS
CRAFTS WITH COUNTRY HEART

UPDATING YOUR FAMILY ROOM
Page 60

GREAT HOME COOKING
15 EASY NEW RECIPES

HEALTH
LIVING TO BE 100!
Page 36

JOYS OF A TWO-COOK KITCHEN

HOME COOKING '90s STYLE

DELICIOUS, STREAMLINED, HEALTHFUL

BY BARBARA JOHNSON

The way we cook and eat keeps changing! We love homemade family meals, but lack time to cook. We want to eat healthfully, yet crave comfort foods.

These recipes let you have it all. Each is handpicked from our just-revised, red-plaid classic New Cook Book, *now at bookstores.*

SO-EASY DINNER!

CHICKEN DIJON

Here's what busy families need—a 30-minute home-cooked meal! Micro-cook even quicker. Either way, this dish gives you more time to spend with people you love.

▼ For a smooth sauce: Stir constantly while adding flour mixture.

Photographs: Mike Dieter and Scott Little. Food stylists: Janet Herwig and Lynn Blanchard

FRESH!

KOHLRABI WITH HONEY BUTTER

Used to be Mom had to coax us to clean the vegetables off our dinner plates. But, no longer! We're eating more vegetables and trying interesting new varieties at astonishing rates. This sweet and lemony vegetable side dish offers one more wonderful excuse to sample yet another tuber: kohlrabi.

◄ What to do with a kohlrabi? Cut off the top. Then, use a sharp knife to pull off strips of the woody peel before slicing the vegetable.

WHOLESOME!

CHOOSE-A-GRAIN CASSEROLE

More than ever we're eating sensibly. And high-fiber foods like whole grains are especially important. For this creamy side dish, use whatever favorite grains you have handy (choose from bulgur, barley, rice, or wheat berries). If you like, cook the entire recipe in your microwave oven in less than 10 minutes!

▼ Sautéing magic: The onion will turn from opaque to translucent as you sauté the colorful vegetable mixture.

BARBECUE!

STEAK AND SPINACH PINWHEELS

Your lucky dinner guests will praise your barbecue talents when you serve this classy hot-off-the-grill entrée. To fix, wrap lean beef flank steak around a robust bacon, spinach, and Parmesan cheese filling; thread on barbecue skewers. Then sizzle on either your charcoal or gas grill to tender, juicy perfection. Now this is one enticing meal!

▲ Pinwheels are easy: From a short side, roll the scored, pounded steak around filling.

LIGHT!

GREEK-STYLE SALADS WITH OIL-FREE DRESSING

Main-dish salads answer the quick dinner call. Toss together your choice of greens with a few ounces of a favorite cooked meat (lamb, pork, chicken, turkey, or beef). Add feta cheese, olives, and tomatoes for a taste of Greece. Then, top off your creation with our healthful zero-fat dressing. Quick, cool, and crisp!

▶ **For paper-thin lamb strips, use a sharp knife to cut lamb chops lengthwise into narrow slices.**

EXOTIC TASTE!

CHOOSE-A-FRUIT SALAD WITH APRICOT-NECTAR DRESSING

Today's grocers carry more exotic fruit—and we carry more home for everyday meals. Put together your favorite combination of the tropical delights in this fast, easy salad. Then, enjoy every silky drizzle of the fruit dressing—made the sensible way with low-fat yogurt.

▲ Papaya savvy: Use a spoon to scoop out the seeds. Then, peel and slice the papaya.

▶ For easy transferring, wrap pastry around rolling pin; unroll onto pie plate.

COMFORTING!

CRUMB-TOPPED PEACH PIE WITH PECAN PASTRY

We crave down-home cooking, but with a twist—like this pie. It's bursting with best-of-season peaches baked in a tempting pecan-laced pastry. Truly sublime!

MICROWAVE SHORTCUT!

OATMEAL BREAD

Baking bread in the microwave age happens with speed. Micro-raise the dough in about a fourth of the usual time. The result? Tender, light, and wholesome loaves.

▼ Press two fingers into dough ½ inch. If impressions remain, go on to shaping.

HEALTHFUL!

VEGETABLE-TOPPED FILLETS

What's on the menu for dinner tonight? More often these days, the answer turns out to be fish. Why? Because fish is both good for you and more readily available than ever before. Fix whatever fish is on special at the market this week in this healthful, adaptable recipe.

▲ A slick trick for fish poaching: Use a spatula to slide fillets into bubbling broth.

COOK AHEAD!

VEGETABLE-PORK SOUP

On crisp fall days, come home and enjoy the enticing aroma of this hearty, nourishing soup. Take advantage of your convenient crockery cooker to make the recipe. When you do, your meal will be ready and waiting the minute you walk in the door.

▲ Layer vegetables first, then meat—that way everything cooks evenly.

BOLD FLAVORS!

ITALIAN-STYLE BURGERS WITH PARSLEY PESTO TOPPING

Burgers never go out of style—they just get better. Italian seasonings and a dousing of pesto punch up this juicy version. Each incredible bite will satisfy anyone's hankering for zesty taste.

▼ To make equal portions, cut mounded meat mixture into fourths or sixths, then shape.

SIMPLIFIED!

ONE-LAYER CHOCOLATE CAKE AND NO-COOK FUDGE FROSTING

Baking scratch cake is a cinch, thanks to our Test Kitchen's revolutionary method. Measure all ingredients into one bowl and mix! Fast and easy, yes. And, what a divine flavor and texture! You can even micro-cook the cake with superb results. Top with the decadent frosting.

▲ About the only thing that isn't new is the doneness test: a clean toothpick!

HOME-BAKED EASE!

APPLE-STREUSEL LADDER LOAF

Re-create Mom's home baking with '90s ease: start with frozen bread dough. The sugar-and-spice apple filling is irresistible!

There's nothing to the ▶ ladder! Alternately fold dough strips over filling, at an angle.

CLASSIC AND CLASSY!

CHOCOLATE CHIP COOKIES; MACADAMIA NUT AND WHITE CHOCOLATE CHUNK COOKIES

Old favorites *can* get better! This sensational cookie shows how. Try the traditional chocolate chip and trendy macadamia variations—sure to satisfy both the nostalgic and sophisticated sides of us all.

Save a step and a bowl! ▶ Dump in both flour and baking soda, rather than combining the two first.

APPLE-STREUSEL LADDER LOAF

Use tart apples like Jonathans, Granny Smiths, or Winesaps for this blue-ribbon bread—

- 1 16-ounce loaf frozen sweet bread dough *or* frozen bread dough, thawed
- 2 tablespoons margarine *or* butter, softened
- ¼ cup packed brown sugar
- 1 tablespoon all-purpose flour
- 1 teaspoon ground cinnamon
- 2 cups finely chopped, peeled apples

Milk
- 2 tablespoons all-purpose flour
- 2 tablespoons sugar
- 1 tablespoon margarine *or* butter
- ¼ cup slivered almonds (optional)

● **Divide bread dough in half.** On a lightly floured surface, roll each half into an 8-inch square. (For easier rolling, let dough rest a few minutes.) Spread *each* square with *1 tablespoon* of the softened margarine or butter.

● **For filling,** in a bowl combine brown sugar, the 1 tablespoon flour, and the cinnamon. Add apples; toss to coat.

● **Spread** *half* of the filling down the center of *each* square. Cutting from the right edge toward the filling, make 2½-inch-long cuts in dough at 1-inch intervals. Repeat from the left edge. Fold strips alternately over filling and fold under ends (see photo, *above left*).

● **Place loaves** on a greased 15x10x1-inch baking pan. Brush with milk. Combine the 2 tablespoons flour and sugar. Cut in the 1 tablespoon margarine or butter till mixture resembles coarse crumbs. Sprinkle *half* of the crumb mixture over *each* loaf. Top with almonds, if desired. Cover and let loaves rise till nearly double (45 to 60 minutes).

● **Bake in a 350° oven** for 30 minutes or till golden. Serve warm. Makes 2 loaves (32 servings).

Nutrition information per serving: *65 cal., 1 g pro., 11 g carbo., 2 g fat, 1 mg chol., 82 mg sodium, 29 mg potassium.*

CHICKEN DIJON

The cream, lemon-pepper seasoning, and Dijon-style mustard provide a superb balance of flavors—

   ¾ cup long grain rice *or* one
      4.5-ounce package herb-flavored
      rice mix
   2 whole medium chicken breasts
      (1½ pounds total), skinned,
      boned, and halved lengthwise
   1 teaspoon lemon-pepper
      seasoning
   ¼ teaspoon onion powder
   2 tablespoons margarine *or* butter
Milk *or* light cream
   2 teaspoons all-purpose flour
   1 tablespoon Dijon-style mustard
Tomato wedges (optional)
Green pepper strips (optional)

● **Cook rice or rice mix** according to package directions.
● **Meanwhile, rinse chicken;** pat dry. Sprinkle both sides of chicken with lemon-pepper seasoning and onion powder. In a skillet cook chicken in hot margarine or butter over medium heat about 12 minutes or till tender and no longer pink, turning occasionally to brown evenly. Transfer to a platter; keep warm.
● **For sauce, measure pan juices;** add milk or light cream to measure ⅔ cup liquid. Return to the skillet. Stir ¼ cup milk or light cream into flour; add to juices mixture (see photo, *page 121*). Stir in the mustard. Cook and stir till thickened and bubbly. Cook and stir for 1 minute more. Spoon *some* sauce over chicken; pass remaining sauce. If desired, garnish with the tomato wedges and green pepper strips. Serve with hot rice. Makes 4 servings.

   Microwave directions: Cook the rice or rice mix according to the package directions.

   Rinse chicken; pat dry. Place the chicken in a 10x6x2-inch microwave-safe baking dish. Sprinkle both sides of chicken with lemon-pepper seasoning and onion powder. *Omit* the margarine or butter. Micro-cook, covered with waxed paper, on 100% power (high) for 4 to 6 minutes (low-wattage oven: 6 to 8 minutes) or till tender and no longer pink, turning chicken over and rearranging once. Transfer chicken to a platter; cover and keep warm.

For sauce, pour pan juices into a 2-cup glass measure; add milk or light cream to measure ½ cup liquid. Stir ¼ cup milk or light cream into flour; add to juices mixture. Stir in the mustard. Cook, uncovered, on high for 2½ to 4 minutes or till mixture is thickened and bubbly, stirring every 30 seconds. Serve as directed.

   Nutrition information per serving with long grain rice: *360 cal., 29 g pro., 30 g carbo., 12 g fat, 82 mg chol., 406 mg sodium, 286 mg potassium. U.S. RDA: 15% thiamine, 65% niacin, 11% iron.*

KOHLRABI WITH HONEY BUTTER

   4 small kohlrabies (about 1 pound),
      peeled and cut into
      ¼-inch-thick strips (3 cups)
      (see photo, *page 122*)
   1 medium carrot, cut into
      ⅛-inch-thick strips (½ cup)
   1 tablespoon snipped chives *or*
      parsley
   ¼ teaspoon finely shredded
      lemon peel
   1 tablespoon lemon juice
   2 teaspoons honey
   ⅛ teaspoon pepper
   1 tablespoon margarine *or* butter
Lemon slices (optional)

● **In a medium saucepan cook** the kohlrabi and carrot, covered, in a small amount of boiling water for 6 to 8 minutes or till crisp-tender. Drain.
● **In a bowl combine** chives or parsley, lemon peel, lemon juice, honey, and pepper. Pour over the hot kohlrabi and carrot; add margarine or butter. Toss to coat. If desired, serve with lemon slices. Makes 4 side-dish servings.

   Microwave directions: In a 1½-quart microwave-safe casserole micro-cook kohlrabi, carrot, and 1 tablespoon *water*, covered, on 100% power (high) for 7 to 9 minutes (low-wattage oven: 10 to 12 minutes) or till crisp-tender, stirring once. Drain. In a bowl combine chives or parsley, lemon peel, lemon juice, honey, and pepper. Pour over hot kohlrabi and carrot; add margarine or butter. Toss to coat. Serve as directed.

   Nutrition information per serving: *74 cal., 2 g pro., 12 g carbo., 3 g fat, 0 mg chol., 61 mg sodium, 436 mg potassium, 4 g dietary fiber. U.S. RDA: 105% vit. A, 80% vit. C.*

STEAK AND SPINACH PINWHEELS

Grill or broil this delectable entrée. Serve with your favorite vegetable and orzo (a ricelike pasta)—

   8 slices bacon
   1 1- to 1½-pound beef flank steak
      or boneless beef top round steak
   1 10-ounce package frozen
      chopped spinach, thawed and
      well drained
   ¼ cup grated Parmesan cheese

● **In a large skillet cook** bacon just till done but not crisp. Drain on paper towels. Score steak by making shallow cuts at 1-inch intervals diagonally across steak in a diamond pattern. Repeat on second side. With a meat mallet, pound the steak into a 12x8-inch rectangle, working from the center to the edges. Sprinkle with *salt* and *pepper*. Arrange bacon lengthwise on steak.
● **Spread spinach over bacon.** Sprinkle with Parmesan cheese. Roll up from a short side (see photo, *page 123*). Secure with wooden toothpicks at 1-inch intervals, starting ½ inch from one end. Cut between toothpicks into eight 1-inch slices.
● **Place, cut side down,** on the unheated rack of a broiler pan. Broil 3 inches from the heat for 6 minutes. Turn; broil 6 to 8 minutes more for medium doneness. Remove picks. Makes 4 servings.

   Grilling directions: Prepare the meat as above. Thread *two* slices onto *each* of 4 long skewers. Grill slices on an uncovered grill directly over *medium* coals for 6 minutes. Turn and grill to desired doneness, allowing 6 to 8 minutes more for medium doneness. Remove toothpicks and skewers.

   Nutrition information per serving: *334 cal., 30 g pro., 2 g carbo., 22 g fat, 77 mg chol., 498 mg sodium, 681 mg potassium, and 1 g dietary fiber. U.S. RDA: 91% vit. A, 12% vit. C, 17% thiamine, 21% riboflavin, 28% niacin, 17% calcium, 25% iron.*

CHOOSE-A-GRAIN CASSEROLE

Garnish with red pepper strips and celery leaves for an attractive finishing touch—

- ½ **cup chopped green *or* sweet red pepper**
- ½ **cup chopped onion**
- ½ **cup chopped celery *or* one 4-ounce can diced green chili peppers, drained**
- 1 **clove garlic, minced**
- 1 **tablespoon margarine *or* butter**
- 1½ **cups cooked rice, bulgur, wheat berries, *or* barley**
- ½ **of an 8-ounce container (½ cup) soft-style cream cheese**
- ¼ **teaspoon salt**
- ¼ **teaspoon pepper**
- ¼ **teaspoon ground cumin, ground coriander, *or* dried basil, crushed**
  Milk
- ½ **cup shredded cheddar cheese (2 ounces)**

● **In a small saucepan cook** green or red pepper, onion, celery (if using instead of chili peppers), and garlic in hot margarine or butter till tender (see photo, *page 122*).

● **Meanwhile, in a bowl combine** chili peppers (if using); cooked rice, bulgur, wheat berries, or barley; cream cheese; salt; pepper; and cumin, coriander, or basil. Stir in onion mixture. Transfer to a 1-quart casserole. Bake, covered, in a 375° oven about 25 minutes or till heated through.

● **If mixture seems stiff, stir in milk,** a tablespoon at a time, to moisten. Sprinkle with cheese. Bake for 2 to 3 minutes more or till cheese melts. Makes 5 or 6 side-dish servings.

Microwave directions: In a 1-quart microwave-safe casserole, microcook green or red pepper, onion, celery (if using instead of chili peppers), garlic, and margarine or butter, covered, on 100% power (high) for 1½ to 2½ minutes (low-wattage oven: 3 to 4 minutes) or till tender, stirring once. Stir in chili peppers (if using); cooked rice, bulgur, wheat berries, or barley; cream cheese; salt; pepper; and cumin, coriander, or basil. Cook, covered, on high for 3 to 5 minutes (low-wattage oven: 4 to 6 minutes) or till heated through, stirring once. If mixture seems stiff, stir in

milk, a tablespoon at a time, to moisten. Sprinkle with cheese. Cover and let stand till cheese melts.

Nutrition information per serving: 231 cal., 6 g pro., 20 g carbo., 14 g fat, 12 mg chol., 479 mg sodium, 192 mg potassium, 1 g dietary fiber. U.S. RDA: 56% vit. A, 56% vit. C, 14% calcium.

GREEK-STYLE SALADS WITH OIL-FREE DRESSING

Our taste testers raved about this salad, prepared with strips of medium-rare lamb. To cook lamb chops this way, broil 3 to 4 inches from the heat for 4 minutes. Turn and broil 4 to 6 minutes more. The cooked chops will be easier to slice if you chill them completely—

- 3 **cups torn curly endive *or* romaine**
- 1½ **cups torn iceberg lettuce *or* spinach**
- 6 **ounces cooked lamb, pork, chicken, turkey, *or* beef, cut into thin strips (see photo, *page 124*)**
- 1 **medium tomato, chopped**
- ½ **of a small cucumber, thinly sliced**
- ½ **cup crumbled feta cheese (2 ounces)**
- 2 **green onions, sliced**
- 6 **radishes, sliced**
- 2 **tablespoons sliced pitted ripe olives**
- 2 **recipes Oil-Free Dressing (see recipe, *right*) *or* ½ cup Vinaigrette (see recipe, *right*)**
- 3 **anchovy fillets, drained, rinsed, and patted dry (optional)**

● **Toss together** curly endive or romaine and lettuce or spinach. Divide greens among 3 salad plates. Arrange meat, tomato, cucumber, feta cheese, green onions, radishes, and olives over greens. Drizzle with Oil-Free Dressing or Vinaigrette. If desired, top with anchovies. Makes 3 main-dish servings.

Nutrition information per serving: 239 cal., 20 g pro., 17 g carbo., 11 g fat, 73 mg chol., 318 mg sodium, 604 mg potassium, and 3 g dietary fiber. U.S. RDA: 44% vit. A, 35% vit. C, 14% thiamine, 24% riboflavin, 20% niacin, 16% calcium, 15% iron.

OIL-FREE DRESSING

Heavy on the herbs, light on the fat—

- 1 **tablespoon powdered fruit pectin**
- ¾ **teaspoon snipped fresh oregano, basil, thyme, tarragon, savory, *or* dillweed *or* ¼ teaspoon dried oregano, basil, thyme, tarragon, savory, *or* dillweed, crushed**
- ½ **teaspoon sugar**
- ⅛ **teaspoon dry mustard**
- ⅛ **teaspoon pepper**
- ¼ **cup water**
- 1 **tablespoon vinegar**
- 1 **small clove garlic, minced**

● **In a mixing bowl combine** pectin, desired herb, sugar, mustard, and pepper. Stir in water, vinegar, and garlic. Cover and store in the refrigerator for up to 3 days. Makes about ½ cup.

Nutrition information per tablespoon: 7 cal., 0 g pro., 2 g carbo., 0 g fat, 0 mg chol., 0 mg sodium, 5 mg potassium.

VINAIGRETTE

A light dressing that's perfect for any of your favorite tossed salads—

- ½ **cup salad oil**
- ⅓ **cup white wine vinegar *or* vinegar**
- 1 **tablespoon sugar**
- 2 **teaspoons snipped fresh thyme, oregano, *or* basil; *or* ½ teaspooon dried thyme, oregano, *or* basil, crushed**
- ½ **teaspoon paprika**
- ¼ **teaspoon dry mustard *or***
- 1 **teaspoon Dijon-style mustard (optional)**
- ⅛ **teaspoon pepper**

● **In a screw-top jar mix** oil; vinegar; sugar; desired herb; paprika; mustard, if desired; and pepper. Cover and shake well. Store in the refrigerator for up to 2 weeks. Shake before serving. Makes ¾ cup.

Nutrition information per tablespoon: 86 cal., 0 g pro., 2 g carbo., 9 g fat, 0 mg chol., 0 mg sodium, 10 mg potassium.

CHOOSE-A-FRUIT SALAD WITH APRICOT-NECTAR DRESSING

Our flashy fruit combination includes sliced carambola (star fruit), raspberries, pineapple, pear, kiwifruit, strawberries, and papaya. For an easy way to seed papaya, see page 125—

4 cups desired fruit (see *below*)
Lemon juice
Leaf lettuce
½ cup Apricot-Nectar Dressing (see recipe, *below*)

● **If necessary, brush** fruit with lemon juice to prevent darkening. On a lettuce-lined platter, arrange fruit. Serve with Apricot-Nectar Dressing. Makes 4 side-dish servings.

Fruit options: Choose any combination of peeled and sliced or cut-up avocados, bananas, kiwifruit, mangoes, melons, papayas, or peaches; sliced or cut-up pineapple, apples, apricots, nectarines, pears, or plums; peeled-and-sectioned oranges, tangerines, or grapefruit; berries (halve any large strawberries); halved and pitted dark sweet cherries; or halved seedless grapes.

Nutrition information per serving: *90 cal., 2 g pro., 21 g carbo., 1 g fat, 1 mg chol., 14 mg sodium, 367 mg potassium, 4 g dietary fiber. U.S. RDA: 20% vit. A, 130% vit. C.*

APRICOT-NECTAR DRESSING

The thickness of yogurt varies from brand to brand. That's why you may need to add more nectar to make a dressing of drizzling consistency—

1 tablespoon brown sugar
⅛ teaspooon ground cinnamon
Dash ground nutmeg
½ cup plain low-fat yogurt
¼ to ½ cup apricot nectar

● **Stir brown sugar,** cinnamon, and nutmeg into yogurt. Add enough of the apricot nectar to make a dressing of drizzling consistency. Stir till smooth. Cover and store in the refrigerator for up to 2 weeks. Makes 1 cup.

Nutrition information per tablespoon: *10 cal., 0 g pro., 2 g carbo., 0 g fat, 0 mg chol., 6 mg sodium, 25 mg potassium.*

CRUMB-TOPPED PEACH PIE WITH PECAN PASTRY

Spice up this wonderful pie by adding ¼ teaspoon ground allspice or ginger to the peach filling—

1 recipe Pecan Pastry (see recipe, *below*)
½ cup sugar
3 tablespoons all-purpose flour
6 cups peaches, peeled, pitted, and thinly sliced
½ cup all-purpose flour
½ cup packed brown sugar
2 tablespoons margarine *or* butter

● **Prepare, roll out, and flute** Pecan Pastry as recipe directs. Set aside.
● **For filling,** in a large mixing bowl stir together sugar and the 3 tablespoons flour. Add peaches and toss till the fruit is coated with sugar mixture. Transfer to the pastry-lined 9-inch pie plate.
● **For topping, combine** the ½ cup flour and brown sugar. Cut in the margarine or butter till mixture resembles coarse crumbs; sprinkle over filling. Cover edge with foil. Bake in a 375° oven for 25 minutes. Remove foil. Bake for 20 to 25 minutes more or till top is golden and fruit is tender. Makes 8 servings.

Nutrition information per serving: *388 cal., 4 g pro., 64 g carbo., 14 g fat, 0 mg chol., 105 mg sodium, 344 mg potassium, and 3 g dietary fiber. U.S. RDA: 16% vit. A, 10% vit. C, 17% thiamine, 11% riboflavin, 15% niacin, 11% iron.*

PECAN PASTRY

1¼ cups all-purpose flour
¼ teaspoon salt
⅓ cup shortening *or* lard
¼ cup finely chopped pecans
3 to 4 tablespoons cold water

● **In a mixing bowl stir together** flour and salt. Cut in shortening or lard till pieces are the size of small peas. Stir in pecans.
● **Sprinkle** *1 tablespoon* water over part of mixture; gently toss with a fork. Push to side of bowl. Repeat till all is moistened. Form dough into a ball.
● **On a lightly floured surface,** flatten dough with hands. Roll dough from center to edges, forming a circle about

12 inches in diameter. Wrap pastry around rolling pin. Unroll onto a 9-inch pie plate (see photo, *page 126*). Ease pastry into pie plate, being careful not to stretch pastry.
● **Trim** to ½ inch beyond edge of pie plate; fold under extra pastry. Make a scalloped or fluted edge. *Do not* prick pastry. Continue as directed for Crumb-Topped Peach Pie with Pecan Pastry.

Micro-Raising Yeast Dough

With a little help from your microwave oven, you may be able to significantly shorten the time it takes to proof (raise) your yeast breads.

Before you begin, check your owner's manual to see if proofing is recommended. (Yeast dough proofing is not recommended in low-wattage microwave ovens.) Or, use this test to check your oven.

Place 2 tablespoons cold stick margarine *(do not use corn oil margarine)* in a custard cup in the center of your oven. Micro-cook, uncovered, on 10% power (low) for 4 minutes. If the margarine doesn't completely melt, your microwave can proof yeast dough. But if the margarine does completely melt, your microwave will kill the yeast before the bread has a chance to rise. If so, you'll have to raise your yeast breads conventionally.

If your oven passed the test, here's how to proceed. While kneading your dough, place 3 cups water in a 4-cup glass measure. Cook on 100% power (high) for 6½ to 8½ minutes or till boiling. Move water to back of oven. Place kneaded dough in a greased microwave-safe bowl, turning once. Cover with waxed paper and place in microwave oven with hot water. Heat dough and water on 10% power (low) for 13 to 15 minutes or till dough has almost doubled (see photo, *page 126*). Punch dough down; shape as directed.

Place shaped dough in 8x4x2-inch microwave-safe loaf dishes. (For round or long loaves that are shaped on baking sheets, or rolls that are shaped in muffin cups, you'll have to do this second proofing step conventionally.) Return to microwave oven with hot water. Cover with waxed paper. Heat on low for 6 to 8 minutes or till nearly doubled.

OATMEAL BREAD

To make a whole wheat and oatmeal version (as we did for the photo on page 126), use 3¾ to 4¼ cups all-purpose flour, 1 cup rolled oats, and 1 cup whole wheat flour—

- 4¼ to 4¾ cups all-purpose flour
- 1 package active dry yeast
- 1¾ cups water
- ⅓ cup packed brown sugar
- 3 tablespoons shortening, margarine, *or* butter
- 1 teaspoon salt
- 2 cups quick-cooking *or* regular rolled oats

● **In a large mixer bowl combine** *2 cups* of the all-purpose flour and the yeast. In a saucepan heat and stir water, brown sugar, shortening, and salt till warm (120° to 130°) and shortening almost melts. Add to the flour mixture. Beat with an electric mixer on low speed for 30 seconds, scraping bowl constantly. Then beat on high speed for 3 minutes. Using a spoon, stir in rolled oats and as much of the remaining flour as you can.

● **Turn out** onto a lightly floured surface. Knead in enough of the remaining flour to make a moderately stiff dough that is smooth and elastic (6 to 8 minutes total). Shape into a ball. Place in a lightly greased bowl; turn once. Cover and let rise in a warm place till double (1 to 1½ hours). (*Or*, to micro-proof dough, see tip box, *page 133*.)

● **Punch dough down.** Turn out onto a lightly floured surface. Divide in half. Cover and let rest for 10 minutes. Meanwhile, lightly grease two 8x4x2-inch loaf pans. Shape each half of the dough into a loaf. Place in pans. Cover and let rise in a warm place till nearly double (45 to 60 minutes).

● **Bake in a 375° oven** 40 to 45 minutes or till done. Cover loosely with foil the last 10 to 20 minutes, if necessary, to prevent overbrowning. Remove from pans; cool. Makes 2 loaves (32 slices).

Nutrition information per slice: 99 cal., 3 g pro., 18 g carbo., 2 g fat, 0 mg chol., 68 mg sodium, 46 mg potassium, and 1 g dietary fiber. U.S. RDA: 10% thiamine.

VEGETABLE-TOPPED FILLETS

Summer squash and zucchini make a colorful vegetable duo. But you can use just one type of squash if you like—

- 1 small yellow summer squash
- 1 small zucchini
- 1 cup sliced fresh mushrooms
- ½ of a small onion, sliced and separated into rings
- 1 clove garlic, minced
- ⅛ teaspoon salt
- 1 14½-ounce can tomatoes, cut up
- 1 tablespoon cornstarch
- ¼ teaspoon dried basil, crushed
- ¼ teaspoon dried oregano, crushed
- Dash bottled hot pepper sauce
- 1 pound fresh *or* frozen skinless sole *or* flounder fillets
- 1 cup chicken broth
- Fresh rosemary sprigs (optional)

● **For sauce,** cut yellow squash and zucchini in half lengthwise, then crosswise into ¼-inch-thick slices. In a medium saucepan stir together the squash, zucchini, mushrooms, onion, garlic, salt, and ¼ cup *water*. Bring to boiling; reduce heat. Simmer, covered, 4 minutes or till vegetables are nearly tender. Drain.

● **Mix** *undrained* tomatoes, cornstarch, basil, oregano, and hot sauce. Stir into vegetable mixture. Cook and stir till bubbly. Cook and stir 2 minutes more.

● **Meanwhile,** measure thickness of the fish. In a large skillet bring chicken broth just to boiling. Carefully add fish (see photo, *page 127*). Return just to boiling; reduce heat.

● **Cover and simmer** till fish flakes easily with a fork. (Allow 4 to 6 minutes per ½-inch thickness for fresh fish; 6 to 9 minutes per ½-inch thickness for frozen fish.) Serve sauce over fish. If desired, garnish with rosemary sprigs. Makes 4 servings.

Microwave directions: Use ½-inch-thick fish fillets. Thaw, if frozen. Cut squash and zucchini as directed.

For sauce, in a 2-quart microwave-safe casserole mix squash, zucchini, mushrooms, onion, garlic, salt, and 2 tablespoons *water*. Micro-cook, covered, on 100% power (high) for 4½ to 5 minutes (low-wattage oven: 6 to 7 minutes) or till vegetables are nearly tender; stir once. Drain. Mix *undrained* tomatoes, cornstarch, basil, oregano, and hot sauce. Stir into vegetables in the casserole. Cook, uncovered, on high for 4 to 6 minutes (low-wattage oven: 6 to 8 minutes) or till bubbly, stirring every 2 minutes. Cook, uncovered, on high for 1 minute more.

Meanwhile, in an 8x8x2-inch baking dish arrange fish; turn under thin portions to make fillets of even thickness. Do not use the chicken broth. Cover with vented clear plastic wrap. Cook on high for 4 to 7 minutes or till fish flakes easily with a fork, giving dish a half-turn once. Serve as directed.

Nutrition information per serving: 162 cal., 25 g pro., 11 g carbo., 2 g fat, 54 mg chol., 520 mg sodium, 909 mg potassium, and 3 g dietary fiber. U.S. RDA: 17% vit. A, 26% vit. C, 14% thiamine, 14% riboflavin, 29% niacin, 10% iron.

VEGETABLE-PORK SOUP

1 pound pork stew meat *or* lamb
   stew meat, cut into ½-inch cubes
1 tablespoon cooking oil
½ cup chopped onion
1 teaspoon paprika
3 cups beef broth
1 cup peeled potatoes cut into
   ½-inch cubes
1 cup loose-pack frozen whole
   kernel corn
1 cup peeled winter squash *or*
   sweet potatoes cut into
   ½-inch cubes
⅔ cup chopped tomato
½ teaspoon garlic salt
⅛ teaspoon pepper
1 cup torn fresh spinach

● **In a large saucepan brown** *half* of
the meat cubes in the hot cooking oil.
Remove meat cubes from the saucepan.
Brown the remaining meat cubes with
the chopped onion and paprika. Drain
off the fat. Return all of the meat mixture to the saucepan.
● **Add the beef broth.** Bring to boiling;
reduce heat. Cover and simmer for 30
minutes. Add the potatoes, whole kernel corn, squash or sweet potatoes,
chopped tomato, garlic salt, and pepper. Return to boiling; reduce heat.
Cover and simmer for 15 to 20 minutes
or till the vegetables are tender.
● **Stir in the torn fresh spinach.** Simmer the mixture for 3 to 5 minutes or
till the spinach is tender. If necessary,
skim the fat from the soup. Makes 4
main-dish servings.

Crockery-cooker directions: In a
large saucepan or skillet brown meat,
onion, and paprika in hot oil as directed
above. In a 3½- or 4-quart electric
crockery cooker layer potatoes, corn,
squash or sweet potatoes, and tomato
(see photo, *page 128*). Place the meat-
onion mixture atop. Combine 2½ cups
beef broth, garlic salt, and pepper. Pour
over the mixture in the crockery cooker. Cover and cook on low-heat setting
for 10 to 12 hours. If necessary, skim fat
from the soup. Stir in the spinach just
before serving.

Nutrition information per serving:
378 cal., 34 g pro., 24 g carbo., 17 g fat, 82
mg chol., 880 mg sodium, 1,039 mg po-
tassium, and 4 g dietary fiber. U.S.
RDA: 35% vit. A, 25% vit. C, 44% thia-
mine, 23% riboflavin, 44% niacin, 15%
iron.

PARSLEY PESTO TOPPING

Depending on the moistness of the pars-
ley, you may need to use 4 tablespoons of
oil to make a pesto of spreading consist-
ency. You also can make this piquant
topper in your food processor—

3 tablespoons cooking oil
2 cups lightly packed snipped
   parsley
2 tablespoons chopped walnuts
1 teaspoon dried basil
1 clove garlic, quartered
¼ cup grated Parmesan cheese

● **Place oil** in a blender container. Add
parsley, walnuts, basil, and garlic. Cover and blend till nearly smooth. Stir in
Parmesan cheese. Serve with Italian-
Style Burgers.

Recipe tip: The easiest way to snip
parsley or other fresh herbs is in a measuring cup or bowl. Place the parsley in
the cup or bowl, and use kitchen shears
to snip the parsley.

ITALIAN-STYLE BURGERS WITH PARSLEY PESTO TOPPING

Serve a thick slice of ripe tomato on
these burgers—

1 beaten egg
2 tablespoons catsup
¾ cup soft bread crumbs (1 slice) *or*
   ¼ cup fine dry bread crumbs
2 tablespoons grated Parmesan
   cheese
2 tablespoons chopped onion *or*
   ¼ teaspoon onion powder
1 tablespoon prepared mustard *or*
   ½ teaspoon dry mustard
¾ teaspoon dried Italian
   seasoning
1 clove garlic, minced, *or*
   ⅛ teaspoon garlic powder
   (optional)
¼ teaspoon salt
¼ teaspoon pepper
1 pound ground beef, ground pork,
   ground veal, *or* ground lamb
4 or 6 hamburger buns, split and
   toasted
1 recipe Parsley Pesto Topping
   (see recipe, *left*)

● **In a mixing bowl combine** egg and
catsup. Stir in bread crumbs, Parmesan
cheese, onion, mustard, Italian seasoning, garlic, salt, and pepper. Add meat;
mix well. Shape meat mixture into four
¾-inch-thick or six ½-inch-thick patties (see photo, *page 128*).
● **Place patties** on the unheated rack
of a broiler pan. Broil 3 to 4 inches from
the heat for 15 to 18 minutes for ¾-inch
patties (10 to 12 minutes for ½-inch
patties) or till no pink remains. Turn
once. Serve patties on hamburger buns
with Parsley Pesto Topping. Makes 4 or
6 servings.

Nutrition information per serving:
580 cal., 31 g pro., 33 g carbo., 36 g fat,
155 mg chol., 768 mg sodium, 542 mg
potassium, 2 g dietary fiber. U.S. RDA:
38% vit. A, 49% vit. C, 22% thiamine,
24% riboflavin, 32% niacin, 25% calci-
um, 38% iron.

ONE-LAYER CHOCOLATE CAKE

Just the right size for a small family—

    1 cup all-purpose flour
    1 cup sugar
    ¼ cup unsweetened cocoa powder
    1 teaspoon baking powder
    ¼ teaspoon baking soda
    ¼ teaspoon salt
    ¾ cup milk
    ¼ cup shortening
    ½ teaspoon vanilla
    1 egg
    1 recipe No-Cook Fudge
       Frosting (see recipe, *right*)

● **In a large mixer bowl combine** the flour, sugar, cocoa powder, baking powder, baking soda, and salt. Add the milk, shortening, and vanilla. Beat the mixture with an electric mixer on low speed till combined. Beat on medium speed for 2 minutes. Add the egg and beat for 2 minutes more. Pour into a greased and floured 9x1½-inch round baking pan.

● **Bake in a 350° oven** for 30 to 35 minutes or till a toothpick inserted near the center comes out clean (see photo, *page 129*). Cool on a wire rack for 10 minutes. Remove the cake from the pan. Cool thoroughly on the rack. Frost with the No-Cook Fudge Frosting. Makes 8 servings.

Microwave directions: (Not recommended for low-wattage ovens.) Prepare batter as directed, *except* substitute softened *margarine* or *butter* for the shortening. Grease the bottom of a 2-quart microwave-safe ring mold; line with waxed paper. Pour batter into the mold. Micro-cook, uncovered, on 50% power (medium) for 10 minutes, giving the dish a quarter-turn every 3 minutes. If the cake is not done, cook on 100% power (high) for 30 seconds to 2 minutes more or till the surface is nearly dry. Cool on a wire rack for 5 minutes. Invert onto a plate; remove the waxed paper. Cool completely.

Hint: To keep a cake cooked in a microwave oven moist, cover the cooled cake with plastic wrap. Better yet, frost the cake.

Nutrition information per serving: *410 cal., 4 g pro., 70 g carbo., 14 g fat, 36 mg chol., 265 mg sodium, 99 mg potassium, 2 g dietary fiber.*

NO-COOK FUDGE FROSTING

After you frost the One-Layer Chocolate Cake, you'll have some frosting left over. Store the remaining frosting, covered, in the refrigerator up to 2 weeks for another use. Before using, let stand at room temperature about 3 hours or till spreadable. (Or, place in moisture- and vapor-proof container; seal, label, and freeze up to 3 months. Before using, thaw and let stand as suggested)—

    4¾ cups sifted powdered sugar
    ½   cup unsweetened cocoa powder
    ½   cup margarine *or* butter,
        softened
    ⅓   cup boiling water
    1   teaspoon vanilla

● **In a bowl mix** powdered sugar and cocoa. Add margarine or butter, boiling water, and vanilla. Beat with electric mixer on low speed till combined. Beat 1 minute on medium speed. Cool 20 to 30 minutes or till of spreading consistency. Recipe frosts tops and sides of two 8- or 9-inch cake layers.

CHOCOLATE CHIP COOKIES

Try the macadamia version with 1 cup white chocolate and 1 cup semisweet chocolate pieces as we did for the photo on page 130—

    ½   cup shortening
    ½   cup margarine *or* butter
    2½ cups all-purpose flour
    1   cup packed brown sugar
    ½   cup sugar
    2   eggs
    1   teaspoon vanilla
    ½   teaspoon baking soda
    1   12-ounce package (2 cups)
        semisweet chocolate pieces
    1   cup chopped walnuts, pecans, *or*
        hazelnuts (filberts) (optional)

● **In a mixing bowl beat** the shortening and margarine or butter with an electric mixer on medium to high speed for 30 seconds. Add about *half* of the flour, the brown sugar, sugar, eggs, vanilla, and baking soda (see photo, *page 130*). Beat mixture till thoroughly combined. Beat in the remaining flour. Stir in chocolate pieces and, if desired, nuts.

● **Drop the dough** by rounded teaspoons 2 inches apart onto an ungreased cookie sheet.

● **Bake in a 375° oven** for 8 to 10 minutes or till edges are lightly browned. Cool cookies on a wire rack. Makes about 60 cookies.

Macadamia Nut and White Chocolate Chunk Cookies: Prepare Chocolate Chip Cookies as directed above, *except* substitute chopped *white baking bars* (or *pieces*) with cocoa butter or *vanilla-flavored confectioners' coating* for the semisweet chocolate pieces. Stir in one 3½-ounce jar *macadamia nuts*, chopped, with the chopped white baking bars or pieces.

Nutrition information per cookie: *99 cal., 1 g pro., 12 g carbo., 5 g fat, 9 mg chol., 31 mg sodium, 39 mg potassium.*

OCTOBER

▲ HERE'S HOW!
Mom has the knack.
And after a few
practice twists, so
will the kids.

1-2-3 TWIST!

Divide dough into 24 pieces; roll pieces into 16-inch ropes. Cross one end of a rope over the other to form a circle, leaving ends free.

Holding one end in each hand, twist once at the point where the dough overlaps. After a couple of twists, you'll be an expert!

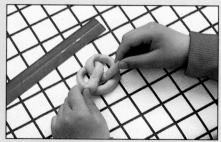

Carefully lift ends across to the opposite edge of the circle. Tuck ends under to make a pretzel shape. Moisten ends; press to seal.

WEEKEND COOKING

ENJOY THE DOING! ENJOY THE TASTING!
ENJOY EACH OTHER!

BY BARBARA GOLDMAN

KITCHEN FUN FOR ALL AGES

EASY PRETZEL SNACKS

Unwind together while you twist up a batch of kid-pleasing pretzels. Then watch junior cooks swell with pride over the results.

◀ **AND NOW, THE PAYOFF!**
Creating your own hand-shaped pretzels is great fun. But nothing beats that first bite!

PLAIN

FANCY!

EXTRA-FANCY!!

PEANUT BUTTER ▶ PRETZEL SNACKS
Take one soft pretzel, add chocolate glaze, then nuts. Wow!

▲ CRANBERRY-PEACH RING
Relax during the weekend with a cup of coffee and a luscious slice of fruit-filled coffee cake. Bread making goes fast when you use quick-rise yeast.

◄ APPLES IN PHYLLO
Outstanding! That's how our tasters rated this apple dessert. You'll think so, too—and it's easy to make with thawed frozen phyllo dough. Top with ice cream and rum sauce—then reap compliments!

THE PLEASURES OF
WEEKEND COOKING
HOME-BAKED TREATS;
ENJOY ANYTIME
A SWEET QUARTET

Go ahead. Pamper yourself a little! The weekend's the time to do it. Prepare one of these goodies at a leisurely pace—or bake up two or three! You can freeze the coffee cake and brownies to satisfy your sweet tooth another day. Then, gather good friends and family around the table—and savor the pleasure of eating together.

Talk about easy—and good! Kids will love making these Brickle Bars. So will adults!

▲ BRICKLE BARS
Quickly mix up these rich brownies in a saucepan, transfer to a baking pan, sprinkle with chocolate and almond brickle pieces, and bake.

◄ CAPPUCCINO TORTE
Sound elaborate? It only looks that way! This torte is fun to make. Just allow for baking, standing, and chilling time some afternoon. Then relish the goodness that night.

141

· MENU ·

Easy Shrimp and
Guacamole Canapés

Stuffed Endive and
Grape Platter

Provençal Pizza

Oriental Sesame-
Noodle Salad

Apricot-Pecan
Tartlets

Ice Cream with
Fruit Topping

▲ THE HELPER
The weekend is a great time for the entire family to get in on the pleasures of cooking—and to encourage budding cooks.

SHARING WITH FRIENDS

A CASUAL PARTY MENU

Enjoy an easygoing weekend get-together! Try new foods and flavors and sharpen your cooking skills with fast-to-fix, serve-yourself appetizers and desserts.

◄ SIMPLY STYLISH
Good food needn't be complicated to look and taste great! These desserts, and the appetizers at far left, are easily done—but taste wonderful!

▲ GREAT PARTY!
Your payoff for a few hours of cooking? Relaxing with good friends and good food.

PEANUT BUTTER PRETZEL SNACKS

```
3 to 3½ cups all-purpose flour
1 package quick-rising active dry
  yeast
1 cup milk
⅓ cup creamy peanut butter
2 tablespoons sugar
1 tablespoon margarine or butter
½ teaspoon salt
1 egg
1 tablespoon water
1 egg white
1 recipe Chocolate Glaze
  (optional)
Chopped peanuts (optional)
```

● **In a large mixing bowl** combine *2 cups* of the flour and the yeast.

● **In a small saucepan heat** milk, peanut butter, sugar, margarine or butter, and salt just till warm (120° to 130°) and margarine or butter is almost melted, stirring constantly. Add milk mixture to flour mixture; add the one whole egg. Using a wooden spoon, mix well. Stir in as much of the remaining flour as you can.

● **Turn out** onto a lightly floured surface. Knead in enough of the remaining flour to make a moderately stiff dough that is smooth and elastic (6 to 8 minutes total). Divide the dough into 4 portions. Cover and let rest for 10 minutes. Divide each portion into 6 pieces. Roll *each* piece of dough into a rope about 16 inches long.

● **Shape each pretzel** by crossing one end of a rope over the other to form a circle, overlapping about 4 inches from each end and leaving ends free (see photos, *page 138*). Take one end of dough in each hand and twist once at the point where the dough overlaps. Carefully lift each end across to the opposite edge of the circle. Tuck ends under edge to make a pretzel shape. Moisten ends; press to seal.

● **Place pretzels** about ½ inch apart on greased baking sheets. Cover and let rise in a warm place till nearly double (about 20 minutes).

● **Meanwhile, in a small bowl stir** together the water and the egg white. Just before baking, brush the pretzels with a little of the egg white mixture.

● **Bake in a 375° oven** for 10 to 12 minutes or till golden brown. Remove from baking sheets. Cool on wire racks. Place pretzels on waxed paper (*or* on a wire rack over waxed paper).

Drizzle pretzels with Chocolate Glaze and sprinkle with chopped peanuts, if desired. Makes 24 pretzels.

Chocolate Glaze: In a small saucepan melt 1 square (1 ounce) *semisweet chocolate* over low heat. Remove from heat. (*Or*, in a 1-cup glass measure micro-cook chocolate, uncovered, on 100% power [high] for 1 to 2 minutes or till soft enough to stir smooth, stirring after every minute during cooking. Chocolate won't look melted till stirred.) Add 1 cup *sifted powdered sugar*. Add enough *hot water* (1 to 2 tablespoons) to make glaze of drizzling consistency.

Nutrition information per pretzel: 96 cal., 4 g pro., 14 g carbo., 3 g fat, 12 mg chol., 77 mg sodium, 66 mg potassium, 1 g dietary fiber.

CRANBERRY-PEACH RING

```
1 recipe Cranberry-Peach Filling
2½ to 3 cups all-purpose flour
1 package quick-rising active dry
  yeast
½ cup margarine or butter
½ cup milk
¼ cup water
2 tablespoons sugar
½ teaspoon salt
1 egg
1 recipe Confectioners' Icing
```

● **Prepare** Cranberry-Peach Filling; set aside.

● **In a large mixer bowl stir** together 1¼ cups of the flour and the yeast. In a small saucepan heat margarine or butter, milk, water, sugar, and salt just till warm (120° to 130°) and margarine is almost melted, stirring constantly.

● **Add to flour mixture; add egg.** Beat with an electric mixer on low speed for 30 seconds, scraping sides of bowl constantly. Beat on high speed for 3 minutes. Using a wooden spoon, stir in as much of the remaining flour as you can. Turn out onto a lightly floured surface. Knead in enough of the remaining flour to make a moderately soft dough that is smooth and elastic (3 to 5 minutes total). Cover dough and let rest for 10 minutes.

● **On a lightly floured surface roll** dough into an 18x10-inch rectangle. Spread the Cranberry-Peach Filling lengthwise down center of dough in a 3-inch-wide strip. On long sides make 3-inch cuts from edge toward center at 1-inch intervals. Starting at one end,

alternately fold opposite strips of dough at an angle across filling. Carefully transfer to a greased baking sheet.

● **Shape into a ring,** stretching slightly to curve; pinch ends together. Cover ring and let rise in a warm place till nearly double (about 30 minutes).

● **Bake in a 375° oven** for 20 to 25 minutes or till golden. If necessary, cover edges with foil during last 10 minutes of baking to prevent overbrowning. Carefully remove from pan and cool on a wire rack about 30 minutes. Drizzle with icing. Serve warm or cool. Makes 1 coffee cake (12 servings).

Cranberry-Peach Filling: In a small saucepan combine 1 cup *cranberries*, 2 tablespoons *sugar*, and 2 tablespoons *water*. Bring to boiling; reduce heat. Simmer, uncovered, about 5 minutes or till cranberries pop. Stir together 1 tablespoon *cold water* and 1 tablespoon *cornstarch*. Add the cornstarch-water mixture to the hot cranberry mixture. Cook and stir till mixture is thickened and bubbly. (Mixture will be very thick at this point.) Remove from heat and stir in ½ cup *peach preserves*. Set aside to cool.

Confectioners' Icing: In a small mixing bowl combine 1 cup sifted *powdered sugar*, ¼ teaspoon *vanilla*, and enough *milk* (about 4 teaspoons) to make of drizzling consistency.

To warm one serving in the microwave oven: Place one serving of the cooled, iced coffee cake on a microwave-safe plate. Heat coffee cake, uncovered, on 100% power (high) for 15 to 20 seconds or till coffee cake is warm.

Freezing directions: Prepare as directed, *except* omit drizzling the coffee cake with Confectioners' Icing. Cover thoroughly with freezer wrap. Label and freeze.

Thaw coffee cake at room temperature for 3 to 4 hours. If you wish to serve coffee cake warm, reheat *thawed uniced* coffee cake in a 350° oven for 15 to 20 minutes. Drizzle with Confectioners' Icing.

Or, to reheat directly from freezer, unwrap *frozen uniced* coffee cake. Place coffee cake on baking sheet; cover with foil. Bake in a 350° oven 1 hour or till heated through. Drizzle with icing.

Nutrition information per serving: 265 cal., 4 g pro., 44 g carbo., 9 g fat, 24 mg chol., 192 mg sodium, 81 mg potassium, 1 g dietary fiber. U.S. RDA: 13% thiamine, 10% riboflavin.

APPLES IN PHYLLO

Here is a glamorous version of a baked apple that's sure to win raves from your guests—

- 4 sheets frozen phyllo dough (18x14-inch rectangles), thawed
- ¼ cup margarine *or* butter, melted
- 6 small tart cooking apples (such as Jonathan or Winesap), peeled and cored
- ¼ cup sugar
- 1 teaspoon ground cinnamon
- ⅓ cup slivered almonds
- Ice cream (optional)
- 1 recipe Rum-Raisin Sauce

● Brush *one* sheet of the phyllo dough with *some* of the melted margarine or butter. (Remove 1 sheet of the phyllo at a time and keep the remaining sheets of phyllo covered with a damp paper towel.) Repeat brushing and layering with the remaining margarine or butter and phyllo.

● Cut phyllo stack lengthwise into 6 strips. Cut strips crosswise into thirds, forming 18 rectangles about 6x2 inches. Gently press 3 rectangles into *each* of 6 greased 6-ounce custard cups so that the entire cup is covered.

● Place a wooden-handled spoon or chopstick on each side of 1 apple to prevent slicing through to the bottom of the apple. Cut apple into thin slices, cutting ¾ of the way to, but not through, the bottom. Repeat with remaining apples.

● In a small bowl combine the sugar and the cinnamon. Place an apple into *each* of the phyllo-lined custard cups. Sprinkle the apples with the sugar-cinnamon mixture. Fill *each* apple cavity with the almonds (a scant tablespoon). Place the custard cups in a 15x10x1-inch baking pan.

● Bake in a 375° oven for 25 to 30 minutes or till the phyllo is golden and the apples are tender. Cool slightly. Carefully slip out the apple desserts onto individual serving plates. If desired, place a small scoop of vanilla ice cream atop *each* apple. Top *each* of the apples with warm or cold Rum-Raisin Sauce. Makes 6 servings.

Rum-Raisin Sauce: In a heavy small saucepan stir together ½ cup *packed brown sugar* and 1 tablespoon *cornstarch.* Stir in ⅓ cup *water* and ⅓ cup *raisins.* Cook and stir over medium heat till thickened and bubbly. Cook and stir for 2 minutes more. Stir in 1 tablespoon rum. Serve the sauce immediately or cover surface with clear plastic wrap; cool.

Nutrition information per serving: 329 cal., 2 g pro., 56 g carbo., 12 g fat, 0 mg chol., 134 mg sodium, 319 mg potassium, 4 g dietary fiber.

BRICKLE BARS

You need just 10 minutes' preparation time and 30 minutes' baking time for this luscious brownie variation—

- ½ cup margarine *or* butter
- 2 squares (2 ounces) unsweetened chocolate
- 1 cup sugar
- 2 eggs
- 1 teaspoon vanilla
- ¾ cup all-purpose flour
- ¾ cup almond brickle pieces
- ½ cup miniature semisweet chocolate pieces

● In a medium saucepan cook and stir margarine or butter and unsweetened chocolate over low heat till melted. Remove from heat; stir in sugar. Add eggs and vanilla; beat *lightly* with a wooden spoon just till combined (*don't overbeat* or brownies will rise too high, then fall). Stir in flour.

● Spread batter in a greased 8x8x2-inch baking pan. Sprinkle almond brickle pieces and chocolate pieces evenly over the top of batter.

● Bake in a 350° oven for 30 minutes. Remove pan from oven and cool brownies in pan on a wire rack. Cut into bars. Makes 16 bars.

Freezing directions: Remove the Brickle Bars from the pan. Wrap the bars thoroughly in freezer wrap. Label and freeze. To serve, let Brickle Bars thaw, covered, at room temperature.

Nutrition information per bar: 230 cal., 2 g pro., 24 g carbo., 15 g fat, 34 mg chol., 98 mg sodium, 76 mg potassium, 1 g dietary fiber. U.S. RDA: 12% thiamine.

CAPPUCCINO TORTE

- 1 recipe Meringue Shell
- 1⅓ cups milk
- 2 to 3 teaspoons instant coffee crystals
- ½ teaspoon finely shredded orange peel
- 1 package 4-serving-size *instant* vanilla pudding mix
- ½ cup whipping cream
- Orange slices, halved (optional)
- Chocolate-covered candy coffee beans (optional)

● Prepare Meringue Shell. Cool.

● Omit the milk called for on the pudding package. In a medium mixing bowl combine the 1⅓ cups milk, coffee crystals, and orange peel. Add pudding mix and beat according to package directions. Beat whipping cream to soft peaks. Immediately fold into pudding.

● Place cooled Meringue Shell on a serving platter. Spoon the filling into the shell. Cover and chill for 3 hours or overnight. (If you like a crisper meringue, serve the same day; for a softer meringue, chill overnight.)

● To serve, arrange orange slices and candy atop, if desired. Serves 10.

Meringue Shell: In a small mixer bowl let 3 *egg whites* stand at room temperature for 1 hour. Meanwhile, cover a baking sheet with plain brown paper or foil; draw a 9-inch circle. Add ½ teaspoon *vanilla* and ¼ teaspoon *cream of tartar* to whites. Beat with electric mixer on medium speed till soft peaks form (tips curl). Add 1 cup *sugar, 2 tablespoons* at a time, beating on high speed till very stiff peaks form (tips stand straight). Using the back of a large metal spoon, spread meringue over circle on paper; shape into a shell, building up sides. Bake in a 300° oven for 50 minutes. Turn off oven; let meringue dry in the oven at least 1 hour. (Do not open oven door.)

Nutrition information per serving: 175 cal., 3 g pro., 31 g carbo., 5 g fat, 19 mg chol., 76 mg sodium, 94 mg potassium.

EASY SHRIMP AND GUACAMOLE CANAPÉS

12 medium fresh *or* frozen peeled, deveined shrimp
¼ cup Italian salad dressing
1 6-ounce container frozen avocado dip (hot 'n' spicy *or* original), thawed
24 melba toast rounds
Chopped tomato, fresh chive sprigs, *or* snipped fresh cilantro (optional)

● **Thaw shrimp,** if frozen.
● **In a 10-inch skillet cook** the shrimp in hot salad dressing over medium-high heat for 3 to 5 minutes or till the shrimp turn pink, stirring constantly. Remove from heat; cool slightly. Transfer shrimp and dressing to a storage container; chill till serving time.
● **To assemble the canapés, spread** about *1 teaspoon* of the avocado dip on *each* melba toast round. (Use any remaining as a dip.)
● **Drain shrimp; cut *each* shrimp** in half lengthwise. Place *one* shrimp half atop each canapé. If desired, top *each* with tomato, chive, or cilantro. If desired, cover and chill up to 3 hours before serving. Makes 24 canapés.

Nutrition information per canapé: 43 cal., 2 g pro., 4 g carbo., 2 g fat, 5 mg chol., 78 mg sodium, 29 mg potassium.

STUFFED ENDIVE AND GRAPE PLATTER

Combine the fantastic flavor duo of pears and blue cheese with a little cream cheese. Spoon the pear-cheese mixture onto delicate Belgian endive leaves and accent with fresh fruit and walnuts. Tastes super and looks gorgeous—

16 to 20 large Belgian endive leaves
1 large ripe pear, peeled, cored, and coarsely chopped *or* shredded and well drained
½ of an 8-ounce package cream cheese, cut up
1 cup crumbled blue cheese (4 ounces)
¼ cup broken walnuts

1 pound seedless red grapes, separated into clusters
2 large oranges, peeled and sectioned
Fresh unpeeled pear slices
Orange *or* lemon juice

● **Separate endive leaves.** Rinse endive in cool water and pat dry.
● **In a food processor bowl** combine coarsely chopped pear and cream cheese; cover and process till smooth. (*Or*, in a small mixer bowl combine shredded, drained pear and cream cheese, beating till well combined.) Reserve *2 tablespoons* of the blue cheese. Stir remaining blue cheese into pear mixture. Cover; chill.
● **Before serving, spoon** or spread pear-cheese mixture onto endive leaves. Top *half* of the filled endive leaves with the reserved blue cheese, the other *half* with walnuts. Mound grape clusters in center of a serving platter. Arrange stuffed endive leaves, orange sections, and pear slices (dipped in orange or lemon juice to prevent browning) around edge of platter. Makes 16 to 20 appetizer servings.

Note: You can make the cheese stuffing a day ahead. Simply cover surface with clear plastic wrap and chill.

Nutrition information per serving: 107 cal., 3 g pro., 11 g carbo., 6 g fat, 14 mg chol., 142 mg sodium, 181 mg potassium, 1 g dietary fiber. U.S. RDA: 26% vit. C.

PROVENÇAL PIZZA

A touch of American ingenuity—frozen bread dough—simplifies a country French version of an Italian pizza—

1 16-ounce loaf frozen bread dough, thawed
4 medium onions, thinly sliced and separated into rings (4 cups)
2 cloves garlic, minced
1 teaspoon dried basil, crushed
1 teaspoon dried oregano, crushed
½ teaspoon fennel seed, crushed
2 tablespoons cooking oil
4 medium tomatoes, peeled, seeded, and chopped
1½ cups shredded part-skim mozzarella cheese
½ of a sweet red pepper, cut into thin strips

½ of a sweet yellow *or* green pepper, cut into thin strips
1 2¼-ounce can sliced, pitted ripe olives, drained

● **On a lightly floured surface** (such as a pastry cloth or countertop) cover the thawed dough and let rest for 5 minutes. Line a 15x10x1-inch baking pan with heavy foil; grease foil on the bottom and sides.
● **Roll the dough** into a 16x12-inch rectangle, allowing the dough to rest if necessary. Press dough onto bottom and up the sides of the prepared pan. Prick bottom and sides of dough with the tines of a fork. Let dough stand for 5 minutes before baking. Bake in a 425° oven about 10 minutes or till dough starts to brown; cool.
● **Meanwhile, in a large skillet** cook the onions, garlic, basil, oregano, and fennel seed, uncovered, in hot oil over medium heat about 20 minutes or till onions are tender but not brown, stirring frequently. Stir in the chopped tomatoes. Cook the vegetable mixture, uncovered, for 10 minutes more, stirring frequently. Spread vegetable mixture over the cooled crust. Sprinkle with shredded mozzarella cheese. Arrange pepper strips on top. Then sprinkle with sliced ripe olives.
● **Freeze for 1½ to 2 hours** or till firm. Using the foil, lift pizza out of baking pan. Cover top of pizza with clear plastic wrap. Wrap in moisture- and vapor-proof wrap; seal wrap, label, and freeze.
● **About 30 minutes before** serving, place the frozen pizza in a 15x10x1-inch baking pan. Remove the top foil and plastic wrap. Fold back bottom foil, leaving pizza edges covered.
● **Bake the pizza in a 425° oven** for 25 to 30 minutes or till crust is brown and topping is heated through. Let pizza stand for 5 minutes; remove foil. Slice; serve pizza warm or at room temperature. Makes 20 appetizer servings.

To serve immediately without freezing: Prepare recipe as directed, *except* after adding toppings, bake pizza immediately, uncovered, in a 425° oven for 12 to 15 minutes.

Nutrition information per serving: 113 cal., 5 g pro., 14 g carbo., 4 g fat, 6 mg chol., 181 mg sodium, 100 mg potassium, 1 g dietary fiber. U.S. RDA: 10% vit. C.

ORIENTAL SESAME-NOODLE SALAD

You'll find soba, a Japanese pasta, in Oriental and specialty food stores—

- 4 ounces buckwheat noodles *(soba) or* whole wheat spaghetti, broken
- 1 small yellow summer squash, halved lengthwise, and cut crosswise into thin slices (1 cup)
- 1 small zucchini, halved lengthwise and cut crosswise into thin slices (1 cup)
- 1 cup halved cherry tomatoes
- ½ cup bean sprouts
- 3 tablespoons sodium-reduced soy sauce
- 2 tablespoons rice vinegar *or* white wine vinegar
- ½ teaspoon grated gingerroot
- ½ teaspoon sesame oil
- Several drops bottled hot pepper sauce (to taste)
- 8 ounces fresh spinach
- 1 tablespoon sliced green onion (optional)
- 1 teaspoon toasted sesame seed (optional)

● **In a large saucepan cook** the noodles according to the package directions. Before draining the pasta, stir in the summer squash, zucchini, and cherry tomatoes. Immediately drain. Rinse the pasta and vegetables under cold water; drain well. Return to the saucepan. Add the bean sprouts.

● **Meanwhile,** in a small mixing bowl combine the soy sauce, vinegar, gingerroot, sesame oil, and hot pepper sauce. Toss with the drained noodles and vegetables. Transfer to a spinach-lined platter. If desired, sprinkle with the sliced green onion and sesame seed. Serve at room temperature or chilled. Makes 8 appetizer servings.

Nutrition information per serving: *81 cal., 4 g pro., 15 g carbo., 1 g fat, 13 mg chol., 265 mg sodium, 342 mg potassium, 1 g dietary fiber. U.S. RDA: 45% vit. A, 26% vit. C, 13% thiamine.*

Serve the Apricot-Pecan Tartlets with ice cream and fruit topping spiked with fruit liqueur.

ICE CREAM WITH FRUIT TOPPING

Just stir a little fruit liqueur into bottled or homemade fruit topping and enjoy over ice cream—

- 1 cup bottled *or* homemade strawberry *or* raspberry ice-cream topping
- 2 to 3 teaspoons strawberry, raspberry, cherry, *or* orange liqueur (optional)
- 1 quart vanilla ice cream

● **Spoon the ice-cream topping** into a small serving bowl. If desired, stir the fruit liqueur into the topping.

● **Scoop the ice cream** into a serving bowl or into individual serving dishes. Serve the fruit topping over the ice cream. Makes 8 servings.

Nutrition information per serving (½ cup ice cream with 2 tablespoons fruit topping): *226 cal., 2 g pro., 38 g carbo., 7 g fat, 30 mg chol., 68 mg sodium, 129 mg potassium. U.S. RDA: 13% vit. C.*

Hint: To make this simple ice-cream dessert even easier to serve for a party, scoop the ice cream into a serving bowl earlier in the day. Freeze, covered, until serving time.

APRICOT-PECAN TARTLETS

- ½ cup margarine *or* butter, softened
- ½ of an 8-ounce package cream cheese, softened
- 1 cup all-purpose flour
- ¾ cup snipped dried apricots
- ¾ cup water
- ⅓ cup chopped pecans
- ¼ cup sugar
- 2 tablespoons orange marmalade
- ½ teaspoon ground cinnamon
- ⅛ teaspoon ground cloves
- 1 recipe Cream Cheese Frosting

● **For pastry,** in a small mixer bowl beat the margarine or butter and *3 ounces* of the cream cheese. (Reserve *1 ounce* of the cream cheese for the Cream Cheese Frosting.) Stir the flour into the margarine mixture. Cover and chill about 1 hour or till mixture is easy to handle. Shape into 1-inch balls. Press onto the bottom and up the sides of ungreased 1¾-inch muffin cups.

● **For filling,** in a small saucepan combine the apricots and the water. Bring apricot-water mixture to boiling; reduce the heat. Cover and simmer mixture for 5 to 8 minutes or till fruit is tender; drain. Stir in the pecans, sugar, marmalade, cinnamon, and cloves. Fill *each* pastry-lined muffin cup with *1 rounded teaspoon* of the apricot-pecan filling.

● **Bake in a 325° oven** for 25 to 30 minutes or till crust is brown and filling is bubbly. Remove tartlets from oven; cool slightly in pans on wire racks. Remove tartlets from pans; cool completely on wire racks. Just before serving, pipe a rosette of Cream Cheese Frosting on each tartlet. Chill any remaining tartlets. Makes 24 tartlets.

Cream Cheese Frosting: In a small mixer bowl beat together the reserved *1 ounce cream cheese* with 1 tablespoon *margarine* or *butter* and ½ teaspoon *vanilla.* Gradually add ½ cup *sifted powdered sugar,* beating till frosting is smooth.

Nutrition information per tartlet: *115 cal., 1 g pro., 13 g carbo., 7 g fat, 5 mg chol., 65 mg sodium, 79 mg potassium, and 1 g dietary fiber. U.S. RDA: 11% vit. A.*

NOVEMBER

TURKEY-ROASTING GUIDE

Here's all you need to know to roast a holiday bird to juicy perfection.

HOW MUCH TO BUY

For a 12-lb.-or-less bird, buy 1 lb. per serving; more than 12 lb., ¾ lb. per serving. For turkey breast (bone-in), buy ⅓ lb. per serving.

THAWING FROZEN TURKEY

Refrigerator thawing: Place wrapped bird on a tray in the refrigerator for 3 to 4 days (24 hours for each 5 lb.).

Cold-water thawing: Place wrapped bird in sink of cold water. Change water every 30 minutes. (Allow 30 minutes per lb.).

BEFORE ROASTING

Unwrap, free legs and tail, then remove the giblets and neck piece from the cavities. Thoroughly rinse bird; pat dry. *Don't stuff bird till you're ready to roast it.*

To stuff the bird, spoon some stuffing *loosely* into neck cavity. Pull neck skin over stuffing; fasten to back of bird with skewer. Place bird, neck side down, in large bowl. *Loosely* spoon stuffing into body cavity; *do not* pack (stuffing would not reach a safe temperature quickly enough). Tuck drumsticks under band of skin across tail or tie legs to tail. Twist wing tips under back.

ROASTING DIRECTIONS

Open or covered roasting pan: Place bird, breast side up, on rack in shallow pan; brush with cooking oil. Push meat thermometer into center of inside thigh muscle so bulb doesn't touch bone.

For **open** roasting, cover bird *loosely* with foil, leaving space between bird and foil. Press foil in lightly at end of drumsticks and neck. Roast in a 325°

oven, basting occasionally. When bird is two-thirds done, cut skin or string between legs. Remove foil the last 30 to 45 minutes to brown.

For **covered** roasting, *do not* add water. Roast, covered with vent open, in 325° oven 20 to 25 minutes per pound.

Uncover; drain, reserving juices. Turn oven to 475°. Roast 20 minutes more or till bird is brown.

Foil-wrapped turkey: *Do not* stuff bird roasted this way. (Because the bird is roasted at a high temperature, the meat will cook before the stuffing reaches a safe temperature.) Wrap *unstuffed* bird, breast side up, in greased, heavy foil. Place in a large shallow roasting pan. Insert meat thermometer in thigh muscle through foil. Roast at 450°. Open foil the last 20 to 30 minutes.

Oven bag turkey: Shake 1 tablespoon all-purpose flour in a turkey-size oven cooking bag. (This prevents the bag from bursting during roasting.) Add bird to bag. Place, breast side up, in a large roasting pan at least 2 inches deep. Close bag with nylon tie. With sharp knife, make six ½-inch slits in top of bag to allow steam to escape. Insert a meat thermometer in thigh muscle through slit in bag. Roast in a 350° oven.

Turkey breast and portions (bone-in): Thaw turkey, if frozen, as directed. Place turkey, skin side up, on rack in shallow roasting pan. Brush with cooking oil. Insert a meat thermometer into center so bulb does not touch bone. Roast, uncovered, in a 325° oven, basting occasionally. Cover loosely with foil to prevent over-browning, if necessary.

TURKEY-ROASTING TIMES

Because birds differ in size, shape, and tenderness, use these roasting times as a general guide.

Type of Turkey	Ready-to-Cook Weight	Oven Temp.	Guide to Roasting Time
Stuffed Whole Turkey* (open roasting)	6–8 lb.	325°	3–3½ hr.
	8–12 lb.	325°	3½–4½ hr.
	12–16 lb.	325°	4–5 hr.
	16–20 lb.	325°	4½–5½ hr.
	20–24 lb.	325°	5–6½ hr.
Unstuffed Foil-Wrapped Turkey	8–10 lb.	450°	1¼–1¾ hr.
	10–12 lb.	450°	1¾–2¼ hr.
	12–16 lb.	450°	2¼–3 hr.
	16–20 lb.	450°	3–3½ hr.
	20–24 lb.	450°	3½–4 hr.
Stuffed Oven Bag Turkey*	12–16 lb.	350°	2½–3 hr.
	16–20 lb.	350°	3–3½ hr.
	20–24 lb.	350°	3½–4 hr.
Turkey Breast and Portions (bone-in)	2–4 lb.	325°	1½–2 hr.
	3–5 lb.	325°	1½–2½ hr.
	5–7 lb.	325°	2–2½ hr.

Testing for doneness: Roast whole turkeys till the thermometer registers 180° to 185° (170° for turkey breast—*do not* overcook). Meat should be fork tender, and juices no longer pink when pierced with a fork. (Pierce thigh meat on whole turkeys.) Remove from oven; cover loosely with foil. Let stand 10 to 15 minutes before carving. Stuffing temperatures should be at least 165°.

*Unstuffed turkeys generally require 30 to 45 minutes less total roasting time than stuffed turkeys.

THE NEW
THANKSGIVING DINNER

BY LISA HOLDERNESS

- **EASY RECIPES, ALL READY IN 4 HOURS**

- **FAVORITE FOODS MADE LIGHTER—SO GOOD!**

MENU

SAVORY GRILLED TURKEY

•

TWO-POTATO SWIRLS

•

WILD RICE AND PROSCIUTTO DRESSING

•

LIME POPPY SEED FRUIT SALAD

•

APPLE-BERRY GINGER PIE

4-HOUR PLAN

FIRST HOUR
- Make pie filling
- Light coals
- Finish pie; bake
- Prep turkey and start grilling

You're on your way!

SECOND HOUR
- Start rice dressing
- Boil and mash potatoes
- Cool pie
- Brush turkey with oil

Smell that turkey yet?

THIRD HOUR
- Finish rice dressing and chill
- Make potato swirls and chill
- Start fruit salads
- Brush turkey with oil

It's almost dinnertime!

FOURTH HOUR
- Arrange salads; chill
- Bake rice dressing and potato swirls
- Set your table and get serving dishes ready
- Cool turkey and carve

Your Thanksgiving dinner's on!

PHOTOGRAPHS: TIM SCHULTZ. FOOD STYLIST: PAT GODSTED

OUTDOOR GRILLING

● Cooking the turkey outdoors leaves your oven free for the rest of the meal. Brush turkey with oil frequently to keep it moist.

EASY PIE MAKING

● A no-fuss pastry lets you fix this pie quickly—leaving plenty of cooling time. For crust, bring extra pastry up over the filling and pleat.

POTATO PIPING

● Bake potatoes next to dressing— both fit and are ready at the same time. For swirls, pipe potatoes into 3-inch circles, 2 layers high.

SAVORY GRILLED TURKEY

Stoke up the grill! After tasting the succulent flavor of turkey, slowly cooked over the coals, you'll make grilling a Thanksgiving tradition—

> 1 9- to 11-pound fresh turkey *or* frozen turkey, thawed
> 4 cloves elephant garlic, halved, *or* 8 to 10 regular cloves garlic
> Cooking oil (about 2 tablespoons)

● **In a covered grill, stack** coals in a pyramid or mound, and ignite. Let coals reach *medium-hot* heat.

● **Meanwhile, rinse the turkey** on the outside, as well as inside the body and neck cavities, removing the neck and giblets. Pat turkey dry with paper towels. Skewer the neck skin to the back. Place garlic in the body cavity. Tuck drumsticks under the band of skin across the tail or tie legs securely to the tail. Twist the wing tips under the back. Insert a meat thermometer into the center of one of the inside thigh muscles, not touching the bone.

● **Using long-handled tongs,** arrange the preheated coals in a circle around a large, disposable drip pan. Test for *medium-hot* heat above the coals. Pour 1 inch of water into the drip pan. Place the turkey, breast side up, on the grill rack directly over the drip pan but not over the coals. (For gas grilling, light the burner on just one side and place the food over a drip pan on the other side. Or, place the drip pan on the grate over the center of the burner. Then, cook the turkey on the grill rack directly over the drip pan. The same temperature tests apply as for charcoal grilling.)

● **Brush turkey** lightly with cooking oil (see photo, page 151). Lower the grill hood. Grill for 2½ to 3 hours or till meat thermometer registers 180° to 185°, brushing occasionally with oil. Add coals and water every 20 to 30 minutes or as necessary. Remove turkey from the grill. Let stand for 15 minutes before carving. Makes 12 servings.

Note: For food safety reasons, these grilling directions are recommended only for unstuffed turkeys.

Microwave head start: You can use your microwave to cut down on cooking time. (This method is not recommended for low-wattage ovens.)

Prepare turkey as directed. Cover wing tips and legs with small pieces of foil. (Check your owner's manual to see if foil use is OK.)

Place turkey, breast side down, on a rack in a microwave-safe baking dish. Brush with cooking oil. Cover with waxed paper. Micro-cook on 100% power (high) for 3 minutes per pound of turkey, giving dish a half-turn once during cooking. Flip the turkey so the breast side is up and brush with cooking oil. Continue to cook, covered, on high for 1½ minutes per pound, giving the dish a half-turn once.

Insert a microwave meat thermometer into the thigh muscle. Cook, covered, on high for 1½ minutes per pound or till thermometer registers 140°, giving dish a half-turn once. Remove the thermometer. Brush the turkey with cooking oil.

Meanwhile, prepare the grill and test coals as directed. Immediately after microwaving, place turkey, breast side up, on the rack over the drip pan but not over the coals. Insert a conventional meat thermometer. Lower the hood. Grill for 50 to 60 minutes or till thermometer registers 180° to 185°, brushing occasionally with cooking oil.

Nutrition information per serving: 285 cal., 46 g pro., 0 g carbo., 10 g fat, 119 mg chol., 109 mg sodium, 465 mg potassium, and 0 g dietary fiber. U.S. RDA: 17% riboflavin, 42% niacin, 15% iron.

For swirls, pipe the potatoes into 3-inch circles, 2 layers high.

TWO-POTATO SWIRLS

Turn holiday "usuals"—mashed potatoes and sweet potatoes—into tempting two-color swirls. These impressive potatoes fit easily into the 4-hour plan—

> 3 large potatoes (6 to 8 ounces each)
> 3 large sweet potatoes *or* yams (6 to 8 ounces each)
> 2 tablespoons milk
> 2 tablespoons margarine *or* butter
> 2 tablespoons orange juice
> 1 tablespoon honey

● **Peel and quarter potatoes.** In separate saucepans cook white potatoes, and sweet potatoes or yams in a small amount of boiling salted water, covered, about 20 minutes or till potatoes are tender. Drain.

● **In a small mixer bowl beat** hot white potatoes with an electric mixer on low speed till almost smooth. Add milk and *1 tablespoon* of the margarine or butter. Continue beating till light and fluffy. Transfer to another bowl.

● **In same mixer bowl beat** hot sweet potatoes with an electric mixer on low speed till almost smooth. Add *remaining* margarine or butter, orange juice, and honey. Continue beating till light and fluffy.

● **Line a baking sheet** with foil; spray with nonstick spray coating. Spoon white potato mixture along one side of a decorating bag fitted with a large star tip. Spoon sweet potato mixture along other side of bag. For swirls, on the prepared baking sheet pipe 3-inch circles of the mixture, starting at the outside and working toward the center, building a peak 2 layers high (see photo, left). Make 8 swirls. Cover loosely with plastic wrap; chill till baking time.

● **Bake, uncovered,** in a 375° oven for 15 to 20 minutes or till the tips are golden and swirls are heated through. Use a wide spatula to carefully transfer the swirls to dinner plates. Makes 8 servings.

Nutrition information per serving: 193 cal., 3 g pro., 38 g carbo., 3 g fat, 0 mg chol., 115 mg sodium, 646 mg potassium, and 4 g dietary fiber. U.S. RDA: 341% vit. A, 43% vit. C, 10% riboflavin.

WILD RICE AND PROSCIUTTO DRESSING

Ask for prosciutto (pro-SHOO-toe) at your supermarket deli counter, or at Italian and specialty markets. The special flavor of this Italian salt-cured ham makes it well worth buying—

⅓ cup wild rice
1¼ cups water
⅓ cup regular brown rice
½ teaspoon instant chicken bouillon granules
1½ cups sliced fresh mushrooms
3 green onions, sliced
1 2-ounce jar sliced pimiento, drained
½ cup broken pecans
2 ounces prosciutto, snipped (½ cup), *or* 3 slices bacon, crisp-cooked, drained, and crumbled
2 tablespoons snipped parsley
¼ cup water

● **In a sieve rinse** wild rice for about 1 minute under *cold* water. In a medium saucepan combine wild rice, the 1¼ cups water, brown rice, and bouillon granules. Bring to boiling; reduce heat. Cover; simmer for 45 minutes. Add mushrooms, onions, and pimiento. Cook, covered, over medium-low heat for 10 minutes more or just till onion is tender, stirring frequently. Stir in the pecans, prosciutto, parsley, and the ¼ cup water.

● **Transfer to a 1-quart casserole.** (If making ahead, chill for up to 24 hours before cooking. Increase cooking time if needed.) Bake, covered, in a 375° oven for 25 to 30 minutes or till heated through. Makes 8 servings.

Microwave directions: Prepare dressing as directed, *except* use a microwave-safe 1-quart casserole. Micro-cook, covered, on 100% power (high) for 6 to 8 minutes (low-wattage ovens: 9 to 11 minutes) or till heated through, carefully stirring once.

Nutrition information per serving: 120 cal., 4 g pro., 14 g carbo., 6 g fat, 4 mg chol., 120 mg sodium, 163 mg potassium, and 2 g dietary fiber. U.S. RDA: 13% vit. C, 11% thiamine.

APPLE-BERRY GINGER PIE

3 cups (12 ounces) cranberries
¾ cup apple juice
1⅓ cups sugar
⅓ cup cornstarch
3 medium cooking apples (such as Jonathan, Winesap, *or* Granny Smith) peeled, cored, and chopped (about 3 cups)
1 tablespoon snipped crystalized ginger *or* ½ teaspoon ground ginger
1½ cups all-purpose flour
½ teaspoon finely shredded orange peel
¼ teaspoon salt
½ cup shortening
4 to 5 tablespoons cold water
Sifted powdered sugar (about 2 teaspoons)

● **In a medium saucepan** stir together the cranberries and apple juice. Cook the cranberry mixture, uncovered, over medium heat for 5 to 8 minutes or till the cranberries begin to pop, stirring occasionally.

● **Combine the sugar** and the cornstarch; stir into the hot cranberry mixture. Cook and stir till mixture is thick and bubbly. Remove from heat. Stir in the apples and ginger. Set aside while preparing the pastry.

● **In a medium mixing bowl** stir together the flour, orange peel, and salt. With a pastry blender or a fork, cut in shortening till pieces are the size of small peas. Sprinkle *1 tablespoon* of the water over *part* of the mixture and gently toss with a fork. Push the moistened mixture to a side of the bowl. Repeat, adding more water, till all of the mixture is moistened. Form the dough into a ball.

● **For pastry,** on a lightly floured surface flatten dough with your hands. Roll dough from center to edges, forming a circle about 15 inches in diameter. Wrap pastry around rolling pin. Unroll onto a 9-inch pie plate. Ease pastry into pie plate, being careful not to stretch pastry. Trim pastry 1½ to 2 inches beyond edge of pie plate.

● **Spread the cranberry mixture** evenly in the pastry-lined pie plate. Bring the crust up over the filling, pleating to fit (see photo, page 151). To prevent overbrowning, cover the edge of the pie with foil. Bake in a 375° oven about 15 minutes. Remove foil from pie. Bake for 30 to 35 minutes more or till pastry is golden. Cool pie on a wire rack. Before serving, sprinkle with powdered sugar. Makes 8 servings.

Nutrition information per serving: 404 cal., 3 g pro., 71 g carbo., 13 g fat, 0 mg chol., 66 mg sodium, 132 mg potassium, and 3 g dietary fiber. U.S. RDA: 12% thiamine.

LIME POPPY SEED FRUIT SALAD

1 recipe Lime Poppy Seed Dressing
Leaf lettuce *or* spinach
3 pears, sliced into thin wedges
1 tablespoon lemon juice
2 cups seedless green *and/or* red grapes, halved
½ cup broken walnuts

● **Prepare** Lime Poppy Seed Dressing.
● **Line 8 salad plates** with leaf lettuce or spinach. In a medium bowl toss pear wedges with lemon juice.
● **Divide and arrange** pear wedges, grapes, and walnuts atop leaf lettuce. Cover and chill till serving time, up to 1 hour. Drizzle with Lime Poppy Seed Dressing. Makes 8 servings.

Lime Poppy Seed Dressing: In a small mixer bowl stir together ⅓ cup *honey,* ¼ teaspoon finely shredded *lime peel,* 3 tablespoons *lime juice,* 1½ teaspoons *poppy seed,* ¼ teaspoon *salt,* and ⅛ teaspoon *ground mace.*

Beat honey mixture with an electric mixer on medium-high speed while gradually adding ¼ cup *salad oil* and 2 tablespoons *walnut oil* or *salad oil.* Continue beating till mixture thickens. Cover; chill. Stir to remix before serving. If, after chilling, mixture becomes too thick to drizzle, let stand at room temperature for 30 minutes. Makes about ¾ cup.

Nutrition information per serving: 254 cal., 2 g pro., 31 g carbo., 0 mg chol., 16 g fat, 66 mg sodium, 232 mg potassium, and 2 g dietary fiber. U.S. RDA: 18% vit. C.

15 EASY, ELEGANT HOLIDAY RECIPES

BY LISA HOLDERNESS

STRUT YOUR STUFF this holiday season! Host a stylish appetizer and dessert party. All the recipes you need are right here—with built-in shortcuts so you can star at your own party with plenty of confidence and flair.

DISTINCTIVE DESSERTS

Share luscious yet light grand finales with friends.

VANILLA CRÈME PASTRIES

Impressive doesn't mean difficult—fill flaky puff pastry with a simple yogurt crème.

These pastries—custom-designed for a hassle-free holiday—rival some of the best that take hours from scratch.

MARSALA ORANGES

This lush dessert takes just three ingredients and 30 minutes!

When your celebration calls for something light, spoon a glistening marsala sauce over juicy, peeled oranges. Serve with chocolaty-rich *Cappuccino Sandwich Flats.*

PUMPKIN RAISIN TART

Truly delectable and easy—what more could you ask for?

Thanksgiving just wouldn't be the same without pumpkin pie! This three-layer tart goes beyond tradition with creamy honey-raisin and nut layers and a quick-fix tart shell from prepared pastry. Dollop with whipped cream and top with nuts to serve.

HOLIDAY RECIPES

FABULOUS FINGER FOOD

Let guests mingle around a savory buffet of assorted appetizers.

SOUTHWESTERN CHILI DIP

It's hot, in more ways than one.

The spice of the party! Lure your friends with this colorful Mexican dip and chips. Once they start munching, they won't stop till this dip is gone!

SPINACH SAUSAGE PIE

And to think it all starts with bread dough!

How do you bid your guests happy holidays in Italian? With a zesty stuffed meat pie! For easy entertaining, make ahead, chill, and heat through at party time. Serve with *Marinated Sun-Dried Tomatoes and Olives.*

BITE-SIZE SMØRREBRØD AND SALMON BAGELETTES

Try our simple topping suggestions to create platters of impressive hors d'oeuvres.

Here's a chance to use your imagination! Mix and match toppings, breads, and spreads for open-face sandwiches. For a stunning party companion, pair Smørrebrød with delicate salmon-topped mini bagels.

BREADS, BARS, and COOKIES

Fill your home with the aroma of fresh-baked goods.

FRUIT-SAFFRON RING AND ALMOND LOAF

Two breads to win you over with their built-in timesavers.
Bring fond memories of holiday baking back to life. These recipes save on time by using a bread mix for one and quick-rise yeast for the other.

CRANBERRY BARS

Bright ruby cranberry sauce makes an easy filling.
When your heart yearns for something down-home delicious, stir together a quick batch of bars—no mixer needed.

3-WAY SHORTBREADS

A platterful of distinctive short-breads—all from one basic recipe.

Buttery Scottish cookies that melt in your mouth! Make three kinds, Shortbread Wedges, Thumbprints, and Pecan Spice Shortbreads, and store in the freezer for last-minute entertaining.

VANILLA CRÈME PASTRIES

Combine puff pastry, available in most grocery stores, with this season's juicy grapes for a charming, simple dessert—

- ½ of a 17¼-ounce package (1 sheet) frozen puff pastry
- ½ cup vanilla yogurt
- ½ cup dairy sour cream
- 1 tablespoon brown sugar
- ¾ cup seedless red *and/or* green grapes, halved
- 2 tablespoons finely chopped pistachio nuts

● **Thaw puff pastry** according to package directions; unfold. Place puff pastry sheet on a baking sheet. With a knife, score into 8 rectangles (4¾ x 2⅜ inches each). Bake in a 375° oven for 20 to 25 minutes or till puffed and golden. Cool on a wire rack. Cut into rectangles along the scored lines.
● **In a small mixing bowl** combine yogurt, sour cream, and brown sugar. Transfer *half* of the yogurt mixture to another bowl. Fold ½ *cup* of the grapes into one portion of the yogurt mixture.
● **To assemble pastries, split** pastry rectangles in half horizontally; spread *each* bottom half with about *2 tablespoons* yogurt-grape mixture. Cap with pastry tops; spoon about *1 tablespoon* yogurt mixture without grapes on top. Top with remaining grapes, cut side down. Sprinkle with nuts. Serve immediately, or cover and chill up to 2 hours. Makes 8.

Nutrition information per pastry: *201 cal., 3 g pro., 19 g carbo., 13 g fat, 7 mg chol., 161 mg sodium, 1 g dietary fiber.*

PUMPKIN RAISIN TART

- 1 9-inch folded refrigerated unbaked piecrust
- 1 8-ounce container soft-style cream cheese with honey *or* plain soft-style cream cheese
- ⅓ cup raisins
- 1 beaten egg yolk
- 1 cup canned pumpkin
- 1 5-ounce can (⅔ cup) evaporated milk
- ⅓ cup sugar
- 3 egg whites
- 1½ teaspoons pumpkin pie spice
- ½ cup finely chopped pecans *or* walnuts
- Whipped cream (optional)
- Finely chopped pecans *or* walnuts (optional)

● **Let piecrust** come to room temperature according to package directions. Preheat a baking sheet in a 375° oven.
● **Meanwhile,** in a small mixing bowl stir together cream cheese, raisins, and egg yolk; set aside. In a medium mixing bowl combine pumpkin, evaporated milk, sugar, egg whites, and pumpkin pie spice.
● **Ease piecrust** into a 10-inch tart or quiche pan. Press edges of piecrust against edges of pan. Sprinkle nuts over pastry. Carefully spoon cream cheese mixture evenly atop nut layer in piecrust. Pour pumpkin mixture atop cream-cheese layer.
● **Place tart** on the preheated baking sheet; bake in the 375° oven for 30 to 35 minutes or till knife inserted off-center comes out clean. Cool on a wire rack. Cover and chill, up to 2 days. (*Or,* wrap in freezer wrap; seal, label, and freeze up to 3 months. To serve, thaw tart, loosely covered, for 24 hours in the refrigerator.)
● **To serve,** if using a tart pan with a removable bottom, remove outer rim of pan and carefully lift tart from pan bottom with a large spatula; slide onto a serving platter. Spoon whipped cream atop tart and sprinkle with chopped nuts, if desired. Makes 8 servings.

Nutrition information per serving: *391 cal., 7 g pro., 35 g carbo., 26 g fat, 40 mg chol., 243 mg sodium, 270 mg potassium, and 2 g dietary fiber. U.S. RDA: 149% vit. A, 11% riboflavin, and 11% calcium.*

CAPPUCCINO SANDWICH FLATS

These dainty, designer sandwich cookies start with purchased chocolate wafers for extra ease—

- 3 tablespoons margarine *or* butter
- 2½ cups sifted powdered sugar
- 2 teaspoons instant coffee crystals *or* 3 tablespoons coffee liqueur
- 1 square (1 ounce) semisweet chocolate, finely shredded
- 1 8½-ounce package chocolate wafers (42 wafers)
- Powdered sugar

● **For filling,** in a small mixer bowl beat margarine or butter with an electric mixer on medium speed about 30 seconds or till softened. Gradually beat in *1 cup* of the sifted powdered sugar. If using coffee granules, dissolve in 2 tablespoons *water.* Beat in coffee mixture or coffee liqueur till smooth. Beat in enough of the remaining 2½ cups powdered sugar to make a very stiff filling (should still be of spreading consistency). Stir in chocolate.
● **To assemble sandwich cookies,** frost the bottom *half* of the cookies with about *2 teaspoons* filling. Top *each* with the remaining unfrosted cookies, bottom side down.
● **Store in an airtight container** at room temperature for up to 2 days or in the freezer for up to 6 months. If frozen, thaw at room temperature for 10 to 15 minutes. Using stencils or a doily, sift powdered sugar atop each sandwich cookie just before serving. Makes 21 sandwich cookies.

Nutrition information per cookie: *119 cal., 1 g pro., 21 g carbo., 4 g fat, 4 mg chol., 35 mg sodium, 26 mg potassium, and 0 g dietary fiber.*

MARSALA ORANGES

    4 oranges
    2 cups sweet marsala *or*
       madeira wine
    ½ cup sugar

● **Using a vegetable peeler,** remove thin layers of peel from the oranges in strips, avoiding the bitter-tasting white membrane. Cut enough of the peel into very thin 2-inch-long strips to make *3 tablespoons.* Using a sharp knife, remove and discard the remaining peel and white membrane from the oranges. Place oranges in a large bowl; set aside.

● **For sauce,** in a medium saucepan combine the orange peel strips, marsala, and sugar. Bring orange-peel mixture to boiling and reduce heat. Simmer, uncovered, for 15 to 20 minutes or till mixture is reduced to *1½ cups.* Cool to room temperature. Pour over oranges, coating each orange. Cover with plastic wrap and chill till serving time, up to 24 hours.

● **Serve the oranges,** whole or halved, with the sauce ladled atop. Makes 4 servings.

Nutrition information per serving: 322 cal., 1 g pro., 51 g carbo., 0 g fat, 0 mg chol., 5 mg sodium, 337 mg potassium, and 3 g dietary fiber. U.S. RDA: 126% vit. C.

SPINACH SAUSAGE PIE

    1 pound bulk Italian sausage
    1 10-ounce package frozen
       chopped spinach, thawed and
       well drained
    1 8-ounce can tomato sauce
    1 4-ounce can sliced mushrooms,
       drained
    ⅓ cup fine dry seasoned bread
       crumbs
    1 2-ounce jar sliced pimiento,
       drained
    1 16-ounce loaf frozen whole
       wheat *or* rye bread dough,
       thawed
    1 tablespoon margarine *or* butter,
       melted

● **For filling,** in a large skillet cook sausage till brown; drain. Stir in the spinach, tomato sauce, mushrooms, bread crumbs, and pimiento; set aside.

● **For crust,** on a lightly floured surface roll *two-thirds* of the bread dough into an 11-inch circle. Carefully place in a greased 9-inch springform pan, patting dough 1 inch up the sides. Add filling.

● **On a lightly floured surface,** roll remaining dough into a 10-inch circle. Cut into 10 to 12 wedges. Arrange wedges atop filling, slightly overlapping edges and sealing ends to bottom crust along edge of pan. Brush top with margarine or butter.

● **Bake in a 375° oven** for 30 to 35 minutes or till crust is golden brown. If necessary, cover with foil the last 10 minutes of baking to prevent overbrowning. Cool on a wire rack 10 minutes. Remove sides of pan. Serve warm. Makes 10 to 12 appetizer servings.

Nutrition information per serving: 235 cal., 9 g pro., 28 g carbo., 9 g fat, 19 mg chol., 653 mg sodium, 278 mg potassium, and 2 g dietary fiber. U.S. RDA: 41% vit. A, 11% vit. C, 24% thiamine, 14% riboflavin, 15% niacin, 13% iron.

MARINATED SUN-DRIED TOMATOES AND OLIVES

Mix together this simple recipe at least four days in advance and chill; the flavors keep getting better over time—

    1 8-ounce jar sun-dried tomatoes
       (oil pack)
    1 6-ounce can pitted ripe
       olives, drained
    ⅓ cup vinegar
    ¼ cup chopped onion
    2 to 3 teaspoons sugar
    1 teaspoon dried oregano,
       crushed

● **In a 1-quart jar** or storage container combine the *undrained* tomatoes, olives, vinegar, onion, sugar, and oregano. Cover and chill thoroughly (at least 4 to 7 days).

● **To serve, drain** olives and tomatoes. Makes 12 to 15 appetizer servings.

Nutrition information per serving: 50 cal., 1 g pro., 3 g carbo., 4 g fat, 0 mg chol., 118 mg sodium, 82 mg potassium, and 1 g dietary fiber.

Bite-Size Smørebrøds

Create a delicious assortment of finger sandwiches with an array of bread cutouts, spreads, and toppings—

● **Breads:** Experiment with several kinds of thinly sliced bread. French baguettes, pumpernickel, and canned brown bread work well. Cut breads into stars, hearts, triangles, or any shape you like with cookie cutters or a paring knife.

● **Spreads:** Top your bread cutouts with a variety of spreads such as mayonnaise or salad dressing, soft-style cream cheese with herbs, plain yogurt, sour cream, herb-flavored butters, and tuna salad.

● **Toppings:** For the final touch, decorate each cutout with savory toppings. Here are some ideas to get you started: thinly sliced cooked deli meats, cooked shrimp, smoked salmon, sliced radishes, sliced cucumbers, edible flowers, shredded carrots, capers, fresh herb sprigs, lettuce, cheese slices, sliced mushrooms, chopped green or sweet red peppers, olives, cooked bacon pieces, pineapple tidbits, feta or blue cheese crumbles, caviar, sliced hard-cooked egg, sliced kiwi fruit, mandarin orange sections, and sliced green onion.

● **The smørrebrød** combinations that are shown on *page 157* include: pumpernickel hearts with dill-spiked cream cheese, smoked salmon, and flat-leaf parsley; French bread triangles with Bibb lettuce, thinly sliced roast beef, radish slices, and capers; rye bread triangles with piped cream cheese, salami, and flat-leaf parsley; and pumpernickel flowers with curry-flavored mayonnaise, cucumber slices, cooked shrimp, and parsley. Plan about 2 smørrebrøds per guest.

Nutrition information per 2 pumpernickel smørrebrøds with curry-flavored mayonnaise, cucumber slices, cooked shrimp, and parsley: 74 cal., 3 g pro., 8 g carbo., 4 g fat, 14 mg chol., 117 mg sodium, 52 mg potassium, and 1 g dietary fiber.

SOUTHWESTERN CHILI DIP

Look for pita chips at your grocery store. Or, to make your own chips, split pita bread into 2 single layers. Cut layers into wedges. If desired, brush pitas lightly with oil or margarine for extra crunch. Bake in a 350° oven for 12 to 15 minutes or till crisp and golden brown—

  2 cups shredded low-fat *or* regular cheddar cheese (8 ounces)
  1 cup reduced-calorie mayonnaise *or* salad dressing
  1 4½-ounce can chopped ripe olives, drained
  1 4-ounce can chopped green chili peppers, drained
  ¼ teaspoon garlic powder
Few drops bottled hot pepper sauce
  1 medium tomato, chopped
  ¼ cup sliced green onions
Pita chips (optional)

● **In a large mixing bowl** stir together the cheddar cheese, the mayonnaise or salad dressing, *half* of the ripe olives, the green chili peppers, garlic powder, and hot pepper sauce till combined. Spread the mixture into a 9-inch quiche dish or pie plate*.

● **Bake in a 350° oven** about 20 minutes or till heated through. Sprinkle with the tomato, remaining olives, and green onion in 3 rings, starting near the outer edge of the dish. Serve warm with pita chips, if desired. Makes 8 to 10 appetizer servings.

Note: Cheese mixture can be covered with plastic wrap and chilled up to 4 hours before baking. Continue as directed; however, baking time may need to increase for thorough heating.

Microwave directions: Prepare as directed, *except* spread cheese mixture into a microwave-safe 9-inch quiche dish or pie plate. Micro-cook, uncovered, on 100% power (high) for 4 to 6 minutes or till heated through, stirring twice. Continue as directed. (This recipe does not give low-wattage microwave oven timings because this size baking dish does not fit in most of the smaller microwave ovens.)

Nutrition information per 2 tablespoons: *201 cal., 9 g pro., 4 g carbo., 17 g fat, 30 mg chol., 519 mg sodium, 105 mg potassium, and 1 g dietary fiber. U.S. RDA: 39% vit. A, 35% vit. C, 25% calcium.*

SALMON BAGELETTES

  1 8-ounce container soft-style cream cheese with salmon
  8 to 10 frozen miniature bagels, thawed, split, and toasted
  1 sprig fresh dill, snipped
  3 or 4 cherry tomatoes, quartered

● **Place cream cheese** in a pastry bag with a medium-size star tip. Pipe about *1 tablespoon* of the cream cheese atop *each* bagel half. Top *half* of the bagel halves with snipped dill, and top the remaining bagel halves with a tomato quarter and snipped dill. Serve immediately, or cover and chill up to 1 hour. Makes 16 to 20 appetizers.

Garden Bagelettes: Prepare the Salmon Bagelettes as directed, *except* substitute one 8-ounce container *soft-style cream cheese with chives and onion* for the cream cheese with salmon. Omit the dill and tomatoes. With a knife, spread about *1 tablespoon* cream cheese atop *each* bagel half. Top each with vegetable cutouts such as *carrot* flowers with *green onion* stems, thinly sliced *radishes,* or chopped *olives.*

Nutrition information per Salmon Bagelette: *48 cal., 1 g pro., 1 g carbo., 5 g fat, 1 mg chol., 35 mg sodium, 27 mg potassium, and 0 g dietary fiber.*

ALMOND LOAF

4¼ to 4¾ cups all-purpose flour
  1 package quick-rising active dry yeast
  1 cup milk
  ⅓ cup sugar
  ⅓ cup margarine *or* butter
  1 teaspoon salt
  2 eggs
  1 12½-ounce can almond cake and pastry filling
  ½ cup miniature semisweet chocolate pieces

● **In a large mixer bowl stir** together *2 cups* of the flour and yeast. In a small saucepan heat milk, sugar, margarine or butter, and salt just till warm (120° to 130°), stirring constantly. Add to flour mixture; add eggs. Beat with an electric mixer on low speed for 30 seconds, scraping sides of bowl constantly.

Beat on high speed for 3 minutes. Using a spoon, stir in as much of the remaining flour as you can.

● **On a lightly floured surface** knead in enough of the remaining flour to make a moderately stiff dough that is smooth and elastic (6 to 8 minutes). Shape into a ball. Place dough in a greased bowl; turn dough once to grease surface. Cover and let the dough rise in a warm place about 20 minutes. Punch dough down; divide in half. Roll half of the dough into a 24x8-inch rectangle. Spread with ½ cup of the almond filling and *2 tablespoons* of the chocolate pieces.

● **Fold dough loosely** from one of the short sides, making about eight 3-inch-wide folds. (This is similar to rolling a jelly roll except you fold the dough instead of rolling it.) Transfer to a baking sheet. Make 2½-inch-long cuts in the dough at ¾-inch intervals on one of the long sides. (*Do not* cut completely through to the other long side of dough roll.) Flip every other cut to the opposite side. Twist each cut in the same direction to expose the filling. Repeat, making a second loaf with the remaining dough, ½ cup filling, and *2 tablespoons* chocolate pieces. Cover loaves and let rise in a warm place till nearly double (about 30 minutes).

● **Bake loaves in a 375° oven** for 18 to 20 minutes or till golden, covering with foil after 10 minutes to prevent overbrowning. Sprinkle each loaf with *half* of the remaining chocolate pieces while the loaf is still warm. Serve warm. Makes 2 loaves, about 10 slices per loaf.

Freezing directions: To freeze, wrap the loaves thoroughly in freezer wrap; seal, label, and freeze loaves up to 8 months.

To serve, thaw loaves in freezer wrap at room temperature for 3 to 4 hours. If you wish to serve the loaves warm, reheat the *thawed* loaves, loosely covered with foil, in a 350° oven for 15 to 20 minutes or till the loaves are completely heated through.

Or, to reheat directly from freezer, unwrap *frozen* loaves. Place loaves on a baking sheet; cover each loosely with foil. Bake in a 350° oven for 1 hour or till heated through.

Nutrition information per slice: *253 cal., 6 g pro., 34 g carbo., 11 g fat, 28 mg chol., 158 mg sodium, 188 mg potassium, and 3 g dietary fiber. U.S. RDA: 15% thiamine, 17% riboflavin, 10% niacin, and 11% iron.*

FRUIT-SAFFRON RING

Like many European holiday breads, this delicious, fruit-speckled ring has a coarse, heavy texture. The bright yellow color comes from the treasured spice, saffron, which also lends a mild bittersweet flavor—

- 1 6-ounce package mixed dried fruit bits
- ¼ cup apple juice
- 1 16-ounce package hot roll mix
- 2 tablespoons sugar
- ⅛ teaspoon ground saffron
- 1 recipe Powdered Sugar Icing

● **In a small bowl combine** fruit and apple juice; let stand 5 minutes, stirring twice.

● **Meanwhile, prepare** roll mix according to package directions, *except* add sugar and saffron along with the flour mixture. Drain the fruit, if necessary, discarding excess liquid. Stir fruit into dough before kneading.

● **On a lightly floured surface form** dough into an 18-inch rope. Place in a greased 10-inch fluted tube pan, pressing ends together (make sure that rope is the same size throughout, especially where ends attach, or ring will bake unevenly). Cover; let rise according to package directions.

● **Bake in a 375° oven** for 20 to 25 minutes or till golden brown. Invert onto a wire rack; cool. Drizzle with Powdered Sugar Icing. Makes 12 servings.

Powdered Sugar Frosting: In a small mixing bowl combine 1 cup sifted *powdered sugar* and 1 to 2 tablespoons *apple juice* to make an icing of drizzling consistency. Makes about ⅓ cup.

Freezing directions: To freeze, wrap uniced ring thoroughly in freezer wrap. Seal, label, and freeze up to 8 months.

Thaw ring, in the freezer wrap, at room temperature for 3 to 4 hours. If you wish to serve ring warm, reheat *thawed uniced* ring, covered with foil, in a 350° oven for 15 to 20 minutes or till heated through. Drizzle with Powdered Sugar Icing.

Nutrition information per serving: 218 cal., 5 g pro., 49 g carbo., 1 g fat, 0 mg chol., 262 mg sodium, 173 mg potassium, and 1 g dietary fiber. U.S. RDA: 17% thiamine, 13% niacin, 10% iron.

CRANBERRY BARS

- 1½ cups all-purpose flour
- 1½ cups quick-cooking rolled oats
- ¾ cup packed brown sugar
- 1 teaspoon finely shredded lemon peel
- ¼ teaspoon baking soda
- ¾ cup margarine *or* butter, melted
- 1 16-ounce can whole cranberry sauce
- ¼ cup finely chopped pecans *or* walnuts

● **In a large mixing bowl** stir together the flour, oats, brown sugar, lemon peel, and baking soda. Stir in the margarine or butter, and mix thoroughly. Reserve *1 cup* of the flour-oat mixture for the topping. Pat the remaining oat mixture into an ungreased 12x7½x2-inch baking pan. Bake in a 350° oven for 20 minutes.

● **Carefully spread** cranberry sauce atop baked crust. Stir nuts into reserved oat mixture. Sprinkle atop cranberry sauce. Lightly pat oat mixture into sauce. Bake for 25 to 30 minutes more or till top is golden. Cool in the pan on a wire rack. Cut into bars. Makes 24.

Freezer directions: Transfer bars to a freezer container or plastic freezer bags; seal, label, and freeze up to 12 months. To serve, thaw 10 to 15 minutes at room temperature.

Nutrition information per bar: 161 cal., 2 g pro., 24 g carbo., 7 g fat, 86 mg sodium, 61 mg potassium, and 1 g dietary fiber.

3-WAY SHORTBREADS

- 1¼ cups all-purpose flour
- 3 tablespoons sugar
- ½ cup butter*

● **For Shortbread Wedges,** in a large mixing bowl stir together the flour and sugar. Cut in butter till mixture resembles fine crumbs. Form mixture into a ball and knead till smooth.

● **On an ungreased cookie sheet** pat or roll dough into an 8-inch circle. For a scalloped edge, with forefinger of one hand, push dough edge between forefinger and thumb of the other hand. Using a sharp knife, cut dough circle into 12 to 16 pie-shape wedges. *Do not* separate wedges. Prick each wedge with a fork, making a design if desired.

● **Bake in a 325° oven** for 25 to 30 minutes or just till edges are light brown. While warm, recut wedges. Remove from pan; cool on a wire rack. Makes 12 to 16 shortbread wedges.

Thumbprints: Prepare dough as directed, *except* shape dough into 1-inch balls instead of wedges. Place 2 inches apart on an ungreased cookie sheet. Using your thumb, press an indentation in center of each cookie. Bake in a 325° oven for 18 minutes or till bottoms are light brown and edges are slightly golden. Immediately spoon ½ teaspoon *fruit preserves* (such as cherry, strawberry, or peach) into *each* indentation. Cool completely, then remove cookies from cookie sheet. Makes 20 to 24.

Pecan Spice Shortbreads: Prepare the dough as directed, *except* substitute *brown sugar* for the sugar and add 1 teaspoon *apple pie spice* to the flour mixture. Pat the dough into an ungreased 9x9x2-inch baking pan.

For shortbread rectangles, cut dough into 1½x1-inch rectangles; do not separate. Top each rectangle with 1 *pecan half,* pressing lightly into dough. Bake in a 325° oven for 23 to 25 minutes or till edges are light brown. While warm, recut rectangles. Sprinkle with powdered sugar. Cool in pan. Makes 54 rectangles.

For shortbread triangles (see photo, *pages 158 and 159),* prepare as directed, *except* sprinkle dough with ¼ cup chopped pecans. Press nuts lightly into dough. Bake in a 325° oven for 23 to 25 minutes. While warm, cut into sixteen 2¼-inch squares. Cut each square diagonally to make triangles. Cool in pan. Drizzle with Vanilla Icing. Makes 32 triangles.

Vanilla Icing: In a small mixing bowl combine ½ cup sifted *powdered sugar* and ¼ teaspoon *vanilla.* Stir in enough *milk* (2 to 3 teaspoons) to make an icing of drizzling consistency.

*Note: These cookies use butter for a richer flavor and stiffer dough. If substituting margarine for butter, you may need to chill dough before shaping.

Freezer directions: Transfer cookies to a freezer container or plastic freezer bags; seal, label, and freeze up to 12 months. To serve, thaw 10 to 15 minutes at room temperature.

Nutrition information per Shortbread Wedge: 127 cal., 1 g pro., 13 g carbo., 8 g fat, 21 mg chol., 78 mg sodium, 15 mg potassium, and 0 g dietary fiber.

HOMEMADE MINCEMEAT
EASY TO FIX; LUSCIOUS IN HOMEBAKED GOODIES

BY BARBARA JOHNSON

Homemade mincemeat is a snap to make with this simple, stream-lined recipe. Make it with fruit exclusively, and skip the peeling. Then, strut your spicy filling in an equally simple coffee bread that begins with convenient hot roll mix or in this luscious bar cookie with crumb topping.

ALL-FRUIT MINCEMEAT

Use a food processor to chop fruit fast—
- **4 cups chopped, unpeeled apples**
- **2 cups raisins, chopped**
- **1 cup snipped dried apricots**
- **1 6-ounce can (¾ cup) frozen apple juice concentrate, thawed**
- **¾ cup water**
- **¼ cup honey**
- **1 teaspoon ground allspice**
- **½ teaspoon salt**
- **2 tablespoons brandy**

In a 4½-quart Dutch oven stir together apples, raisins, apricots, apple juice concentrate, water, honey, allspice, and salt. Bring to boiling; reduce heat. Cover and simmer for 50 minutes, stirring occasionally. Uncover and simmer for 10 to 15 minutes more or till liquid has nearly evaporated, stirring occasionally. Stir in brandy. To store, cover and chill. Use in Mincemeat-Filled Crumb Bars and Mincemeat Coffee Bread. Makes about 4 cups.

MINCEMEAT-FILLED CRUMB BARS

A great choice for gift mailings; these bars weather the shipping well—
- **3½ cups all-purpose flour**
- **1 cup finely chopped walnuts**
- **1½ cups margarine *or* butter**
- **1¼ cups sifted powdered sugar**
- **2 cups All-Fruit Mincemeat**
- **1 tablespoon all-purpose flour**

Stir together the 3½ cups flour and the walnuts; set aside. In a large mixer bowl beat the margarine or butter with

Bake a batch for the holidays.

Start with a convenient hot roll mix.

an electric mixer on medium speed till softened. Add the powdered sugar and beat till the mixture is fluffy. Add flour-walnut mixture and beat at low speed till mixture is well combined.

Press *two-thirds* of the flour mixture onto the bottom of an ungreased 13x9x2-inch baking pan. Reserve remaining flour mixture. Spread the All-Fruit Mincemeat on top. Stir the 1 tablespoon flour into remaining crumb mixture; sprinkle over top. Bake in a 375° oven for 25 to 30 minutes or till crumbs are golden. Cool completely. Cut into bars. Makes 48 bars.

Nutrition information per bar: 133 cal., 2 g pro., 16 g carbo., 7 g fat, 0 mg chol., 80 mg sodium, 1 g dietary fiber.

MINCEMEAT COFFEE BREAD

Serve one coffee bread now; wrap, seal, label, and freeze the other, unglazed, to enjoy later—
- **1 16-ounce package hot roll mix**
- **¾ cup water**
- **2 cups All-Fruit Mincemeat**
- **Nonstick spray coating**
   • • •
- **1 cup sifted powdered sugar**
- **¼ teaspoon vanilla**
- **Milk**

Prepare the hot roll mix according to the package directions, *except* use the ¾ cup water and stir ½ cup of the All-Fruit Mincemeat into the hot roll mix along with the water. Cover and let rise till the dough is double (about 30 minutes). Punch the dough down. Cover and let rest for 10 minutes.

Spray two 8x1½-inch round baking pans with nonstick spray coating. Cut off and reserve *one-third* of the dough. Divide the remaining dough evenly between the prepared pans; pat dough evenly onto the bottoms of the pans. Spread *half* of the remaining mincemeat (¾ *cup*) over the top of the dough in *each* pan.

On a lightly floured surface, divide reserved dough in half. Roll *each* into a 30-inch rope. (If dough seems too elastic, cover and let rest for a few minutes.) Coil loosely over the top of the mincemeat, starting in center of *each* pan. Cover and let rise till nearly double (about 30 minutes).

Bake in a 375° oven for 20 to 25 minutes or till tops sound hollow when tapped. Cover with foil during the last 10 minutes of baking to prevent over-browning. Cool slightly on a wire rack.

Meanwhile, for glaze, in a small mixing bowl stir together powdered sugar and vanilla. Add enough milk (about *1 tablespoon*) to make of drizzling consistency. Drizzle over loaves. Makes 2 loaves, 12 servings each.

Nutrition information per serving: 129 cal., 3 g pro., 30 g carbo., 0 g fat, 0 mg chol., 155 mg sodium, and 2 g dietary fiber.

DECEMBER

A FAMILY FEAST

When It's Your Turn to Fix Christmas Dinner

BY BARBARA JOHNSON

Your family is coming for Christmas dinner. Don't panic! Let our menu help you pull off your biggest meal of the year with style, spirit, and ease. Whether you're having six or 20, our microwave shortcuts and make-ahead hints ensure this gala will be your biggest and best.

❧

Menu

Pork Roast with Pesto Stuffing

•

Potatoes Supreme

•

Sesame Holiday Vegetables

•

Winter Greens with Cranberry Vinaigrette

•

Spiral Breadsticks

•

Steamed Cranberry-Cherry Pudding With Vanilla Cream

•

Linzer Apple Torte

PHOTOGRAPHS: SCOTT LITTLE. FOOD STYLIST: JANET HERWIG

FIXING THE FAMILY FEAST *Everything You*

Your family's holiday feast is guaranteed to be a smashing success. This menu plan, fine-tuned in our Test Kitchen, tells you everything you need to know. We go way beyond the basics, offering important hints, tips, strategies, shortcuts, and pointers that'll save you time and make you look like a seasoned cook even if you've never fixed a single Christmas dinner. So, let's get cooking!

To easily carve the stuffed pork roast, cut between the ribs. Each rib, along with its meat and pocket of stuffing, is a serving.

For a stunning look, pipe potato mixture into dishes with an up-and-down motion. To order a pastry bag and large star tip, see page 131.

EXPANDING THE MENU

How to serve 6, 12, or 20

The recipes are geared for 6 servings. And, you won't need any special equipment—just a basic oven and stovetop. (If you have a microwave oven, great! It'll make things even easier.) Having a bigger crowd? Take heart—we've thought of that, too!

- **For 12 servings**

Double batches—they're the key to serving 12 guests. Make two of every main course recipe: pork roasts, rolls, vegetables, and potatoes. And, assemble *two* large platters of salad. For dessert, just one recipe of both pudding and torte will do. There'll be enough for 12 and probably leftovers to enjoy, too.

- **For 20 servings**

Feeding 20 folks is a bit more involved, but still manageable. (Even more so if someone offers to help. Be sure to accept!) The end of each recipe specifies how to expand that dish to serve 20. Briefly, here's how:

Cook either two *larger* pork rib roasts (stuffed) *or* one large boneless pork loin roast (unstuffed, served with pesto sauce). Make triple recipes of the vegetables, rolls, and salad.

You'll need a triple recipe of potatoes. But, don't panic about peeling 8 pounds of them. Use frozen hash brown potatoes instead, as a clever shortcut.

Again, you'll have plenty of dessert to serve 20. But, no leftovers!

Pork Roast with Pesto Stuffing

If you know the entrée is under control, the rest comes easy. That's why we suggest you tend to the roast first. (Bake everything else later alongside the roast.) Stuff the meat about 3 hours before mealtime (or, depending on how many folks you're having, enough time before dinner for your roast to cook).

To serve a perfect roast, invest in a meat thermometer. Our Test Kitchen always finds that's the best way to tell when a roast is done. Push the thermometer tip into the center of the meat at whatever point looks thickest. Don't leave the thermometer touching bone—that will throw off the reading.

Set the roast in a pan, put the pan on the lowest oven rack, and start roasting. Soon the aroma will fill your home!

- **Shopping tip:**

Call your butcher to order the roast a few days before you plan to shop. Ask the butcher to loosen the backbone. It'll make carving at the dinner table a whole lot easier.

- **Make-ahead hint:**

Make and chill the stuffing and cut the pockets in the roast ahead of time. But, actually spoon the stuffing into the meat right before roasting.

- **Carving pointer:**

You can carve the roast more easily and attractively if you let it stand about 15 minutes after roasting.

Potatoes Supreme

Impressive looking, yes—but, oh, so simple to make! Peel, cut up, cook, and mash potatoes, adding cream cheese.

Now you choose how fancy to make them: Pipe the potatoes through a decorating tip into small soufflé dishes or spoon into small soufflé dishes. Either way, sprinkle on the crunchy golden topping. Then, put the potatoes in the oven about a half hour before you plan to eat dinner. (If fixed ahead, cover and chill the potatoes till baking time.)

- **Shopping tip:**

Choose potatoes with a mealy texture (such as russets or round white potatoes) for this recipe. Our Test Kitchen finds that they mash up best.

- **Make-ahead hint:**

To save yourself the "stage fright" of piping these potatoes in front of an audience of in-laws, you can prepare the potato mixture up to 24 hours beforehand. Simply cover and chill.

- **Microwave shortcut:**

Use microwave-safe soufflé dishes or a casserole, and you can do the final heating in the microwave oven.

Need to Know to Pull It Off Sensationally

To seed an avocado, cut the avocado in half lengthwise, then twist and gently separate the halves. Tap the seed with the sharp edge of the knife. Twist and lift the seed out.

Let the kids have fun pulling the chopsticks out of the breadsticks at the dinner table!

To create a colorful splash, spoon the vegetable combo around the roast on the serving platter.

Winter Greens with Cranberry Vinaigrette

Either fix this beautiful salad on Christmas morning or up to a day ahead. Shake up the easy vinaigrette and stow it in the refrigerator. Then, start rinsing and assembling the greens and vegetables. (Hold off on the avocado, though. Cut the avocado right before serving so it doesn't turn brown.)

Now, cover the platter with plastic wrap and chill; everything will be crisp and crunchy for dinner.

● **Shopping tip:**

Ideally, the avocados you buy should yield to gentle pressure when you squeeze them. In reality, however, the avocados at the store are usually firm. So, you'll need to let them ripen at room temperature. To short-cut ripening, we suggest putting the avocados in a paper bag at room temperature. Once the avocados are perfectly ripe, store them in your refrigerator.

● **Make-ahead hint:**

Rinse, drain, and pat dry both greens and vegetables right after you cart them home from the supermarket. There'll be less to do at dinnertime—and more chance to enjoy your guests—if you assemble and chill the salad platter up to 24 hours ahead.

Spiral Breadsticks

The easiest recipe yet! Pull out a tube of refrigerated breadsticks, some chopsticks or metal skewers, and several of your favorite seasonings (sesame seed, poppy seed, paprika, lemon-pepper seasoning, or the like).

We found the breadsticks were easier to pull off when we greased the chopsticks or skewers. So, wind *half* of the breadsticks around those greased rods. Then, tie the remaining breadsticks into knots as the recipe directs. Brush them all with milk (for a luscious golden color!) and sprinkle with seasonings. Bake, beginning about the last 15 minutes that the roast is in the oven.

● **Make-ahead tip:**

For the ultimate in organization, bake the rolls the day ahead. Then, simply wrap in foil and reheat just before dinner.

● **Microwave shortcut:**

By using wooden chopsticks, we found that you can reheat the rolls in your microwave oven. However, we did notice that the rolls weren't as crisp as freshly baked bread.

Sesame Holiday Vegetables

This vegetable dish comes together in a flash. Rinse and cut up fresh fennel bulbs and celery. (Fennel bulbs taste like licorice and look like large onions, but with celery-stalk-like sections. Lucky enough to get fennel with tops? Save the tops to use later.)

About the time the roast comes out of the oven, start cooking the vegetables. Meanwhile, sauté the sesame seed coating. Toss both mixtures together when they're done (about serving time).

● **Shopping tip:**

Look for fennel bulbs with fresh, bright-green tops. You can use these feathery sprigs to line the meat platter. When fennel with tops isn't available, pick up some fresh dill or parsley to use on the platter.

● **Make-ahead hint:**

To save time on Christmas Day, you can slice the fennel and celery up to 24 hours ahead of time. Store, covered, in separate containers in the refrigerator.

● **Microwave shortcut:**

The vegetables require lots less watching and stirring if you cook them in the microwave oven.

GRAND FINALE
Putting on the Finishing Touches

To make the decorative orange peel star (used as a garnish on the Vanilla Cream), simply press a star-shape cutter into a piece of orange peel.

Glaze the torte with the melted preserves, then add the sugar-topped stars up to several hours before serving.

Steamed Cranberry-Cherry Pudding with Vanilla Cream

● **Make-ahead hint:**

You *can* make and serve this recipe all on the day of your dinner. But, we suggest you make your life easier and steam the pudding ahead (up to 5 days before). On the day of your dinner, start resteaming about 30 minutes before you sit down to eat. That way, the pudding will be perfectly warm at dessert time. Between courses, whip the cream and fold in the yogurt.

● **Shopping tip:**

After several tests, our Test Kitchen concluded that firm-textured bread such as French or Italian works best in this recipe. Soft-textured bread simply sinks under the weight of the fruit and custard, creating a shorter, more compact, and less attractive pudding.

Look for dried cherries and cranberries at gourmet or specialty food stores.

● **Presentation pointer:**

Tall, thin molds; short, squatty ones. We tried all kinds and shapes. Hands down, this steamed pudding looks the most striking when made in a tall, tower-type mold!

Linzer Apple Torte

● **Make-ahead hint:**

As with the pudding, we suggest you make this torte ahead of time, leaving only the finishing touches for the day of your dinner. Stir together the crust, cook the filling, and bake both the pastry stars and torte a day or two ahead.

Up to several hours before serving, glaze the torte with the melted preserves and top with the pastry stars.

● **Shopping tip:**

Our Test Kitchen suggests choosing apples that are best for baking. Some of those varieties are: Golden Delicious, Red Rome, Winesap, Granny Smith, and Jonathan.

● **Microwave shortcut:**

In seconds, melt the preserves in your microwave oven before spooning them over the torte.

PORK ROAST WITH PESTO STUFFING

- ½ cup plain croutons, slightly crushed
- ½ cup purchased pesto sauce
- ¼ cup chopped sun-dried tomatoes* or pimiento
- 1 3- to 4-pound pork loin center rib roast, backbone loosened (6 ribs total)

● **For stuffing,** combine croutons, pesto, and sun-dried tomatoes. Set aside.
● **Place roast,** rib side down, on cutting surface. On the meaty side, cut a 3½-inch-long and 1-inch-deep pocket above each rib, making 6 pockets total. Spoon stuffing into pockets. Place roast, rib side down, in a shallow roasting pan. Sprinkle with a little *salt* and *pepper.* Insert a meat thermometer into the thickest part of the roast, making sure the bulb does not touch the bone.
● **Roast in a 325° oven** for 1½ to 2¼ hours or till thermometer registers 160°. Cover loosely with foil after 1 hour to prevent overbrowning. For easier carving, let roast stand, covered, for 15 minutes. If desired, use fennel bulb tops to line serving platter. To serve, slice roast between ribs. Serves 6.

For 12 servings: Prepare as directed, except double the recipe, making 2 stuffed roasts.

For 20 servings: Prepare stuffing as directed, except use 1¾ cups croutons, 1¾ cups purchased pesto sauce, and ¾ cup chopped sun-dried tomatoes. Cut 20 pockets total in *two 6- to 7-pound pork loin center rib roasts, backbone loosened* (10 ribs each). Stuff roasts and sprinkle with *salt* and *pepper;* insert a meat thermometer in each. Roast in a 325° oven 2½ to 3 hours or till thermometers register 160°. Cover loosely with foil after 1 hour to prevent overbrowning. Serve as directed.

For 20 servings, an easier way: Simplify preparation for a large gathering by roasting two unstuffed boneless roasts and serving with pesto sauce.

For sauce, in a bowl stir together 1¾ cups purchased pesto sauce and ¾ cup chopped sun-dried tomatoes* or pimiento. Cover; chill at least 2 hours.

Place two 3- to 4-pound *boneless pork top loin roasts,* doubled, rolled, and tied, in a shallow roasting pan. Sprinkle with *salt* and *pepper.* Insert a meat thermometer in each roast. Roast in a 325° oven 1¾ to 2¾ hours or till thermometers register 160°. Cover loosely with foil after 1 hour to prevent overbrowning.

Note: If using oil-packed sun-dried tomatoes, drain and chop. If using dry-packed sun-dried tomatoes, pour boiling water over chopped tomatoes; let stand for 2 minutes. Drain.

Nutrition information per serving: *363 cal., 30 g pro., 5 g carbo., 23 g fat, 82 mg chol., 200 mg sodium, 555 mg potassium, 1 g dietary fiber. U.S. RDA: 17% vit. C, 45% thiamine, 23% riboflavin, 27% niacin, 20% iron.*

POTATOES SUPREME

- Nonstick spray coating
- 6 medium potatoes (2 pounds)
- ½ of an 8-ounce container soft-style cream cheese with chives and onion
- ¼ teaspoon salt
- Milk (about ⅓ cup)
- 2 egg whites *or* 1 egg
- 1 tablespoon grated Parmesan cheese
- 1 tablespoon fine dry bread crumbs
- 2 teaspoons margarine *or* butter, melted

● **Spray** 6 individual soufflé dishes with nonstick spray coating. Set aside.
● **Peel and cut up** potatoes. Cook, covered, in boiling salted water for 10 to 15 minutes or till tender. Drain. Mash with an electric mixer on low speed. Add cream cheese, salt, and dash *pepper.* Gradually beat in enough of the milk to make potato mixture light and fluffy. Beat in egg whites or whole egg.
● **Spoon** potato mixture into a pastry bag fitted with a large star tip; pipe into dishes. (*Or,* simply spoon potato mixture into dishes, mounding on the top.)

● **In a small dish combine** Parmesan cheese, dry bread crumbs, and margarine; sprinkle over potatoes. If desired, cover and chill for up to 24 hours.
● **Bake in a 325° oven** for 25 to 30 minutes (30 to 35 minutes for chilled dishes) or till heated through. Makes 6 servings.

For 12 servings: Prepare Potatoes Supreme as directed, *except* double recipe, using 12 individual soufflé dishes.

For 20 servings: Spray two 12x7½x2-inch baking dishes with *nonstick spray coating.* Set aside.

In a 6-quart Dutch oven bring 6 cups *salted water* to boiling. Add two 32-ounce packages *loose-pack frozen hash brown potatoes.* Return to boiling. Cover and boil about 7 minutes or till tender. Drain.

Transfer *half* of the potatoes to a large mixer bowl. Mash with an electric mixer on low to medium speed. Add ¾ cup soft-style cream cheese with chives and onion, ¼ teaspoon salt, and ¼ teaspoon pepper. If necessary, gradually beat in a small amount of *milk* to make potatoes light and fluffy. Beat in 3 egg whites. Spoon most of the mixture into prepared dish, reserving some to pipe on the top, if desired.

Repeat mashing with remaining potatoes, another ¾ cup soft-style cream cheese with chives and onion, ¼ teaspoon salt, ¼ teaspoon pepper, and *milk,* if necessary. Beat in 3 egg whites. Spoon most into prepared dish, piping on top layer, if desired.

Combine ¼ cup grated Parmesan cheese, ¼ cup fine dry bread crumbs, and 3 tablespoons melted margarine; sprinkle atop potatoes. (If desired, cover and chill the dishes for up to 24 hours.)

To serve, bake in a 325° oven about 30 minutes (45 to 50 minutes for chilled baking dishes) or till heated through.

To do the final heating in your microwave oven: Cover baking dishes with vented plastic wrap. Micro-cook, one dish at a time, on 100% power (high) for 7 to 9 minutes (12 to 14 minutes for chilled dishes) or till heated through, giving dish a half-turn once.

Nutrition information per serving: *211 cal., 6 g pro., 28 g carbo., 9 g fat, 2 mg chol., 210 mg sodium, 780 mg potassium, 2 g dietary fiber. U.S. RDA: 31% vit. C, 11% niacin.*

SESAME HOLIDAY VEGETABLES

2 small fennel bulbs (about 6
  ounces each), cut into thin
  wedges
1 16-ounce package loose-pack
  frozen mixed broccoli, baby
  carrots, and water chestnuts
½ cup sliced celery
1 tablespoon sesame seed
1 tablespoon olive oil
1 tablespoon lemon juice
¼ teaspoon salt
¼ teaspoon pepper

● **In a large saucepan cook** fennel in a
small amount of boiling water, covered,
for 3 minutes. Add frozen vegetables
and celery. Return to boiling; reduce
heat. Cover and simmer 7 to 9 minutes
or till the vegetables are tender. Drain.
● **Meanwhile,** in a small skillet cook
sesame seed in hot olive oil for 1 to 2
minutes or till light brown. Remove
from heat. Carefully add lemon juice,
salt, and pepper.
● **Pour sesame mixture** over drained
vegetable mixture. Stir gently till coated. If desired, serve on a platter with
pork roast. Makes 6 servings.

*Microwave cooking directions
for 6 servings:* In a 2-quart microwave-
safe casserole, micro-cook the fennel
with 2 tablespoons *water,* covered, on
100% power (high) for 3 minutes. Add
the frozen vegetables and sliced celery.
Micro-cook, covered, for 8 to 10 minutes
or till crisp-tender. Meanwhile, prepare
the sesame mixture as directed. Drain
vegetables. Pour sesame mixture over
the vegetables. Gently stir till coated.
(Recipe not recommended for low-wattage microwave ovens.)

For 12 servings: Prepare Sesame
Holiday Vegetables as directed for on
the range top, *except* double the recipe.

For 20 servings: In a very large
kettle or 6- to 8-quart Dutch oven, cook
4 large fennel bulbs (about *1 pound
each*), cut into thin, halved wedges, in 4
cups boiling *water,* covered, for 3 minutes. Add *three 16-ounce packages* loose-
pack frozen mixed broccoli, baby
carrots, and water chestnuts and *2 cups*
sliced celery. Return to boiling; reduce
heat. Cover and simmer for 8 to 10 minutes or till tender. Drain.

Meanwhile, in a small saucepan or
skillet cook *¼ cup* sesame seed in *2 tablespoons* hot olive oil and 2 tablespoons *margarine* or *butter* for 1 to 2

minutes or just till seeds are light
brown. Remove from heat. Carefully
add ¼ cup lemon juice, ½ *teaspoon* salt,
and ½ *teaspoon* pepper. Pour sesame
mixture over drained vegetables. Stir
gently till coated. Serve as directed.

Nutrition information per serving:
*39 cal., 1 g pro., 3 g carbo., 3 g fat, 0 mg
chol., 143 mg sodium, 199 mg potassium, 3 g dietary fiber.*

WINTER GREENS
WITH CRANBERRY VINAIGRETTE

½ cup cranberry juice cocktail
2 tablespoons salad oil
1 tablespoon red wine vinegar
1 teaspoon sugar
½ teaspoon salt
1 small head romaine *or* leaf
  lettuce
1 head Belgian endive
1 cucumber, thinly bias-sliced
1 cup fresh enoki mushrooms
  (3½ ounces)
1 sweet red pepper, cut into thin
  bite-size strips*
½ cup alfalfa sprouts
1 avocado
Lemon juice

● **For dressing,** in a screw-top jar combine cranberry juice cocktail, oil, vinegar, sugar, and salt. Cover and shake
well. Chill till serving time.
● **Meanwhile, rinse** romaine and endive; pat dry. Line a platter with some
of the romaine and all of the endive.
Coarsely shred remaining romaine;
spread over platter. Arrange cucumber, mushrooms, red pepper, and
sprouts on lettuce-lined platter. If desired, cover and chill for up to 24 hours.
● **To serve,** halve, seed, peel, and thinly slice avocado; brush slices with lemon juice. Add avocado to platter. Shake
dressing; serve with salad. Serves 6.

For 12 servings: Prepare Winter
Greens with Cranberry Vinaigrette as
directed, *except* double the recipe.

For 20 servings: Prepare dressing
as directed, using *2 cups* cranberry
juice cocktail, ½ *cup* salad oil, *¼ cup*
red wine vinegar, *1 tablespoon* sugar,
and *1½ teaspoon* salt. Prepare salad as
directed, using 2 very large or 3 large
serving platters, *2 large heads* romaine,
3 heads Belgian endive, *4* cucumbers, *3
cups* fresh enoki mushrooms, *4* sweet
red peppers, *2 cups* alfalfa sprouts, and
4 avocados.

*Note: For softer looking red pepper strips, blanch the pepper strips in
boiling water for 1 to 2 minutes. Drain
well and chill completely.

Nutrition information per serving:
*192 cal., 4 g pro., 24 g carbo., 11 g fat, 0
mg chol., 203 mg sodium, 871 mg potassium, 3 g dietary fiber. U.S. RDA: 70%
vit. A, 113% vit. C, 14% thiamine, 21%
riboflavin, 19% niacin, 11% iron.*

SPIRAL BREADSTICKS

1 package (8) refrigerated
  breadsticks
8 10- to 12-inch metal skewers *or*
  wooden chopsticks
2 teaspoons milk
½ teaspoon sesame seed, poppy
  seed, paprika, *or* lemon-pepper
  seasoning

● **Unwind dough** to form strips. Cut *4*
of the strips in half crosswise; tie into
knots. Place on a greased baking sheet.
● **Cut** remaining *4* dough strips in half
lengthwise. Grease skewers or chopsticks. Roll *one* strip around *each* skewer or chopstick, stretching dough
slightly and leaving about ¼ inch of
space between dough twists. Place on
the greased baking sheet, tucking ends
of dough under to secure.
● **Brush all rolls** with milk; sprinkle
with your choice of seed or seasoning.
● **Bake in a 325° oven** for 15 to 20 minutes or till golden. Transfer to a wire
rack. Serve warm. Or, cool completely
and store in a moisture- and vaporproof
container.
● **To reheat,** wrap breadsticks in foil
and place in a 325° oven for 10 to 15
minutes or till warm. Or, place eight
bowknots or spirals on microwave-safe
paper towels. Micro-cook, uncovered,
on 100% power (high) for 20 to 30 seconds or till warm. Repeat as necessary
till all the bowknots and spirals are
heated. Makes 16 rolls.

For 12 servings: Prepare Spiral
Breadsticks as directed, *except* double
the recipe.

For 20 servings: Prepare Spiral
Breadsticks as directed, *except* triple
the recipe.

*Nutrition information per roll: 51
cal., 2 g pro., 8 g carbo., 1 g fat, 0 mg
chol., 117 mg sodium, 13 mg potassium,
0 g dietary fiber. U.S. RDA: 50%
thiamine.*

STEAMED CRANBERRY-CHERRY PUDDING WITH VANILLA CREAM

Layers of rich custard enhance today's new delicacies—dried cranberries and dried cherries. If desired, use just cherries or cranberries (1 cup total)—

- 4 beaten egg yolks
- 2 cups milk
- ½ cup sugar
- ¼ teaspoon salt
- 2 teaspoons vanilla
- 1 teaspoon finely shredded orange peel
- 1 cup orange juice
- ½ cup dried cherries
- ½ cup dried cranberries
- ½ cup light raisins
- 21 slices firm-texture white bread (such as French or Italian)
- 8 candied red cherries, halved
- ½ cup pecan halves
- 1 recipe Vanilla Cream

Orange peel star* (optional)

●**For custard,** in a heavy medium saucepan combine egg yolks, milk, sugar, and salt. Cook and stir constantly over medium heat till mixture coats a metal spoon. (Eggs easily overcook so be sure to use medium heat. Stir the mixture using a figure-eight motion to ensure even cooking. The stirred custard should be cooked in about 10 to 12 minutes.) Remove from heat; cool at once by placing pan in a sink of ice water and stirring for 1 to 2 minutes. Stir in vanilla and shredded orange peel. Cover surface with clear plastic wrap.

●**In a small saucepan heat** orange juice just to boiling. Remove from heat. Stir in dried cherries, cranberries, and raisins. Set aside.

●**With a serrated knife, remove** crusts from bread slices; reserve crusts for another use. Cut bread into ½-inch cubes. (You should have about *13 cups* bread cubes.) In a very large bowl combine custard and bread cubes; toss together.

●**Grease** a 2- to 2½-quart heatproof tower-type mold (with or without tube). Drain fruit, reserving juice. Arrange candied cherry halves in bottom of mold, cut side up. Top with *1 cup* of the bread-custard mixture. Sprinkle with *3 tablespoons* of the reserved juice. Add *half* of the pecans and *half* of the drained fruit on top, arranging some of

the pecans and fruit near the edge of the mold. Add *half* of the remaining bread-custard mixture, *4 tablespoons* of the reserved juice, and the remaining pecans and fruit. Add a last layer of bread mixture and sprinkle with *3 tablespoons* of the reserved juice, pressing with the back of a spoon. (Discard any remaining juice.)

●**Cover mold tightly** with foil. Place mold on a rack in a deep kettle; add *boiling* water to kettle to a depth of 1 inch. Return water to boiling; reduce heat so water simmers. Cover kettle, and steam pudding for 1¼ to 1½ hours or till puffed slightly and pudding springs back when touched, adding more *boiling* water to kettle as needed.

●**Remove mold from kettle;** let stand for 10 minutes. Carefully unmold pudding onto a serving platter.** Slice with a serrated knife, and serve warm with Vanilla Cream topped with an orange peel star, if desired. Makes 12 servings.

Reheating directions: If desired, cover and chill unmolded steamed pudding for up to 5 days. To heat, return pudding to same mold. Cover and resteam for 45 to 60 minutes or till warm. Let stand for 10 minutes; unmold and serve as directed.

Vanilla Cream: Just before serving, in a small mixer bowl beat 1 cup *whipping cream* and 2 tablespoons *sugar* just till soft peaks begin to form. Fold whipped cream into ½ cup *vanilla yogurt.* Serve immediately, decorated with an orange peel star, if desired. Makes about 2 cups.

To make orange peel star: Press a 1½-inch star-shape hors d'oeuvre cutter into a piece of orange peel.

Nutrition information per serving with 2 tablespoons Vanilla Cream: *368 cal., 8 g pro., 51 g carbo., 15 g fat, 123 mg chol., 323 mg sodium, 300 mg potassium, 2 g dietary fiber. U.S. RDA: 11% vit. A, 13% vit. C, 19% thiamine, 14% niacin, 11% calcium.*

LINZER APPLE TORTE

- 1½ cups all-purpose flour
- 1 cup ground hazelnuts (filberts) *or* almonds
- ⅓ cup sugar
- ¼ teaspoon ground cinnamon
- ½ cup margarine *or* butter
- 1 beaten egg

- ¼ cup margarine *or* butter
- 2 pounds apples *or* pears, peeled, cored, and sliced (6 cups)
- 1 tablespoon lemon juice
- ⅓ cup sugar
- 2 tablespoons all-purpose flour
- ⅛ teaspoon ground nutmeg
- ½ cup red raspberry preserves, melted*

Sugar (optional)

●**For crust,** in a mixing bowl stir together the 1½ cups flour, hazelnuts, ⅓ cup sugar, and cinnamon. Cut in the ½ cup margarine or butter till mixture resembles small peas. Add egg, stirring to blend well.

●**Reserve** *one-fourth* of the crust. Press the remaining crust onto the bottom and 1¼ inches up the sides of a 9-inch springform pan; set aside.

●**In a large saucepan melt** the ¼ cup margarine or butter; add apples and lemon juice. Cook, stirring gently, for 3 to 5 minutes or till apples are barely tender. Remove from heat.

●**In a small mixing bowl stir together** the remaining ⅓ cup sugar, the 2 tablespoons flour, and nutmeg; stir into apple mixture. Spread mixture evenly in the crust.

●**Bake in a 375° oven** for 35 to 40 minutes or till crust is brown. Cool on a rack. If desired, cover and store at room temperature for up to 24 hours. Or, cover and chill for up to several days.

●**Meanwhile,** form reserved crust into a ball; roll ⅛ inch thick. Cut into 1½-inch star shapes (about 10 stars total). Transfer stars to a baking sheet. Sprinkle with sugar, if desired. Bake in a 375° oven for 5 to 6 minutes or till light brown; cool. If desired, store in a tightly covered container at room temperature for up to several days.

●**At serving time,** remove pan sides from torte. Spread melted preserves over top of torte. Top with baked pastry stars. Let stand till preserves set up. Makes 8 to 10 servings.

To microwave-melt preserves: Place preserves in a microwave-safe dish. Micro-cook, uncovered, on 100% power (high) about 30 seconds or till melted.

Nutrition information per serving: *531 cal., 6 g pro., 65 g carbo., 30 g fat, 34 mg chol., 214 mg sodium, 233 mg potassium, 4 g dietary fiber. U.S. RDA: 16% vit. A, 18% thiamine, 12% iron.*

OYSTERS YEAR-ROUND

HOW TO BUY, SHUCK, AND SAVOR THEM

By Joy Taylor

Oysters are now available throughout the year! Buying and shucking them isn't as tough as you think—just follow our step-by-step instructions. Then, pop 'em into your mouth raw or try our super-simple recipe. Either is a grand way to savor these sea delicacies!

OYSTER-BUYING TIPS:

- **To confirm an oyster's freshness,** give the shell a tap. A truly fresh one will close its shell up tight.
- **Oysters in the shell** are usually sold by the dozen or by the bag. A bag contains about one bushel.
- **Fresh shucked oysters** can be purchased by the pint. Look for clear, not cloudy, liquid surrounding the oyster meat.
- **Three dozen oysters** in the shell equals about 1 pint of shucked oysters.
- **One dozen oysters** in the shell equals two appetizer servings.
- **Live oysters in the shell** last seven to 10 days on ice in the refrigerator; shucked oysters, a week when chilled.
- **Commercially frozen and canned oysters** may be used in oyster recipes, but the recipes won't taste quite the same as using fresh oysters. Always cook frozen or canned oysters.
- **Home freezing of oysters** is not recommended because the oyster flavor, texture, and color deteriorate.
- **Have the proper equipment** on hand to shuck your oysters. Use an oyster knife, a heavy piece of metal with a safety guard and a sturdy blade designed to open oysters. Wear a heavy work or garden glove to prevent the knife from poking your hand.
- **Cook oysters** till they are plump and firm, and edges begin to curl.

SCOTT LITTLE

SERVE OYSTERS AU GRATIN in their own dishes—the shells!

SHUCKING OYSTERS

CLEANING
To clean live oysters, scrub the shells with a scrub brush under cold running water.

OPENING
Using an oyster knife, insert the tip between shells, twisting to pry open. With blade, separate the top shell and muscle. Remove and discard the top shell.

SHUCKING
Slide knife under oyster to sever the muscle from the bottom shell. Rinse oyster, discarding any bits of shell. Rinse and use shell for serving the oyster.

OYSTERS AU GRATIN

- 20 oysters in shells
- 2 tablespoons finely chopped onion
- 1 tablespoon margarine
- 2 tablespoons all-purpose flour
- 1 8-ounce bottle clam juice
- 2 tablespoons grated Parmesan cheese
- ¼ cup fine dry Italian bread crumbs
- ¼ cup grated Parmesan cheese
- 2 tablespoons margarine, melted
- 1 tablespoon snipped cilantro *or* parsley
- Dash bottled hot pepper sauce

Thoroughly clean, open, and shuck oysters as directed in tip box, *below left.* Place oysters in rinsed and dried bottom shell halves.

For sauce, in a small saucepan cook onion in 1 tablespoon hot margarine till tender. Stir in flour. Add clam juice. Cook and stir till thickened and bubbly. Remove from heat. Stir in the 2 tablespoons cheese. Combine bread crumbs, the ¼ cup cheese, the 2 tablespoons melted margarine, cilantro, and hot pepper sauce. Spoon a *scant tablespoon* of the sauce over each oyster; sprinkle *1 teaspoon* of the crumb mixture atop.

Line a shallow pan with *rock salt* to a depth of ½ inch. (*Or,* use crumpled foil to keep shells from tipping.) Arrange oysters atop salt or crumpled foil. Bake in a 450° oven about 10 minutes or till heated through. Makes 4 appetizer servings or 2 main-dish servings.

Nutrition information per appetizer serving: 215 cal., 12 g pro., 12 g carbo., 13 g fat, 46 mg chol., 607 mg sodium, 123 mg potassium, 0 g dietary fiber. U.S. RDA: 13% vit. A, 36% vit. C, 10% thiamine, 12% riboflavin, 11% niacin, 21% calcium, 24% iron.

Holiday SWEETS

With Love from Grandma's Kitchen

⚘

BY BARBARA GOLDMAN

"BECAUSE I LOVE TRADITIONS!" explains Winnifred Jardine. So the Salt Lake City grandmom accounts for her candy- and cookie-making sessions with her grandchildren—and for dozens of Christmas sweets.

"I'd love my grandkids to remember these good times, and I do all I can to make them happen. I set up a date, and have ingredients on hand. It doesn't always come off perfectly," laughs this go-with-the-flow grandma, "but we're making traditions."

CHRISTMAS HUDDLE
Fun-loving Stuart and Winnifred Jardine cozy up with the six youngest of 10 Jardine grandkids for a casual family portrait.

GINGER DUET
Ginger-haired Liz makes superb ginger cookies. "Better than I make," brags her proud grandmom.

HOLIDAY SWEETS

Candy-making has been part of Winnifred's Christmas ever since she was a girl in Ames, Iowa. A former newspaper food editor, she has never given up the candy-making tradition. Melt-in-your-mouth caramels and nougats are the sugarplum stars in her household, and not just at holiday time.

"In the middle of summer," she laughs, "the grandkids will walk into the house and ask, 'Grandma, do you have a caramel?'"

TOFFEE TIME
Winn dips toffee into melted chocolate, daughter Ann covers it with nuts, and granddaughter Sarah gets ready to sample!

①
WINNIFRED'S NOUGATS

②
CREAMY CARAMELS

③
LICORICE CARAMELS

④
ELEGANT TOFFEE

IT'S EASY! JUST LIKE THIS!
Big sister Emily shows Griffin how to wrap caramels so that they'll pack neatly in a gift box.

WINNIFRED'S NOUGATS

Winn's two-step method allows you the option of making the first part ahead—

PART 1
1½ cups sugar
1¼ cups light corn syrup
¼ cup water
2 large egg whites

• **In a heavy 3-quart saucepan** combine sugar, syrup, and water; mix well. Cook over medium-high heat to boiling, stirring constantly with a wooden spoon to dissolve sugar. This should take 5 to 7 minutes. Avoid splashing mixture on sides of pan to prevent sugar crystals from forming. Carefully clip a candy thermometer to side of pan.
• **Cook over medium heat,** without stirring, to soft-ball stage (238°). Mixture should boil at a moderate, steady rate over entire surface. (Watch closely; mixture reaches soft-ball stage in 5 to 6 minutes.) Remove from heat; remove thermometer from saucepan.

Cook candy mixture (Part 1) to 238°; the mixture should boil at a moderate, steady rate.

• **In a large mixer bowl** *immediately* beat egg whites with a sturdy, free-standing electric mixer (do *not* use hand mixer) on medium speed till soft peaks form (tips curl). *Gradually* pour hot syrup in thin stream (slightly less than ⅛-inch diameter) over egg whites, beating with electric mixer on medium speed. This should take 2 to 3 minutes.
• **After all syrup is added,** continue beating till mixture reaches consistency of marshmallow crème. This should take 5 to 7 minutes. Let stand at room temperature while preparing Part 2. (*Or,* chill in the refrigerator. Mixture will keep several days in refrigerator if well covered with foil or waxed paper.)

After adding hot syrup to the beaten egg whites, beat to consistency of marshmallow crème.

PART 2
3 cups sugar
3 cups light corn syrup
½ cup butter (not margarine), melted
1 tablespoon vanilla
3 cups slivered almonds (¾ pound), toasted
¼ teaspoon salt (optional)

If candy from Part 1 has been stored in the refrigerator, let it stand at room temperature while preparing Part 2. Line two 8x8x2-inch baking pans with foil, extending the foil over the edges of pan. Butter the foil; sprinkle with a small amount of *cornstarch*. Set aside.
• **In a heavy 3-quart saucepan** combine sugar and corn syrup. Cook over medium heat, stirring constantly, till sugar dissolves and mixture boils, about 10 minutes. Without stirring, continue to cook till mixture reaches soft-crack stage (272°), 13 to 15 minutes. (Mixture should boil at a moderate, steady rate over entire surface.)
• **Meanwhile, place candy** from Part 1 in a lightly buttered 4-quart bowl. Pour hot candy (Part 2) into bowl all at once. Mix with a wooden spoon till blended. Thoroughly stir in melted butter and vanilla. Stir in almonds and salt.
• **Quickly turn nougat mixture** into prepared pans. Let stand for several hours. Nougat may vary a little in firmness from one batch to another. If mix-

Pour the hot candy mixture (Part 2) over the cooled candy mixture (Part 1) all at once.

ture is a little soft and sticky, chill a few minutes before cutting.
• **Use foil to lift candy out of pan** onto a cutting board. Peel foil away; discard. With a sharp buttered knife, cut candy into 4 squares; cut each square into 16 pieces, making 64 pieces. Wrap in waxed paper. (If candy is sticky, rub cut edges with *cornstarch*, dusting off excess before wrapping.) Repeat with remaining pan. Keep in a covered container in a cool place, or in refrigerator. Makes 128 pieces (4½ to 5 pounds).

With a buttered knife cut candy into 4 squares; cut each square into 16 equal pieces.

To wrap: Tear off 6-inch strips of waxed paper. Cut strips into 4-inch widths, making pieces 6x4 inches. Roll nougat in length of paper. Fold flaps *under*. Set into boxes, flaps underneath.
Nutrition information per piece: *81 cal., 1 g pro., 16 g carbo., 2 g fat, 2 mg chol., 16 mg sodium, 21 mg potassium.*

Tips For Success In Making Candy

- **Read candy recipes thoroughly** before you begin to cook. See what equipment you'll need. Note how much attention and time are required to cook, beat, and cool the candy. Allow plenty of time to prepare the recipe.
- **Assemble all equipment,** and measure all of your ingredients before you begin to cook.
- **Don't make substitutions** for basic ingredients or alter the ingredient amounts in your candy recipes.
- **Use a heavy saucepan** to cook candies. High-quality aluminum pans are a good choice because they conduct heat evenly.
- **Stir constantly but gently** as you cook the mixture to dissolve the sugar, so it won't splash on the sides of the pan. You want to prevent sugar crystals from forming on the sides of the pan and clumping together. A wooden spoon works best for stirring.
- **To prevent crystal formation,** occasionally wash down the sides of the saucepan with a pastry brush dipped in a little water. Or, cover the saucepan and cook for 30 to 45 seconds if some of the candy mixture splashes on the sides of the pan. As the steam condenses, it will dissolve any crystals that may have formed on the pan sides. But watch carefully so your candy doesn't boil over!
- **Use a candy thermometer** for accuracy in cooking candy to the correct degree of doneness. Clip the thermometer to the side of your saucepan after the sugar is dissolved. For an accurate reading, make sure the bulb of the candy thermometer is completely covered with boiling liquid, not just with foam.

And make sure the bulb of the thermometer doesn't touch the bottom or sides of the pan.
- **Check the accuracy** of your candy thermometer before every use.

To check a thermometer's accuracy: Place the thermometer in a saucepan of boiling water for a few minutes. Read the temperature. If it registers above or below 212°, add or subtract the same number of degrees from the recipe temperature and cook to *that* temperature. For instance, if your thermometer reads 209° rather than 212°, cook the candy 3 degrees *lower* than the recipe states.
- **Boil candy mixtures** at a moderate, steady rate, so the mixture bubbles moderately and evenly over the entire surface. Occasionally you may have to lower or raise the suggested temperature in order to do this, as every range top cooks differently. Cooking the candy mixture too quickly or too slowly may cause the candy to become too hard or too soft.

ELEGANT TOFFEE

Winn coats this luscious toffee on both sides with milk chocolate, then dips it into ground walnuts. No wonder it disappears so fast—

- 1 cup unblanched whole almonds
- 1 cup butter (may use half margarine)
- 1 cup sugar
- ½ teaspoon vanilla
- ¼ teaspoon salt
- 1 12-ounce package real milk-chocolate pieces
- ½ pound walnuts (2 generous cups), finely ground

- **On a foil-lined baking sheet** arrange the almonds in a single layer over an area measuring 12x7 inches; set aside.
- **In a heavy 2-quart saucepan** combine butter, sugar, vanilla, and salt. Cook over high heat, stirring constantly with a clean, dry, wooden spoon till butter is melted. Continue cooking and stirring for 5 to 7 minutes or till candy is the color of unblanched almonds. *Immediately* pour candy, without scraping pan, over almonds, covering all nuts. Cool completely.
- **Meanwhile,** in the top part of a double boiler, melt chocolate over hot (not boiling) water. (*Or,* melt chocolate in a heavy saucepan over low heat stirring constantly; or in a microwave oven in a 1-cup glass measure, uncovered, on 100% power (high) for 1 to 2 minutes or till chocolate is soft enough to stir smooth, stirring every minute.) Break toffee into large pieces. Set top part of double boiler containing chocolate on work surface. Place ground walnuts in a large bowl near the chocolate.
- **Using a fork,** dip each piece of toffee in the melted chocolate, spreading chocolate over toffee in a thin, even layer. Scrape off excess chocolate with another fork. Using two other forks, coat each piece very lightly with ground walnuts. Place on foil or waxed paper to set. Break into serving-size pieces. Store in a tightly covered container in the refrigerator. Makes 2 pounds or 25 pieces.

Nutrition information per piece: 227 cal., 3 g pro., 15 g carbo., 18 g fat, 21 mg chol., 103 mg sodium, 120 mg potassium, 1 g dietary fiber.

CREAMY CARAMELS

Winn says that waiting 3 minutes between adding each ¼ cup of cream makes these caramels extra creamy. But if you don't have time to wait, don't worry. They'll still turn out almost as creamy. Either way, you can't lose—

- 3 **cups whipping cream**
- ½ **of a 14-ounce can (⅔ cup)** *sweetened condensed* **milk**
- 2 **cups sugar**
- 2 **cups light corn syrup**
- ¼ **teaspoon salt**
- 1 **cup broken walnuts**
- 2 **teaspoons vanilla**

● **Line** an 8x8x2-inch baking pan with foil, extending foil over edges of pan. Butter the foil; set aside.

● **In the top of a double boiler** combine whipping cream and sweetened condensed milk. Heat over gently boiling water (upper pan should not touch water) till warm; reduce heat to lowest setting to keep cream warm.

● **In a heavy 3-quart saucepan** combine the sugar, corn syrup, and salt; mix well.

● **Cook over medium-high heat** to boiling, stirring constantly with a wooden spoon to dissolve sugar. Avoid splashing the mixture on sides of pan. Cook for 1 minute more. Reduce heat to medium.

● **Carefully clip** the candy thermometer to the side of the pan. Very slowly add the warm cream mixture to the syrup, about ¼ cup at a time, stirring well after each addition. It will take 10 to 15 minutes for the total addition. (For a creamier caramel, stir for about 3 minutes after adding each ¼ cup of the cream. Winnifred allows about 45 minutes to add all of the cream.) Continue to cook candy mixture, stirring frequently, till the candy thermometer registers 242°. The mixture should boil at a moderate, steady rate over the entire surface. From the time you start to

add cream to the point of the thermometer reaching 242°, it will take a total cooking time of 45 to 55 minutes.

● **Remove the candy mixture** from the heat; remove the candy thermometer from the saucepan. Immediately stir in the walnuts and vanilla. Quickly pour mixture, without scraping pan, into the buttered-foil-lined pan. Allow to stand for several hours till set. (Caramel varies somewhat in firmness. If it seems a little soft, refrigerate for a few minutes before cutting. If it is firmer than you like, keep it at room temperature before cutting.)

● **Use foil to lift the candy** out of the pan onto a cutting board. Peel away foil; discard. With a buttered sharp knife, immediately cut the candy into 4 squares. Cut each square into 16 pieces, making 64 pieces total. (If not cut shortly after being removed from the pan, the candy may soften a little and the caramels may lose the clean rigidity that gives them their nice shape.) Wrap each caramel individually in waxed paper. Store in a covered plastic container in a cool place. Makes 64 pieces (about 3½ pounds).

Chocolate Caramels: Prepare Creamy Caramels as directed, *except* add 3 squares (3 ounces) *unsweetened chocolate*, cut up, after adding cream mixture to syrup; stir till melted. Continue to cook candy mixture, stirring frequently, till candy thermometer registers 242°. Continue as directed.

To wrap caramels: Tear off 6-inch strips of waxed paper; cut each strip into 4-inch widths, making pieces 6x4 inches. Roll caramel in length of paper; fold flaps *under*. Set caramels into gift boxes with flaps underneath. The caramels will pack neatly and stay tightly wrapped.

Nutrition information per piece: *114 cal., 1 g pro., 16 g carbo., 6 g fat, 16 mg chol., 23 mg sodium, 30 mg potassium.*

There's more than one way to eat a creamy caramel.

High-Altitude Adjustments in Making Candy

If you live at an altitude above 1,000 feet, you will need to make adjustments in your candy recipes' cooking temperatures. The cooking temperatures that are given in these recipes are for sea level. A rule of thumb when cooking candies at high altitude is to decrease the temperature in a candy recipe 2 degrees for each 1,000 feet of elevation. That's because rapid evaporation causes candies to concentrate more quickly at high altitudes. However, it is far more accurate to determine the temperature adjustment needed for your *particular* altitude before you prepare a candy recipe.

To do this, follow the same instructions given for checking your thermometer's accuracy (see *"To check a thermometer's accuracy," page 181*). At higher altitudes your thermometer will register less than 212° in boiling water. Simply subtract from your recipe's cooking temperature the number of degrees less than 212° that your thermometer registers. For example, if the thermometer registers 204°, subtract 8° (212° minus 204°) from the temperature in the recipe.

LICORICE CARAMELS

A mild, unbelievably delicious licorice flavor. You'll find black and red paste for coloring these candies in specialty and cake-decorating stores. The black caramels also make great Halloween treats—

1 cup butter (not margarine)
2 cups sugar
1 14-ounce can (1¼ cups) *sweetened condensed* milk
1 cup light corn syrup
⅛ teaspoon salt
1 teaspoon anise extract
½ teaspoon black *or* red coloring paste

● **Line** a 9x9x2-inch baking pan with foil, extending foil over the edges of pan. Butter the foil; set aside.
● **In a heavy 3-quart saucepan** melt the butter over low heat. Add the sugar, sweetened condensed milk, corn syrup, and salt; mix well. Carefully clip a candy thermometer to side of the pan.
● **Cook over medium heat,** stirring frequently, till candy thermometer registers 244°, firm-ball stage. The mixture should boil at a moderate, steady rate over entire surface. Reaching firm-ball stage should take 15 to 20 minutes. (Mixture scorches easily.) Remove from heat; remove candy thermometer from saucepan. Add anise extract and coloring; stir to mix.
● **Quickly pour candy,** without scraping, into the buttered-foil-lined pan. Cool for several hours or till firm. Use foil to lift candy out of pan onto cutting board. Peel foil away; discard. With a buttered sharp knife, cut immediately into 1-inch squares; wrap individually in waxed paper. Makes 81 pieces (about 2¾ pounds).

To wrap caramels: Tear off 6-inch strips of waxed paper; cut each strip into 4-inch widths, making pieces 6x4 inches. Roll caramel in length of paper; fold flaps *under.* Set caramels into gift boxes with flaps underneath. The caramels will pack neatly and stay tightly wrapped.

Nutrition information per piece:
84 cal., 1 g pro., 13 g carbo., 3 g fat, 10 mg chol., 24 mg sodium, 24 mg potassium.

BIG SOFT GINGER COOKIES

These cookies soften even more a day after baking. The big soft ginger cookies, with their spicy aroma and taste, are a Jardine trademark. The family takes them as hostess gifts and sends them in care packages to students—

2¼ cups all-purpose flour
2 teaspoons ground ginger
1 teaspoon baking soda
¾ teaspoon ground cinnamon
½ teaspoon ground cloves
¼ teaspoon salt (optional)
¾ cup margarine, butter, *or* shortening
1 cup sugar
1 egg
¼ cup molasses
2 tablespoons sugar

● **Combine** the flour; ginger; soda; cinnamon; cloves; and salt, if desired. Set aside.
● **In a large mixing bowl** beat margarine, butter, or shortening with an electric mixer on low speed for 30 seconds to soften. Gradually add the 1 cup sugar; beat till fluffy. Add egg and molasses; beat well. Stir flour mixture into beaten mixture.
● **Shape into 1½-inch balls** (1 heaping tablespoon dough each). Roll in the remaining 2 tablespoons sugar and place on an ungreased cookie sheet about 2½ inches apart.
● **Bake in a 350° oven** about 10 minutes or till light brown and still puffed. (Do not overbake.) Let stand for 2 minutes before transferring to a wire rack. Cool. Makes 24 three-inch cookies.

Nutrition information per cookie:
142 cal., 2 g pro., 21 g carbo., 6 g fat, 11 mg chol., 118 mg sodium, 56 mg potassium.

BROWNED BUTTER COOKIES

A delicate cake-soft cookie frosted with browned butter icing—

2½ cups all-purpose flour
1 teaspoon baking soda
½ teaspoon baking powder
¼ teaspoon salt
1½ cups packed brown sugar
½ cup margarine *or* butter
2 eggs
1 teaspoon vanilla
1 cup dairy sour cream
1 cup coarsely chopped walnuts
1 recipe Browned Butter Icing

● **Combine** the flour, soda, baking powder, and salt; set aside.
● **In a large mixing bowl** combine brown sugar and margarine or butter; beat with an electric mixer on medium speed till well combined. Beat in eggs and vanilla till fluffy. Add flour mixture to beaten mixture along with the sour cream, mixing well. Stir in walnuts. Drop by teaspoonfuls onto a greased cookie sheet.
● **Bake in a 350° oven** about 10 minutes or till set. Transfer cookies to a wire rack. Cool; frost with Browned Butter Icing. Makes 56 cookies.

Browned Butter Icing: In a small saucepan heat ¼ cup *butter* (not margarine) over medium heat till butter turns the color of light brown sugar. Remove from heat. Stir in 2 cups *sifted powdered sugar* and enough *boiling water* (1 to 2 tablespoons) to make icing smooth and of spreading consistency. Frost cookies immediately. If frosting becomes grainy, soften with a few more drops of hot water.

Nutrition information per cookie:
104 cal., 1 g pro., 14 g carbo., 5 g fat, 14 mg chol., 66 mg sodium, 46 mg potassium.

PEPPER COOKIES

½ cup margarine *or* butter
½ cup sugar
½ cup dark corn syrup
1½ teaspoons vinegar
1 slightly beaten egg
2¼ cups all-purpose flour
½ teaspoon baking soda
½ teaspoon ground ginger
½ teaspoon ground cinnamon
½ teaspoon ground cloves
¼ teaspoon pepper

● **In a medium saucepan melt** margarine or butter. Add sugar, corn syrup, and vinegar. Bring *just* to boiling; remove mixture immediately from heat and cool to room temperature. Stir in the egg.

● **Combine** flour, soda, ginger, cinnamon, cloves, and pepper; stir into egg mixture, mixing well. Cover and refrigerate for several hours or overnight.

● **Divide dough into 4 portions.** Chill till ready to roll out. On a lightly floured surface roll dough very thin (less than ⅛ inch thick); cut into desired shapes with cookie cutters. Place on a greased cookie sheet.

● **Bake at 375°** for 4 to 5 minutes or till edges are lightly browned. Immediately transfer to a rack; cool. Store in airtight containers. Recipe is easily doubled. Makes 120 two-inch cookies.

Nutrition information per cookie: 24 cal., 0 g pro., 4 g carbo., 1 g fat, 2 mg chol., 15 mg sodium, 4 mg potassium.

Liz holds a plate of Honey Sand Balls while Grandpa holds the baby.

HONEY SAND BALLS

1 cup butter (not margarine), softened
½ cup sifted powdered sugar
2 tablespoons honey
2 cups all-purpose flour
¾ cup chopped walnuts
1 teaspoon vanilla
¼ teaspoon salt
Sifted powdered sugar

● **In a large mixing bowl beat** together butter, the ½ cup powdered sugar, and honey. Add flour, nuts, vanilla, and salt; mix thoroughly, using hands if necessary. Shape into 1-inch balls. Place 1½ inches apart on a greased cookie sheet.

● **Bake in a 325° oven** for 14 to 16 minutes or till the cookies are very lightly browned. While cookies are still warm, roll them in powdered sugar. Cool. Roll cookies in powdered sugar again. Makes 48 cookies.

Nutrition information per cookie: 76 cal., 1 g pro., 7 g carbo., 5 g fat, 10 mg chol., 50 mg sodium, 16 mg potassium.

HOLIDAY TEA RINGS

4¼ to 4¾ cups all-purpose flour
1 package active dry yeast
1 cup milk
½ cup margarine *or* butter
½ cup sugar
¾ teaspoon salt
3 eggs
⅓ cup margarine *or* butter, melted
½ cup sugar
½ cup candied red cherries, chopped*
½ cup candied green cherries, chopped*
½ cup candied pineapple, chopped*
½ cup chopped pecans
1 recipe Rum Icing

In a large mixer bowl stir together *2 cups* of the all-purpose flour and the yeast.

● **In a medium saucepan heat** the milk, the *½ cup* margarine or butter, the ½ cup sugar, and the salt till warm (120° to 130°). Add the milk mixture and the eggs to the flour mixture. Beat with an electric mixer on low speed for 30 seconds, scraping the sides of the bowl. Beat on high speed for 3 minutes. Using a wooden spoon, stir in as much of the remaining flour as you can.

● **Cover and refrigerate the dough** for 6 to 24 hours. Stir down dough.

● **Grease 3 pans,** using either 9-inch pie plates, 8x1½-inch round baking pans, or 9x1½-inch round baking pans; set aside.

● **Divide the dough** into 3 portions. On a lightly floured surface, roll one portion into a rectangle, about 14x8 inches. Brush the rectangle of dough with *one-third* of the melted margarine or butter. Sprinkle rectangle with *one-third* of the remaining ½ cup sugar. Sprinkle with *one-third* of the candied cherries, the candied pineapple, and the nuts.

● **Roll rectangle of dough up loosely** starting from a long side; pinch edges together. Shape the roll into a circle, pinching the ends together. Place the circle of dough in a prepared pie plate or in a baking pan. Using scissors, cut from the outer edge almost through to the center at 1-inch intervals; twist each 1-inch piece a half-turn to the left to form a tea ring. Repeat with the 2 remaining portions of dough to make 2 more tea rings.

● **Cover lightly** with plastic wrap; allow the dough to rise for 6 to 24 hours in the refrigerator. Bake tea rings in a 375° oven about 20 minutes or till light brown. Transfer to a wire rack. Brush tea rings with Rum Icing while hot. Serve tea rings warm or at room temperature. (Or, to freeze, wrap the cooled tea rings thoroughly in freezer wrap; seal, label, and freeze. Store tea rings for up to 3 months in the freezer. To serve, thaw tea rings overnight at room temperature.) Makes 3 tea rings (24 servings).

Rum Icing: In a small mixing bowl stir together 1 cup *sifted powdered sugar,* ¼ teaspoon *rum extract,* and enough *hot water* (about 1 to 2 tablespoons) to make of icing consistency.

Note: You may substitute 1½ cups of diced mixed candied fruits and peels for the candied cherries and candied pineapple.

Nutrition information per serving: 258 cal., 4 g pro., 40 g carbo., 10 g fat, 32 mg chol., 156 mg sodium, 116 mg potassium, 1 g dietary fiber. U.S. RDA: 14% thiamine.

HOMEMADE CINNAMON ROLLS
OUR GOOF-PROOF METHOD ENSURES FABULOUS RESULTS

BY JOY TAYLOR

Some things in life are just best when they're homemade. And, cinnamon rolls, warm from your oven, top the list. As the aroma drifts from the kitchen, your family will clamor for a fresh-baked sample.

Seconds will be just as popular. Simply wrap and freeze half the batch, then thaw and glaze to enjoy.

JUMBO CINNAMON ROLLS

- 4¼ to 4¾ cups all-purpose flour
- 1 package active dry yeast
- 1¼ cups milk
- ¼ cup granulated sugar
- ¼ cup margarine *or* butter
- 1 teaspoon salt
- 2 eggs

• • •

- 6 tablespoons margarine *or* butter, softened
- ½ cup packed brown sugar
- 2 teaspoons ground cinnamon
- 1 recipe Maple Nut Glaze *or* Powdered Sugar Glaze

Step 1: In a large mixer bowl combine *1½ cups* of the all-purpose flour and yeast. Heat the milk, granulated sugar, the ¼ cup margarine or butter, and salt just till mixture is warm (120° to 130°) and the margarine is almost melted, stirring constantly.

Step 2: Add milk mixture to flour mixture; add eggs. Beat with an electric mixer on low speed for 30 seconds; scrape sides of bowl constantly. Beat on high speed for 3 minutes. Using a spoon, stir in as much of the remaining flour as you can. (Dough will be soft.) Turn dough out onto a lightly floured surface. Knead in enough of the remaining flour to make a moderately soft dough (3 to 5 minutes total). Shape dough into a ball.

Every once in a while, treat your family to the superb taste of these foolproof homemade cinnamon rolls.

PHOTOGRAPHS: SCOTT LITTLE

(A) Moisten: Brushing dough edges with water makes them easier to seal.

(B) Cut: To slice easily, pull thread quickly around roll as if tying a knot.

Step 3: Place dough in a lightly greased bowl; turn once. Cover; let rise in a warm place till double (about 1 to 1½ hours). (The dough is ready for shaping when you can lightly and quickly press two fingers ½ inch into dough and indentation remains.)

Step 4: Punch dough down. On a lightly floured surface divide dough in half; shape each half into a smooth ball. Cover; let rest for 10 minutes.

Step 5: On lightly floured surface roll *half* the dough to 12x8 inches. Spread with *3 tablespoons* softened margarine. Combine brown sugar and cinnamon; sprinkle *half* over rectangle. Roll up from a short side. Seal edges (*see photo A*). Make a second roll with remaining dough, margarine, and sugar mixture.

Step 6: Slice each dough roll into 8 pieces (*see photo B*). Arrange slices, cut-side down, in a greased 13x9x2-inch baking pan. Cover; let rise till nearly double (about 30 minutes).

Step 7: Bake rolls in a 350° oven for 25 to 30 minutes or till light brown. Invert at once onto a wire rack. Cool slightly. Drizzle rolls with Maple Nut Glaze or Powdered Sugar Glaze. Serve warm. Makes 16 rolls.

Maple Nut Glaze: In small bowl combine 1 cup sifted *powdered sugar*, 2 tablespoons *maple syrup* or ½ teaspoon *maple extract*, and enough *water* or *milk* (2 to 3 teaspoons) for drizzling consistency. Stir in ¼ cup coarsely chopped *pecans*.

Powdered Sugar Glaze: Combine 1 cup sifted *powdered sugar*, 1 teaspoon *vanilla*, and enough *milk* (about 3 to 4 teaspoons) for drizzling consistency.

Nutrition information per roll with Maple Nut Glaze: 289 cal., 5 g pro., 45 g carbo., 10 g fat, 36 mg chol., 239 mg sodium, 120 mg potassium, and 1 g dietary fiber. U.S. RDA: 17% thiamine, 13% riboflavin, 10% niacin, and 12% iron.

FREEZING AND REHEATING

● Bake and cool rolls as directed; *do not* glaze. Wrap in moisture- and vaporproof wrap. Seal, label, and freeze for up to 3 months.

● To reheat in a conventional oven, wrap frozen rolls in foil. Place in a 350° oven for 20 to 25 minutes or till warm. Drizzle with your choice of glaze.

● To reheat in a microwave oven, wrap *2* of the frozen rolls in microwave-safe paper towels. Micro-cook on 100% power (high) for 1 to 1½ minutes or till warm. Drizzle with glaze.

GOOD GOSH, WINTER SQUASH!
NEW VARIETIES TO PICK FROM

BY JOY TAYLOR

The supermarket produce section is hot! New fruits and vegetables and new varieties of old ones brighten this grocery cart stop. This time of year, the hottest choices include all kinds of winter squash, some of which actually are available all year long.

Each variety looks and tastes unique, but all are nutritious—high in fiber and vitamins, low in calories, and fat free.

Serve them elegantly when entertaining or prepare them simply for family meals. Here's a guide to help you pick and choose.

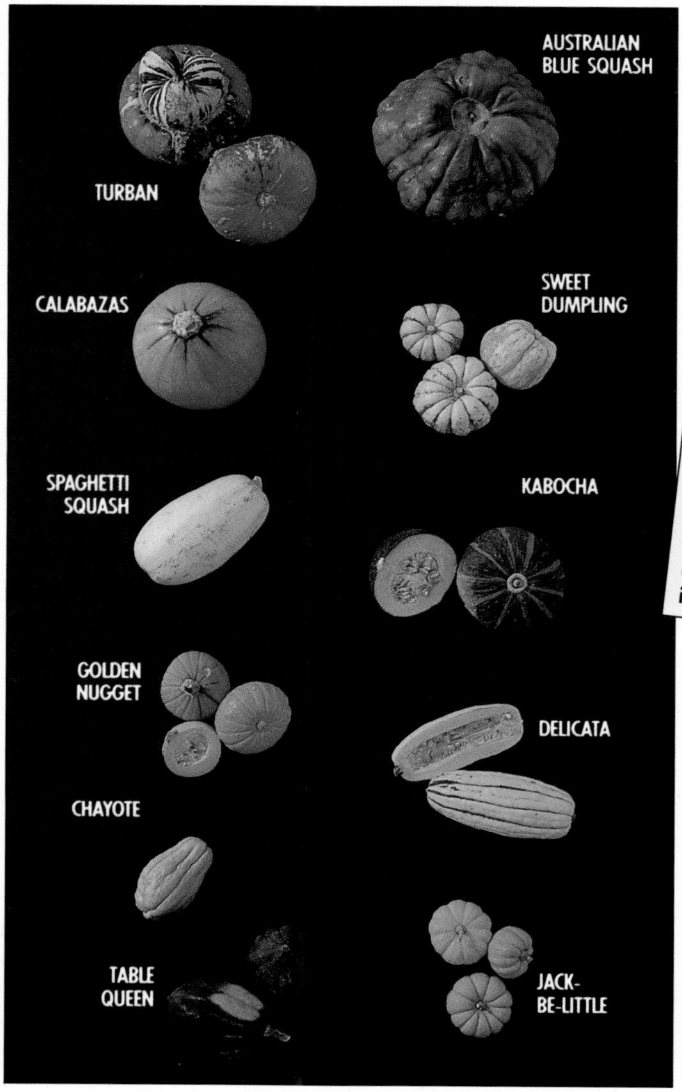

● **Australian Blue Squash** tastes better than it looks. Inside this large lumpy, bluish-gray squash, the flesh is orange, sweet, and flavorful.

● **Calabazas** is also known as West Indian Pumpkin, Cuban Squash, and Toadback. This squash is large and rounded with an orange-yellow flesh that is fine-grained, sweet, and moist.

● **Chayote,** a popular Cajun and Mexican vegetable, is also called Mirliton, Choko, and vegetable pear. Pear-shaped with pale green, irregularly furrowed skin, it has one inedible seed in the center. The flavor is a mild cross between apple and cucumber.

● **Delicata or Sweet Potato Squash** resembles a miniature watermelon with green- and yellow-striped skin. The flavor is slightly cornlike.

● **Golden Nugget** looks like a small golden pumpkin. This hard-skinned squash has a smooth-textured orange

AUSTRALIAN BLUE SQUASH

TURBAN

CALABAZAS

SWEET DUMPLING

SPAGHETTI SQUASH

KABOCHA

GOLDEN NUGGET

DELICATA

CHAYOTE

TABLE QUEEN

JACK-BE-LITTLE

flesh with a slightly sweet, true squash flavor. Cook this squash whole and unpeeled because it is so difficult to split open when uncooked.

● **Jack-Be-Little** tastes almost like pumpkin. The biggest mistake you may make is thinking that these jack-o'-lantern look-alikes are just ornamental. Their size makes them perfect for a single serving, and also for stuffing.

● **Kabocha** is a generic grouping as well as a specific marketing name for many strains of Japanese pumpkins and winter squash. It has an excellent flavor and an almost fiberless texture. If using this squash in a recipe, use less sugar and more liquid, because it is sweet and dry.

● **Spaghetti Squash** is now more popular than ever. When cooked, the flesh of this oval, golden-yellow squash forms pale, spaghettilike strands that taste sweet and mild.

● **Sweet Dumpling** is a miniature pumpkin-shaped squash that can vary in color from pale yellow to cream colored with vertical green stripes. Perfect for a single serving, the cooked flesh is like sweet-tasting pumpkin.

● **Table Queen,** an acorn squash variety, is now more abundant. It is acorn-shaped with smooth glossy skin, tender orange flesh, and a large cavity—ideal for stuffing.

● **Turban,** sometimes called Buttercup, comes in bizarre shapes with intriguing colors, which makes them popular ornamentals. The orange flesh of the turban is one of the sweetest tasting of the squash varieties.

SCOTT LITTLE

BY JOY TAYLOR

Nutty and Nice!

NEW FANCY RICE THAT'S WORTH THE PRICE

There's rice. And then there's *aromatic rice!* More than ever before, basmati, Texmati™, Wild Pecan®, and popcorn rice show up in fancy food shops and in mail-order catalogs. While simmering, each smells like toasting nuts or popping corn. And their nutty taste lives up to that tantalizing aroma.

Use the basic cooking directions below when you plan to serve aromatic rice as a simple side dish. Or sample any one of them in Rice Pilaf Supreme.

TYPES OF AROMATIC RICES

● *Basmati rice:* If rice were judged for beauty, this would be one of the winners. The slender, white grains are a staple in Indian cooking.
● *Texmati™ rice:* This rice is the Texas-grown version of basmati. It looks and tastes quite similar to basmati rice. Both rices cook up very fluffy.
● *Wild Pecan® rice:* No nuts here! The pecanlike aroma and taste name this delicious rice. The grains look like brown rice.
● *Popcorn rice:* You'll think of popcorn when you smell the rice cooking!

HOW TO COOK

To cook, follow individual package directions. Or, use 2 cups water or broth to 1 cup rice. Cover and simmer. Allow 20 to 25 minutes cooking time till the rice is tender and all of the liquid is absorbed.

Rice Pilaf Supreme made with basmati rice. Try it with a simple fish or meat entrée.

SCOTT LITTLE

RICE PILAF SUPREME

The earthy flavor of the mushrooms blends with the taste of the rice for a heavenly result. You can change this recipe over and over again by varying the vegetables and seasonings each time you make it—
  ¼ cup dried mushrooms
  ● ● ●
  1 shallot, finely chopped
  2 tablespoons margarine *or* butter
  1 cup basmati, Texamati™, Wild Pecan®, *or* popcorn rice
  1½ cups chicken broth
  ½ cup dry white wine *or* apple juice
  ½ cup sliced celery
  ● ● ●
  2 cups torn spinach leaves
  1 2-ounce jar diced pimiento, drained

Soak the dried mushrooms in enough *hot water* to cover for 30 minutes. Drain; remove and discard stems. Chop the mushrooms.

In a 2-quart saucepan cook the shallot in hot margarine or butter till tender but not brown. Add the rice; cook and stir the shallot-rice mixture over medium heat for 2 minutes or till the rice is light brown.

Carefully pour in the chicken broth and the wine or juice; add the chopped mushrooms and celery. Bring the mixture to boiling; reduce heat. Cover and simmer mixture for 20 to 25 minutes or till the rice is tender and the liquid is absorbed. Stir in the torn spinach and pimiento. Serve pilaf immediately. Makes 6 to 8 side-dish servings.

Nutrition information per serving: 187 cal., 4 g pro., 29 g carbo., 4 g fat, 0 mg chol., 263 mg sodium, 279 mg potassium, and 1 g dietary fiber. U.S. RDA: 30% vit. A, 11% vit. C, 11% thiamine, 12% niacin, 10% iron.

MAIL ORDER SOURCES

● **Dean & Deluca, 800/221-7714.** Wild Pecan® rice (7 ounces), $2.05. Basmati rice (1 pound), $2.85, plus shipping.
● **Walnut Acres, 800/433-3998.** Basmati rice (1 pound), $1.79, plus shipping to destinations east of the Mississippi.
● **Texmati™ Rice, 800/232-RICE.** Texmati™ rice (1 pound), $2.00 plus shipping.
● **Community Kitchens, 800/535-9901.** Popcorn rice (8 ounces), $2.50, plus shipping.

INDEX

D-F

Index

S

Index

Microwave Wattage

All microwave recipes were tested in countertop microwave ovens that provide 600 to 700 watts of cooking power. The cooking times are approximate because microwave ovens vary by manufacturer.

Nutrition Analysis

Some nutrient information is given by gram weight per serving. The United States Recommended Daily Allowances (U.S. RDAs) for selected vitamins and minerals are given in the recipes when the value exceeds 10 percent. The U.S. RDAs tell the amounts of certain nutrients necessary to meet the dietary needs of most healthy people.

To obtain the nutrition analysis of each recipe, the following guidelines were used:

● When ingredient options appear in a recipe, the analysis was calculated using the first ingredient choice.

● Optional ingredients were omitted in the analyses.

● The nutrition analyses for recipes calling for fresh ingredients were calculated using the measurements for raw fruits, vegetables, and meats.

● If a recipe gives optional serving sizes (such as "Makes 6 to 8 servings"), the nutrition analysis was calculated using the first choice.